Social Housing in Performance

Methuen Drama Engage offers original reflections about key practitioners, movements and genres in the fields of modern theatre and performance. Each volume in the series seeks to challenge mainstream critical thought through original and interdisciplinary perspectives on the body of work under examination. By questioning existing critical paradigms, it is hoped that each volume will open up fresh approaches and suggest avenues for further exploration.

Series Editors
Mark Taylor-Batty
University of Leeds, UK

Enoch Brater
University of Michigan, USA

Titles
Adaptation in Contemporary Theatre
by Frances Babbage
ISBN 978-1-4725-3142-1

Authenticity in Contemporary Theatre and Performance
by Daniel Schulze
ISBN 978-1-3500-0096-4

Beat Drama: Playwrights and Performances of the 'Howl' Generation
edited by Deborah R. Geis
ISBN 978-1-472-56787-1

Drama and Digital Arts Cultures
by David Cameron, Michael Anderson and Rebecca Wotzko
ISBN 978-1-472-59219-4

Social and Political Theatre in 21st-Century Britain: Staging Crisis
by Vicky Angelaki
ISBN 978-1-474-21316-5

Theatre in the Dark: Shadow, Gloom and Blackout in Contemporary Theatre
edited by Adam Alston and Martin Welton
ISBN 978-1-4742-5118-1

Watching War on the Twenty-First-Century Stage: Spectacles of Conflict
by Clare Finburgh
ISBN 978-1-472-59866-0

Fiery Temporalities in Theatre and Performance: The Initiation of History
by Maurya Wickstrom
ISBN 978-1-4742-8169-0

Robert Lepage/Ex Machina: Revolutions in Theatrical Space
by James Reynolds
ISBN 978-1-4742-7609-2

Social Housing in Performance

The English Council Estate on and off Stage

Katie Beswick

Series Editors
Enoch Brater and Mark Taylor-Batty

methuen | drama

LONDON • NEW YORK • OXFORD • NEW DELHI • SYDNEY

METHUEN DRAMA
Bloomsbury Publishing Plc
50 Bedford Square, London, WC1B 3DP, UK
1385 Broadway, New York, NY 10018, USA

BLOOMSBURY, METHUEN DRAMA and the Methuen Drama logo are
trademarks of Bloomsbury Publishing Plc

First published in Great Britain 2019

Series design by Louise Dugdale
Cover image © Michael C. Smith, www.mikesm.co.uk

A catalogue record for this book is available from the British Library.

A catalog record for this book is available from the Library of Congress.

ISBN: HB: 978-1-4742-8521-6
ePDF: 978-1-4742-8520-9
eBook: 978-1-4742-8519-3

Series: Methuen Drama Engage

Typeset by Newgen KnowledgeWorks Pvt. Ltd., Chennai, India
Printed and bound in Great Britain

To find out more about our authors and books visit www.bloomsbury.com
and sign up for our newsletters.

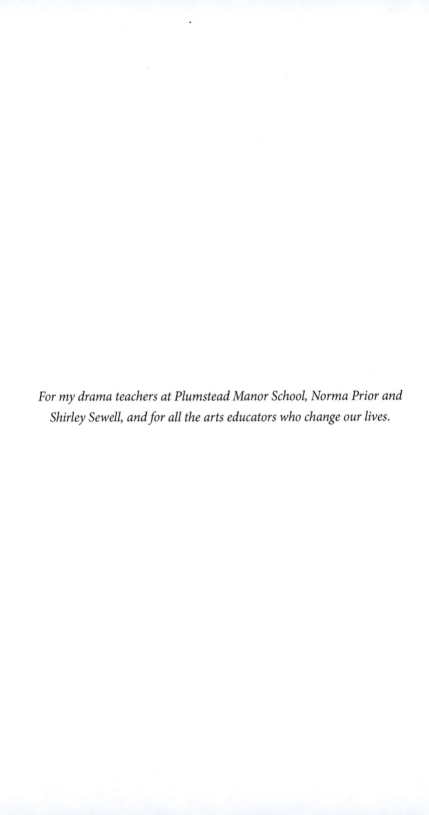

For my drama teachers at Plumstead Manor School, Norma Prior and Shirley Sewell, and for all the arts educators who change our lives.

Contents

Acknowledgements

Social Housing in Performance is the result of work I have carried out across three institutions, and I am thankful for the support, advice, encouragement and kindness of my colleagues at each.

I am particularly grateful to Joslin McKinney and Mick Wallis at the University of Leeds, who supervised the PhD that laid the groundwork for this book. They pushed me intellectually and made the doctoral process fun and much easier than it might have been with less encouraging mentors. Thanks also to David Shearing who was my rock for the duration of the PhD and who continues to inspire and support me.

At Queen Mary University of London, I am indebted to Shane Boyle, Bridget Escolme, Jen Harvie and Caoimhe McAvinchey who all helped in one way or another with the proposal that became *Social Housing in Performance*. I am also grateful for the support of colleagues at the Centre of Studies for Home, particularly Richard Baxter and Olivia Sheringham.

I'd like to thank the Centre for Performance Histories and Cultures at the University of Exeter, where my colleagues have tirelessly read and offered feedback on drafts. Special mentions to: Adrian Curtin, Graham Ley, Jane Milling, Kate Newey, Evelyn O'Malley, Michael Pearce, Kara Reilly, Peter Thompson and Cathy Turner.

Thanks to the artists and institutions who have helped by taking an interest in my project, agreeing to interviews, answering questions over Twitter, giving me permission to quote from emails and conversations, inviting me to participate in talks and events and offering documentation of their work: Battersea Arts Centre, Bola Agbaje, Jane English, Fourthland, Rosalind Fowler, Jordan McKenzie, Conrad Murray, The National Theatre, The National Youth Theatre, Ben Power, David Roberts, The Royal Court Theatre, Paul Sng, SPID Theatre Company, Simon Stephens, Adelle Stripe, Kate Tempest and Andrea Luka Zimmerman.

Thanks also to Charlotte Bell, my sister Holly Beswick, Claire Chambers, Maria Delgado, Dave O'Brien and Trish Reid. And to the series editors and Mark Dudgeon and Lara Bateman at Bloomsbury.

I'd like to offer a special and huge acknowledgement to my brother Billy, who read every single draft of every chapter as I wrote it and gave insightful feedback every time. I literally couldn't have done this without you. Well, not *literally*.

And finally to my mum and dad, as always. For everything.

Three places: A preface

Linnet Close, Thamesmead, London, 1984

A red banister in a stairwell; curtains undulate in the wind. I'm not walking on the stairs – I'm looking up at the stairs, as if I've just woken and someone is carrying me.

Then there's wallpaper with brown flowers.

Years later, when I describe this memory to my mother, she tells me I'm remembering being carried to our flat from the bottom of the block we lived in when I was a baby. I find a picture – it's of Mum, much younger, opening a bottle of wine. That's the wallpaper from my memory behind her.

When I was about two years old we moved – my parents had secured a mortgage on a house a few miles away. I've never been back to visit the estate, but I think it's still there.

*

Harvey Gardens, Charlton, London, 1996

I'm sitting on a low wall, dressed in my school uniform and a denim jacket. It's dark and cold. The bricks are icy; when I move they scratch at the back of my legs, pulling ladders through my tights.

I'm staying overnight at my friend Sarah's. Her estate is made up of redbrick houses positioned around small lawns (we call them 'greens').

Sarah's house faces the football ground. They've got leather settees and a makeshift conservatory her dad calls a 'lean to'.

We are in the square behind the house. There's a group of teenagers, older than us and more sophisticated. Sarah knows them all by name. I'm a stranger, desperate to be included. One of the boys is talking about a TV show called *Game On*. He makes a joke about sex. Someone hands me a bottle of Hooch. It tastes like lemonade.

It's thrilling.

*

Lordship South, Hackney, London, 2007

All the blocks are named after trees, though there are few trees on the estate. I'm carrying a bag full of papers and a folder I keep dropping. Everybody tells me this is the worst estate in Hackney ('Careful. That boy was shot last week and the police haven't found the gun yet'). But it's my favourite because it's so contained and right by the park. When I ring the buzzer the residents let me in without using the intercom to check who it is.

The front room smells of damp; it's freezing – even though it is summer, and warm outside.

There are three generations of women. The grandmother is huge and hyper-alert, she's sitting on the sofa, wearing a woollen hat and gloves. She doesn't get up or greet me.

'I've come about the rent', I say.

She looks me up and down and kisses her teeth. 'How old are you?'

'I'm twenty-three.'

'You don't look twenty-three!' She falls about laughing. 'You look teenaged!'

*

This book explores contemporary representations of the English social housing estate – or 'council estate' – in theatre and performance practices and beyond. Above, I have mapped my own council estate journey in the form of three memory fragments. These memories recall something of my lived experience of estates up until the start of my research, as an infant resident, a visitor and a housing officer. At different points I have both 'belonged' to estates and felt 'outside' of them. My experience of living, playing and working on council estates was informed by the performance practices I was involved in throughout my childhood and early adult life, and the representations of estates that were ubiquitous in television and the news media during this period.

Although I was not always conscious of how representations shaped my experiences, once I started working on estates, subsidizing my (sporadic) acting work by collecting rent arrears for a local authority, the relationship between the lived and the represented began to preoccupy my working life. How are spaces created as we live them? What role does representation play in how we perceive places? Can performance change the ways we think about contested space? These are the questions I began this research project hoping to explore.

I have opened this book by recollecting moments from my own practice of estates because, throughout the course of this project, estate residents, local authority staff, friends and strangers I have discussed the project with have often insisted I validate my interest in council estates. Perhaps because of the contentious place council estates occupy in the British psyche, and the often exploitative representations of estates and their residents that exist across the press, the academy and the media, estate denizens have been suspicious of my motivations. While I do not wish to contribute to the fetishization of 'authentic' experience, which – as I later propose – often underwrites the creation of dominant, negative council estate discourse, I want to acknowledge the importance of my experiences in shaping this research project.

My memory fragments encompass something of the position that has informed this book and reflect the journey that prompted a fascination with estates worthy of a lengthy study.

Introduction: The council estate, definitions and parameters

A council estate: first thing that comes to a lot of people's heads – the first thing that would come to my head – is a block of flats. Like, a couple of blocks and a park. That's pretty much a council estate to me. That's a lot of council estates.

(Interview with estate visitor, November 2010)

*

Well, certain things that people stereotype are true. But then other things ... it's not as bad as people make it out. You had certain stereotypical things – like because I lived in Peckham some people used to be scared that, like, 'oh my God, I'd never go to Peckham', or something like that. But when you actually live [on an estate], it's not, it's not as bad.

(Interview with estate resident, November 2010)

*

You can't call it a 'council estate' Katie, that's offensive. You should call it a housing estate instead.

(Conversation with housing officer, July 2009)

*

In January 2016, as I began work on this book in earnest, David Cameron, then prime minister of the United Kingdom, wrote an article, published in the *Sunday Times*, outlining how the bulldozing of 'sink estates' was at the heart of his vision for a 'social turnaround'. He argued that, despite the efforts of families to build 'warm and welcoming homes' within them, Britain's large-scale social housing estates were 'entrenching poverty'. Cameron offered a description of his understanding of life on 'the worst estates' in Britain:

step outside … and you're confronted by concrete slabs dropped from on high, brutal high-rise towers and dark alleyways that are a gift to criminals and drug dealers. The police often talk about the importance of designing out crime, but these estates designed it in. Decades of neglect have led to gangs, ghettos and antisocial behaviour. And poverty has become entrenched, because those who could afford to move have understandably done so.

(Cameron 2016)

Cameron's article was the latest in a succession of attacks on social housing made by the Coalition and Conservative governments for which he served as prime minister. These included, among other things, legislation aimed at phasing out secure lifetime tenancies for social renters and levying a 'tax' on social rented accommodation deemed to provide residents with a spare bedroom (the so-called 'spare bedroom tax' discussed in more detail below). These moves were often justified by wider ideological attacks on social housing and its presumed users. Underpinning the rationale for the policies I mentioned above, for example, was the figure of the 'shirker' or 'scrounger' – the archetypal lazy, welfare-dependent council estate resident who is invoked to suggest that welfare benefits encourage and facilitate the lifestyles of people who offer nothing back to society (Jowitt 2013, Shildrick 2018). However, the rhetoric of Cameron's article appeals to familiar conceptions of estate life beyond those propagated by his government. Rather, he draws upon widespread understandings about British social housing estates perpetuated across the political spectrum (see Labour prime minister Tony Blair's 1997 'forgotten people' speech at the Aylesbury estate for example (Minton 2017: 65, Slater 2018: 882)) and in popular representations in film, on television, in newspapers, in music videos and online. In such representations, council estates are regularly positioned as dangerous, inhospitable and violent: as corrupt and corrupting spaces that produce a morally inferior, criminal underclass that is lazy, 'lacking' (McKenzie 2015) and dependent on welfare benefits. As author Lynsey Hanley argued in response to Cameron's article, such logic 'wilfully turns cause and effect on its head, citing mental ill-health, drug use and family difficulties as causes of poverty and not the reverse' (Hanley 2016). This kind of derogatory rhetoric works as part of a dominant discourse[1] to create the council estate resident as 'other' – as the deviant, criminal, working-class figure whom the middle class define themselves in opposition to (Lawler 2005: 133). As journalist Owen Jones (2011) suggests, this 'demonization of the working class' has a spatial element, with the derogatory term for the white working class, 'chav', often considered as an acronym for 'council housed and violent' (8).[2]

'Council estate', then, is a British[3] term that usually refers to individual large-scale social housing projects, which are iconic (if rapidly vanishing) features of the United Kingdom's urban landscape. However, it is also used colloquially to refer collectively and descriptively to these places. The term is often applied to imply the social stigma attached to estates and the 'otherness' of estate residents. But 'council estate' is not always applied pejoratively; it is also used by residents of estates to describe their homes and more generally by members of the public to refer to areas of social housing.[4] It is this very disjuncture between the mundane, everyday living of estates and the dominant stigmas attached to the archetypal or 'generic' council estate that makes these spaces such prominent features of British socio-spatial history.

This book is concerned with representations of the council estate, with a focus on England,[5] and particularly with exploring the relationship between representation and reality in performative, theatrical and artistic representations of estates. As Kearns et al. (2013) suggest, there has been limited research concerned with understanding how the reputation of areas is created and maintained 'through transmission processes' (2013: 579). Although social scientists have drawn attention to the damaging effects negative representations have on estates and their residents (see Reay and Lucy 2000, Pearce and Milne 2010, Shildrick 2018), and although arts and humanities scholars have explored the role of arts practices in problematic gentrification and redevelopment processes (see Harris 2012, Harvie 2013, Bell 2014a), there was, until now, no published book-length study that solely examined the myriad ways that *representations* of estates operate within the dominant discourse.[6] As a performance scholar, I have been especially interested to explore how council estates are conceptualized on stage and to understand how performative representations work as 'transmission processes', creating and contesting our understandings of estate space; reinforcing and also resisting negative conceptions of the council estate that circulate within and beyond popular and political discourse. In this way, this book deals with the 'idea' of the council estate, drawing attention to representational practices in a context that remains under-explored. This book seeks to reveal the effects of such practices on estates and their residents.

Social Housing in Performance is the result of almost a decade of research into council estates, council estate representation and council estate performance, but as I indicate in the preface, it is also, inevitably, informed by my earlier practice of estates as a resident, visitor and housing officer. Thus, the analysis is underpinned by an autoethnographic methodology, as I draw on my lived experience to enrich and illuminate my enquiry throughout the book. Ellis et al. (2011) define autoethnographic research and writing as that which 'seeks to describe and systematically analyze (graphy) personal experience (auto) in order to understand cultural experience (ethno)'. In keeping with this broad definition of autoethnography, my foregrounding of my own estate experience is at once a subjective method of reading based on my lived knowledge of estates and a methodological frame I am using to understand the wider cultural significance of estate representation. This autoethnographic approach extends the work of writers such as Lynsey Hanley (2007) and Lisa McKenzie (2015), who have used their personal experience of living on estates as a method for writing about them. However, although I believe that (auto)ethnography importantly offers access to voices and perspectives often suppressed within popular media and academic discourses, I do not wish to conflate autoethnography with 'authenticity'. The fetishization of the 'authentic' in representations of working-class lives and experiences has inflected the production of much estate representation in recent decades. As I will later argue, although this concern with the 'authentic' has afforded estate residents a voice within the public discourse, it has also worked to reinforce existing negative ideas about estates and to load estate artists with a burden of representation that fosters the exploitation and misinterpretation of working-class voices.

Thus, the overarching aim of *Social Housing in Performance* is to explore the role theatrical and other (newspaper, television, film, visual art) representational practices might play in 'producing' (Lefebvre 1991) estate spaces. I do not suggest representational practices operate on a binary of resistance to/reinforcement of dominant narratives, but I am interested in exploring the complex and often paradoxical ways that representations operate both to challenge *and* to sustain dominant understandings about estates, and to feed into the daily practice of estate 'place'.

Although this book is focused on England,[7] its contents have wider implications. A tangential aim of the study has been to begin to articulate how the local and national concerns and practices I discuss have global resonances and international implications. Michael Pearce argues in his book exploring black British theatre that a transnational perspective enables an exploration of relational global spaces, while rooting the enquiry in nationally specific contexts (2017), an approach I hope to foster here.

While the politics of race that Pearce illuminates are not wholly transferrable to this context (although estate space does, as we will see, have racial dimensions), it is nonetheless important, in a climate where national concerns resonate globally, that we are able to conceptualize ostensibly local practices within their transnational context. This transnational perspective makes it possible to more readily understand, adopt and apply diverse strategies for addressing local articulations of global injustice.

My research has developed during a volatile and difficult time in the international landscape of housing provision. As David Harvey (2008) points out, the Western, neoliberal trend towards owner occupation became a global concern throughout the 2000s. The collapse of the sub-prime mortgage market was widely reported to have played a significant role in the 2008 financial crisis and subsequent global recession. Across the world, many people who had been unable to keep up with mortgage repayments found themselves under threat of eviction or repossession.

The culture of speculative development, whereby homes are built by developers for a profit and sold to buyers as units of individual financial investment, has resulted in a situation where those without the economic means to buy their own property are displaced and disenfranchised. The characterization of this type of displacement shifts from country to country (as explored by Harvey 2008), but housing nonetheless remains in crisis across the globe. In 2011, in cities across the world – including Amsterdam, Hong Kong, London and New York – people disenchanted with the neoliberal era of capitalism chose to respond to the state of the financial system with 'Occupy' protests. Protesters took over public spaces in makeshift tented dwellings, symbolically referencing the fact that the recession had threatened the individual right to basic shelter. As the proliferation of literature on subjects relating to housing conditions (see Harvey 2008, Engel 2011, Watt and Minton 2017) demonstrates, housing has become an increasing area of academic interest.

The council estate and the crisis of social housing

'Social housing'[8] is a term that has gained currency since the late twentieth century (Reeves 2005: 2); it is used to refer to subsidized rented housing provision usually provided to individuals and families who cannot afford to buy their own homes or rent privately. In the United Kingdom, as elsewhere, social housing is in crisis. There are numerous reasons for this, including the fact that owner occupation has become a status benchmark and has been promoted as an efficient and low-risk way of ensuring financial security. Other causes of the crisis of social housing in the United Kingdom include a shortage of truly affordable housing exacerbated by the Right to Buy policy (legislation introduced by the Conservative government, then led by Margaret Thatcher, in the Housing Act 1980, which enabled residents to buy their council homes at a discounted price) and subsequent buy-to-let mortgages that have placed former council housing in the private rental market; government policies that have capped housing benefit and sought to eliminate secure tenancies; the reputation of council estates as conducive to crime; and speculative redevelopment (see Minton 2017). The redevelopment of social housing is part of a wider trend towards urban regeneration, whereby successive Labour, Coalition and Conservative governments have incentivized private building provision. Since at least the 2000s urban regeneration has particularly implicated council estates – the demolition and total redevelopment of estate sites has featured as a key part of many urban regeneration projects. Redevelopments taking place on estates have often involved the removal of existing tenants from their homes and either the complete erasure of social renters through the reselling of 'developed' properties to those who can afford them or, more commonly, mixed tenure developments. Mixed tenure developments include dwellings for sale, private rental and social housing – the redevelopments of the Park Hill estate in Sheffield and the Ferrier estate in Kidbrooke, London (now 'Kidbrooke Village') are examples of this. In these kinds of projects, provision for social housing is often hugely reduced; thus, those people moving out of their homes while the redevelopment takes place have no guarantee of being moved back (see e.g. Minton 2017, ASH 2017a for more detailed analyses).

As Ray Forrest and Alan Murie's work demonstrates, the crisis of social housing has been escalating for several decades, as there has been a movement from a position where owner occupation was a predominantly

> middle-class tenure, high-quality council housing was used by the affluent working class and private landlordism catered for the poorest sections of the population towards one where council housing serves the vulnerable, low paid and marginalized population with a highly stratified and differentiated home ownership as mass tenure.
>
> (Forrest and Murie 1985: 106)

In the decades since Forrest and Murie wrote this, there has been a further shift, with a huge expansion in the private rental market, a decrease in both social housing tenure and owner occupation, particularly for first-time buyers, and a greater reliance on landlords to provide housing for both the working classes and the vulnerable poor (Ministry of Housing, Communities and Local Government 2017, Minton 2017). The crisis of social housing has particularly implicated the council estate because estates and estate residents are often referenced, both directly and indirectly, in political rhetoric regarding the welfare state. For example, in 2013 the Coalition government introduced the 'under-occupation penalty' policy – popularly known as the 'spare bedroom tax'[9] – a reduction in housing benefit for any claimants who were deemed to have a 'spare bedroom'. The council estate was especially implicated in the spare bedroom tax because the cuts only affected those renting their property from a local authority or housing association; private renters were not subject to similar cuts to their housing benefit.[10] In 2016, further policy interventions were proposed that would effectively phase out the tradition of social housing as a long-term housing solution for families and individuals. The Housing Bill proposed to end secure and long-term tenancies and introduce 'pay to stay', where 'high-income' residents (those earning over £40,000 in London and £30,000 elsewhere) would be charged market rate for their properties – although pay to stay was not implemented, it indicates the loaded and high-stakes ways in which public debates about social housing are played out.

As a 2010 report published by the Joseph Rowntree Foundation argued, the stigma attached to estate residency, reinforced by continual changes to the policy and governance of estate spaces, has had a damaging impact on the self-esteem and morale of estate residents – leading them to feel they have little control in effecting change in their own lives (Pearce and Milne 2010: 1, see also Shildrick 2018: 791). This is compounded by the fact that residents have a limited voice in terms of their own representation. Council estate residents' lives are often reduced to the stereotypical negative depictions seen in the popular representations discussed later in the book; these often ignore the complexities of the individual lives of residents, which are layered with the same capacity for joy, fear, sorrow, celebration and fulfilment as any human life.

In the early stages of my research, I consciously avoided the term 'council estate'. This was, in part, because of the negative associations with the term outlined above. But I also eschewed it because the phrase 'social housing estate' now has more contemporary currency. This is because the council (or 'local authority') is no longer the primary manager of social housing. Many estates are now owned or managed by housing associations, arms-length management organizations or, more rarely, other types of Registered Social Landlord (such as charities or housing co-operatives). In addition, many of the estates that would once have been referred to as 'council' are made up of mixed tenure homes because of redevelopments or changes to policy regarding standard tenancies and because residents have purchased their social rented properties under the Right to Buy – as I indicate above, many of these were sold on and have ended up being rented on the private market. This means those living on estates might be local authority or housing association tenants on introductory, secure, non-secure, flexible, fixed term or assured tenancies; private renters; freeholders or leaseholders (who own the lease, but not the freehold, to their property), the latter of whose tenure is 'particularly complex since legally they are simultaneously property owners and local authority tenants' (Lees and Ferreri 2016: 15). Additionally there are likely to be those who illegally sublet their property from another tenant, and occasionally those who are squatting.

However, despite the inaccuracy of the term 'council estate' in encompassing the current management and practice of social housing estates, as I have progressed with this project I have found that 'council estate' is most often used in popular media and artistic representations of social housing. The term has also proved the most provocative and stimulating in the various conversations I have had with residents, audience members, artists and scholars throughout the course of this project. The use of the term 'council estate' in a contemporary context, as I discuss throughout this study, is both loaded and contentious. Because this research project has focused on *representation* and because there is necessarily a gap between what is presented in the press, popular media and in artistic and performance practice and the reality (or otherwise) that it purports to present, I have chosen to use the term council estate (or estate) to refer to the contested spaces described above. This is because, despite the pejorative connotations of the phrase, it is exactly this loaded *notion* – the idea of the 'generic place' of the council estate – that dominates contemporary engagements with these sites.

Estates in representation

Council estates have been the subject of popular, academic and government concern almost since their wide-scale inception (see e.g. National Council of Social Service 1938, Jephcott 1971, Damer 1974, Miller 1988, Power 1999, Ravetz 2001, Hanley 2007, Hatherley 2008, McKenzie 2015). They remain an area of public interest. As I suggested above, estates also regularly feature as the setting for popular representations in music video ('Council Estate of Mind' by Skinny Man 2004, 'Council Estate' by Tricky 2008, 'Ill Manors' by Plan B 2011), in film (*Nil by Mouth* 1997, *Fish Tank* 2009, *Tyrannosaur* 2011), on television (*Only Fools and Horses* 1981–2003, *Top Boy* 2011 and 2013, *Raised by Wolves* 2013–2016) and in literature (Sue Townsend's *The Queen and I* 1992, Monica Ali's *Brick Lane* 2007, Richard Milward's *Ten Storey Love Song* 2009). Very often, these representations contain narratives that highlight the negative attributes of estate life and the 'otherness' of estate residents. However, at the same time they also often, paradoxically, celebrate and sometimes fetishize the strategies of survivorship and resistance with which estate residents navigate the complexities of the social and political conditions that structure their lives.

In addition to its prolific invocation in British policy and popular culture, the council estate is also a prominent setting for theatrical performance practices. Council estate performance has proliferated since the turn of the twenty-first century as a result of a growing interest in urban space and the lives and culture of so-called 'marginalized' groups. This is partly an effect of the 'social' and 'spatial' turns in arts scholarship and performance practice, which are themselves partly a result of wider shifts towards socially engaged arts practices, influenced by the New Labour social inclusion agenda and subsequent Arts Council England funding preferences, such as those set out in the strategic framework report *Achieving Great Art for Everyone* (Arts Council England 2010 and 2013).[11] Examples of theatrical council estate performance practices will, of course, be discussed throughout the book, but indicatively they include mainstream productions such as Roy Williams's *Fallout* (Royal Court 2003), Arinze Kene's *God's Property* (Soho/The Albany 2013, see Beswick 2015) and Anna Jordan's *Yen* (Royal Court/Royal Exchange 2016); applied practices such as the University of Nottingham's *The Forgotten Estate Project* (see Jones et al. 2013), Box Clever's *Puck of the Estate* (2009–2012) and the National Youth Theatre's *The Block* (2010, see Beswick 2011a); and site-specific practices such as Jordan McKenzie's *Lock Up Performance Art* (Approach estate, Bethnal Green 2011–2013), SPID Theatre Company's *23176* (Kensal House estate 2008, see Beswick 2011b, 2016a, 2016b) and *The Market Estate Project* (Market Estate Islington 2010).

The stories we tell and hear about ourselves are important. As several sociological studies of urban council estates have indicated, residents have a profound need to narrate their lives positively and to respond to the mostly negative stories that circulate about their lives in popular culture (Reay and Lucey 2000, Watt 2006). In her book *Getting By: Estates Class and Culture in Austerity Britain,* McKenzie (2015) explains how surviving day-to-day life on a council estate includes engaging in meaning-making activities that attribute value to local practices and make the day-to-day experiences of poverty bearable (103–146). Telling a story that speaks back to stigmatizing narratives, she illuminates the logic that led a young mother to spend £25 of her small weekly budget on designer sunglasses. McKenzie writes,

> Those who live on council estates are often accused of having big television sets, state-of-the-art smart phones, expensive clothing, and that they spend their money (or rather, as 'they' see it, the state's money) on frivolity. Anyone who has ever had to live for any extended amount of time with very little knows how weary you become. You see others' lifestyles around you and through the media, and you are not allowed to join in. You live in a society that values high-branded and designer items such as Gucci,

BlackBerry and Apple, but you are financially excluded from joining in. You are devalued for who you are and where you live, and like anyone else, you want to feel good about yourself. You want to be valued.

(McKenzie 2015: 110)

In the following chapters of this book I will unpick the complex and complicated ways that representational stories work within divergent value systems, seeking to understand the relationship between contested spaces and the representations that operate on and through those spaces in one way or another.

The council estate as conceptualized in this book is a generic place associated with a supposed 'underclass': with crime, diverse ethnicity, poverty and deprivation. Although it is not the case that all representations of estates work to reinforce negative stereotypes, the archetypal council estate has become the British conception of what E. V. Walter termed the 'dreadful enclosure'. Walter argued that

> in all parts of the world, some urban spaces are identified totally with danger, pain and chaos ... certain milieux gather reputations for moral inferiority, squalor, violence, and social pathology, and consequently they objectify the fantasy of the dreadful enclosure.
>
> (Walter 1972 in Damer 1974: 221)

My conceptualization of the generic council estate includes an acknowledgement of the estate place as 'dreadful enclosure'. However, my conceptualization also resonates with Richardson and Skott-Myhre's (2012) definition of the 'hood' as a multiple, shifting, global site of urban marginality that comprises paradoxical narratives of struggle and survival that are both limiting and liberating, I return to these ideas in Chapter 1.

Council estateness

A typical British council estate is made up of various types of homes – commonly including flats in tower blocks, terraced houses and maisonettes – the majority of which were built between 1919 and the late 1970s.[12] These estates were initially intended to provide housing for Britain's large working classes: not only re-housing the poor from urban slums but also offering desirable accommodation to fairly well-off families and individuals. However, in the late twentieth century and throughout the beginning of twenty-first century, the political landscape of social housing has changed, leading the generic council estate to become 'reified' (McKenzie 2015), with a 'fixed' identity that structures the reputations of individual estates. As Paul Watt notes, this identity is bound up with conceptions of the (poor) 'working class', 'despite the general erosion of cohesive, clear-cut class identities and images' (2008: 347).

The 'fixity' of identity commonly attached to council estates has contributed to the emergence of these places as contested and contentious sites. Although there has been a long-standing tradition of concern over the lives and lifestyles of those who live on estates (see Ravetz 2001, Hanley 2007), government policies over the past three decades have led to increased distrust of social renters. Changing policies have shaped the way that council estates are practiced and perceived and have contributed to the (generic) council estate becoming an increasingly complex place. This complexity is compounded by the dominant media discourse where the estate is often portrayed as a dreadful enclosure with those who live there positioned as equally dreadful. McKenzie (2009) demonstrates that working-class bodies and spaces are coded by cultural signifiers as tasteless, repulsive and vulgar. She notes that there is little effort made to change perceptions of working-class people and their environments in the neoliberal political system because structures of power rely upon blaming the poor for their position and de-valuing the networks and systems that they have in place to support themselves (see also Skeggs 2005).

Despite my use of the generic term, I acknowledge that individual estates do have individualized identities and practices (see e.g. Parker 1983 and McKenzie 2015 for nuanced accounts of life on specific estates). In academic discourse on council estates, scholars have noted that individual identities also often manifest negatively as residents and locals view a single estate as more 'dreadful' than others in the area (Damer 1974, Ravetz 2001, Hanley 2007, Rogaly and Taylor 2011, Kearns et al. 2013). Estate performances too often work with ideas of localized estate identity. Rachel De-lahay's play *The Westbridge* (Royal Court 2011) explores individual estate identity by juxtaposing the life of a young mixed race couple and their friend, who have moved to a private flat adjacent to the fictional Westbridge estate, with the lives of their friends and family who still live on the estate. For all the characters, the Westbridge features as a significant factor in their personal and collective identities in spite of the different social, cultural and ethnic backgrounds they come from.

Nonetheless, despite the particular character of individual estates, within popular representation the term 'council estate' is regularly used to indicate these places as a collective. This generic conception of the council estate works to homogenize and reify these spaces and their residents in the British psyche. Although the deeply problematic implications of this reified version are the central concern of this study, it is important to acknowledge that the dominant stigmatizing narratives of local and collective estate identity are not necessarily grounded only in fiction. Social problems *do* exist on individual estates where criminal and anti-social behaviour happens (as it does elsewhere). Nonetheless, the causal correlation between the council estate and criminality often suggested in representation is reductive, as Bola Agbaje, playwright and author of council estate plays *Gone Too Far* (Royal Court 2007), *Off the Endz* (Royal Court 2010) and *Concrete Jungle* (Hammersmith 2011) who has also worked as a housing officer, implied during an interview I carried out with her:

> I manage street properties. And the same social issues [exist] on street properties that people face on estates. There's still issues on streets. I have streets where there's issues of gang culture, there's issues of anti-social behaviour and all that stuff that people associate mainly with estates happens on street properties. So you can't then just say 'it's the area', you have to then look at the wider problem and say okay, what [are] the issues within the family home ... And 99% of the time, there are so many different underlying problems.
>
> (Interview with Bola Agbaje July 2011)

Agbaje's discussion of her work as a housing officer suggests the role that the 'idea' of the council estate plays in intersectional narratives of poverty, crime and anti-social behaviour. She suggests how the council estate has become an ideological container for issues relating to race (gang culture), class (poverty) and gender (family relationships, single mothers, domestic violence and hyper-masculinity), which are conflated, collapsed and spatialized in popular representation. This characterization creates a phenomenon I will refer to as 'council estateness' – where the term 'council estate' has become a shorthand for social decay and failure.

Alison Ravetz has suggested that the council estate is part of the British psyche; she notes that 'there can be few British people unable to recognize what is or is not a council estate' (2001: 177). This statement refers to the importance of council estates in the evolution of twentieth-century urban space and to the central role that the development of council housing has played in housing policy over the last century. But, despite Ravetz's assertion about their recognizablility, it is difficult to pinpoint a coherent design uniformity that encompasses all estates – although specific design principles contributed to the architecture of the council estates of the twentieth century, including, notably, the Garden City principle, which influenced the layout of many pre-war estates[13] and brutalism. Nonetheless, as Ravetz's statement suggests, council estates are recognizable for reasons beyond their design – there are also definable yet intangible qualities, essential features of estate*ness*, which construct the estate's reputation and structure the quality of its enduring presence in political and social consciousness.

The council estate's supposed pathology derives from a variety of, often negative, preconceptions about particular types of estates, such as the organization of the modernist estate, with its secluded corners and hidden walkways providing ideal conditions for crime, and particular types of people portrayed as residents in the popular press and on television, film and live performance. However, it over-simplifies the picture to blame negative representations by the media and popular press for the estate's reputation. Criticism of social housing is ubiquitous at all levels of British society. Mistrust of social renting is widespread, as exemplified by the shifting attitudes of policy-makers and political commentators towards social housing and its users. However, social housing users themselves are also often derisive of the policies and procedures that surround the day-to-day running of the sector. In my own work as a housing officer and in the ethnographic placement I undertook at a local authority as part of this research project, I found that the perception of council housing as inefficient, corrupt and 'failed' in terms of the objectives early policies set out to achieve were common in both tenants and local authority staff.

Peter King (2006) maintains that the policies that have influenced the development and management of social housing throughout the twentieth and early twenty-first centuries have been unsuccessful. He argues that these have, for the most part, presumed the users of social housing to be vulnerable and incapable of organizing their own affairs. King suggests that the Right to Buy policy, by giving tenants the economic privilege of ownership, was the only policy that achieved what it set out to achieve – namely a change in the relationship between residents and their homes. King suggests that social housing as it is currently organized in the United Kingdom is unsustainable and advocates a move towards owner occupation. This kind of perspective has driven recent policy developments regarding social housing.

But to see the council estate only as a failed experiment ignores the fact that in many (if not most) cases estates provide families and individuals with good quality, highly desirable homes that they would otherwise be unable to afford and which, like residents of other types of homes, they become very attached to (Watt 2006: 784–785). In a narrative of local perceptions of Leeds' much-maligned Quarry Hill estate (demolished in 1978), Ravetz points out that 'stigmatization was a crude caricature of a living environment that was in many ways satisfactory' (Ravetz 2001: 173). Residents of the (now demolished) Ferrier estate in Kidbrooke, south east London, demonstrated their passionate attachment to their homes in a campaign against Greenwich council, attempting to intervene in the planned 'regeneration' of the area – an event that playwright Lucy Beacon based her 2013 play *Demolition* (Angelic Tales New Writing Festival, Theatre Royal Stratford East) on.

As Will Montgomery (2011) points out, mass provision of council housing in the United Kingdom was initially conceived as a utopian ideal. Its 'failure' was a result of poor implementation of the visions of architects such as Le Corbusier, van der Rohe and Gropius, with 'cheap, system-built council buildings of the 1960s and 1970s [that] were poorly designed – barely designed at all in many cases' (447). This poor implementation arguably accelerated the dystopian view of council estates that has come to dominate these spaces, with the collapse of Ronan Point, a twenty-two-storey tower block in Newham, East London, in May 1968, widely believed to have been the tipping point in public opinion, which began 'to turn decisively against council estate modernism' (Montgomery 2011: 446). The Ronan Point disaster was also addressed through theatre practice; Joan Littlewood and John Wells staged a 'satirical treatment' of the inquiry into the incident in the 1968 performance *The Projector* (Holdsworth 2006: 40).

What I am calling 'council estateness', then, encompasses the negative attributes of the council estate's reputation. The concept of council estateness reveals the uncomfortable tension between the fetishized fantasy of the 'dreadful enclosure' archetype and the day-to-day practice of estates by residents – which includes both scepticism towards the system and attachment to their homes and communities, such as might be experienced by private renters and home owners.

Gallagher and Neelands argue that

> The city, like a play, is a space where everything means more than one thing. It is an objective thought and a subjective experience, a charged and symbolic thing as well as a real, material, lived, reality.
>
> (Gallagher and Neelands 2011: 152)

The generic council estate, as an iconic feature of British towns and cities, a pertinent social symbol and a range of 'real' places, might also be considered a space where 'everything means more than one thing'. Therefore despite the definability of 'council estateness', as the debates above indicate, a simple definition of the archetypal council estate is not possible. This is because each estate is different and because the 'council estate', as a generic place, is a complex system.

The complex council estate

Mick Wallis (using Hunt and Melrose 2005) defines a complex system as one that has seven principal characteristics (Wallis 2009: 144–146). The generic council estate is a complex system, which can be mapped onto these seven characteristics, as demonstrated below.

1. *A system which comprises many elements*

In addition to the physical elements of the various incarnations of the council estate – including dwellings (houses, flats, maisonettes), public and recreational spaces (walkways, grassy areas, public squares, community halls) and local amenities (markets, public houses, convenience stores) – there are numerous organizational and functional elements that contribute to the council estate as a system. At a macro-level, the government's Ministry of Housing, Communities and Local Government (formerly the Department for Communities and Local Government) oversees the operation of housing on estates at the time of writing. At a local level, elements that contribute to the council estate system include the individual bodies that play a part in the organization of everyday life on council estates – such as community groups and Tenants and Residents Associations (TRAs)[14] – and the housing associations or local authorities and their staff who oversee the day-to-day management of individual estates. The individual households and their residents also constitute elements within the overall system.

2. *The elements interact in a rich, other-than-linear way*

The interactions between the various elements comprising the council estate are inevitably 'other-than-linear'. Within the separate elements outlined above, there are formal structures at play that function to oversee the organization of the estate space. For example, at the local authority where I worked before embarking on this project, individual departments offered specialized management in the discrete areas that contributed to the day-to-day running of estates, including rent collection, repairs, voids (empty properties), anti-social behaviour and cleaning. Most housing associations and local authorities will have similar systems in place to govern the running of their properties (Reeves 2005). Invariably, the work of staff within different departments intersects and crosses over with other formal and informal 'elements'. For example, housing officers working in the rents department of a local authority may have to liaise with voids officers where squatters or subletters have moved into an empty property; in a case like this, conflict with the persons residing in the property may also complicate a linear interaction.

In Katherine Wright's (2011) PhD, she explored the rich informal networks that exist on an estate in Leeds. Her work highlights ways that tenants work both within and outside of formal networks to navigate daily life on the council estate. For example, sporadic or non-existent interaction with organizations such as community groups is often supplemented by regular interactions with friends or family as people navigate the various networks they have available to manage their lives.

3. *There are feedback loops*

Both formal and informal 'feedback loops' exist on the council estate. Informal feedback loops are multiple and difficult to map, but might include conversations in which neighbours resolve a dispute, or the way that a large family utilize the rooms in their property to ensure all members have a sleeping space. McKenzie describes a feedback loop that she refers to as 'estatism': the disadvantages experienced by estate residents, causing them to seek safety in the bounded location of the estate, and often leading to local networks of crime whereby the residents create informal structures through which to survive economically. '[Estatism] is a reciprocal dynamic of fear, prejudice, and resentment protecting those who engage in it to some degrees but also causing immense amounts of damage' (2009: 269).

Formal feedback loops include the many opportunities for 'consultation' provided by the management bodies responsible for running estates, such as regular TRA meetings (see above) and formal complaints procedures, where action might be taken to resolve issues raised by residents regarding the management of their estate. There are also national regulations that comprise part of the feedback loop social landlords must adhere to. From April 2010 to April 2012, for example (see Social Housing Regulator 2011), under the Regulatory Framework for Social Housing, all social housing providers were required to report on their performance against six national standards (Tenant Service Authority 2009).

The representation of the council estate in media and artistic forms also constitutes a 'feedback loop'. As we will see below, these forms of representation work as a method by which social housing is assessed, understood and practiced. Academic research such as this book and the studies cited within it also work as part of the multiple feedback loops at play within the council estate system.

4. *Each element responds to local influences and cannot know the total system*

Despite attempts to communicate across the multiple and layered elements that make up the estate – via some of the formal feedback systems outlined above – it is axiomatic that such a complex system will evade holistic knowledge by a single element. Pearce and Milne (2010) have noted that policy-makers' lack of understanding about the lived experience of estate space is often problematic when it comes to making and implementing policy. They suggest that a lack of experiential knowledge about council estate residents and spaces often leads to the exacerbation of the social problems that exist in such places (2–4).

5. *A system which is open/co-extensive*

As Wallis suggests, any system that involves human agents will be both open to outside influences and 'co-extensive with an evolving cultural context' (2009: 144–145). In the case of the council estate, cultural evolution can be mapped directly through many of the elements which comprise the system – including architectural, political, personal and, as I demonstrate in this book, artistic developments.

6. *Complex systems have a history*

The personal, geographical and political histories that circulate in relation to the council estate are mapped through a number of academic and artistic sources (many of these are referenced in this book); for example, Lynsey Hanley's *Estates: An Intimate History* (2007) offers both a personal and a sociopolitical overview of the history of the British council estate.

7. *Complex systems operate far from equilibrium*

The deep and continued tensions surrounding the operation of estates mean that, almost since their inception, such places have operated far from equilibrium. The ongoing instability of social housing – both in terms of its social and political viability and its physical form (as evidenced by the many redevelopments and demolitions of estates that have taken place in the past three decades, not to mention disasters such as the horrific Grenfell Tower fire in 2017, discussed in more detail in Chapter 3) – creates instability for residents. This instability means that the council estate is a site that is ideally placed to operate as what cultural critic bell hooks refers to as a 'space of resistance' (1990: 145), where artistic and critical interventions may be well placed to articulate and challenge the structural injustices that create and exacerbate inequality.

Council estate performance: A taxonomy

Throughout this book I refer to 'council estate performance' to describe a range of cultural practices. For the purposes of clarity, I offer below an indicative taxonomy of council estate performance, which suggests the kinds of practices this phrase is intended to encompass – although I emphasize that this taxonomy is indicative as there are necessarily crossovers between the various categories and indeed categories that might be added (commercial performances, such as the musical *Everybody's Talking About Jamie* (Sheffield Crucible/Apollo Theatre 2017), don't easily map onto my model).

Narrative-driven, theatrical representations of the council estate tend to foreground the estate as home-space, as the notion of dwelling in a 'dreadful enclosure' provides a particular dramatic tension. In mainstream productions, this is often because the estate provides a recognizable space where social issues of national concern – such as drug use, racism, sexuality and crime – can be contained and explored. Mainstream council estate performance is often presented in social realist forms, which echo dominant representations of the council estate on screen media such as film and television (see Chapter 2 for a more detailed discussion). It is difficult for social realist theatre practices to break free of the dominant estate discourse that circulates in popular culture. However, theatre *does* offer possibilities for intervention and reimagining. Experimentations with form and content on the mainstream stage, and the emphasis on residents as authors in various applied, interventionist and located practices, offer methods for the delivery of counter-narratives, and for residents to participate in discourses about their homes.

A taxonomy of council estate performance:

1. **Mainstream council estate performance**: plays written by a named playwright or playwrights, set on estates, that are performed in subsidized building-based theatres, that usually require payment for viewing and that often exist after the performance in the form of a separate published play text.

   E.g. Jonathan Harvey's *Beautiful Thing* (Bush Theatre 1993), Ché Walker's *Fleshwound* (Royal Court Theatre 2003), Janice Okoh's *Three Birds* (Royal Exchange Theatre Manchester 2013)

2. **Issue-based council estate plays**: plays, often ostensibly mainstream in their form, but which are primarily concerned with highlighting a specific estate-based social issue and might or might not be performed in a subsidized theatre building, and might or might not charge for entry.

   E.g. Akran Creative's *Estate of Mind* (Alhambra Studio 2009), Lucy Beacon's *Demolition* (Theatre Royal Stratford East 2013), Cressida Brown's *Re:Home* (The Yard 2016)

3. **Applied council estate performance**: performance practices that involve outreach or grass-roots work, conceived by established organizations, either with estate residents or with estates as their focus.

    E.g. *The Block* (National Youth Theatre 2010), *Puck of the Estate* (Box Clever 2012), *The Boy's Project* (Bryony Kimmings Ltd 2014–2016, suspended due to lack of funding)

4. **Located council estate performance**: performance work taking place on council estate sites.

    i. **Site-specific**: performances taking place on specific estates that are devised or written for those sites and cannot be performed elsewhere.

        E.g. *Sixteen* (SPID 2008), *SLICK* (National Youth Theatre 2011), *The Forgotten Estate Project* (University of Nottingham 2012)

    ii. **Site-generic**: performances designed for generic estate sites that might move between sites.

        E.g. *Super Human* (SPID 2008), *Noise Project* (South London Gallery 2012), *Summer Scheme* (SPLASH Arts, ongoing)

    iii. **Community-based site-specific**: performance and other artwork that is staged on specific estates and is made by or with the resident community.

        E.g. *A Life, A Presence, Like the Air* (Caitlin Shepherd and collaborators 2017), David Robert's work on Balfron Tower (see Roberts 2018), The Drawing Shed (ongoing)

5. **Located arts practices 'as' council estate performance**: installations and located visual artworks, in estates, that might be framed 'as' performance in one way or another.

    E.g. *I Am Here* (Fugitive Images 2009–2014), *The Market Estate Project* (Various artists 2010), *I Wish To Communicate With You* (Goodwin Development Trust 2017)

6. **Resident-artist led**: performance works or events made on estates or elsewhere by professional artists who are also estate residents.

    E.g. *Lock Up Performance Art* (Jordan McKenzie 2011–2013), 'Look at the E(s)tate We're In' (Jordan McKenzie/Live Art Development Agency 2013), *Neighbourhood Watching* (Michael Needham, ongoing)

7. **Estate protest**: activism and protest events making 'performative' use of estate space, actively resisting policy changes and redevelopments that impact estates. This category might also include artistic practices (films, plays, artworks etc.) produced as part of or in response to such protests.

E.g. the Focus E15 campaign's occupation of the Carpenters estate in Newham, London, and the performances based on this occupation, *E15* (Lung Theatre 2015) and *Land of the Three Towers* (You Should See the Other Guy 2016); Steve Ball and Rastko Novaković's *Concrete Heart Land* (2016), a film that records the resistance to and criticism of the redevelopment of the Heygate estate in Southwark, London

8. **Quotidian estate performance**: encompassing everyday performative practices – including both the daily practices of estate residents and their representation in 'everyday' media such as the newspaper press, on film, on the internet and on television

In the context of national and global housing crises, the role of critics and artists is crucial – both in drawing attention to the injustices caused by a broken housing system and in imagining new ways that housing might function for those without the means to buy or rent privately. My investigation uses specific case studies from a range of practices to offer a critical exploration of how performance mediates and produces the council estate. This type of critical perspective is useful in shedding light on the variety of ways that performance and performative practices might intervene in popular discourse and operate both within and against the conditions of a neoliberal global landscape.

Why spatiality? Methodology and theoretical frameworks

I frame this book as a spatial study. This is not only because it focuses on a specific type of what I refer to as 'generic place', but also because it is concerned with understanding how theatre and performance practices operate spatially. Specifically, I am concerned with examining the role of performance in what Lefebvre calls the 'production of space' (1991). The production of space is the continual interaction between the perceived, the conceived and the lived elements of space; as Nadine Holdsworth outlines, Lefebvre, 'explores how spaces are never empty but always loaded with meanings actively produced and re-circulated through dynamic social practices' (2007: 296). I am concerned with how theatre and performance operate as dynamic social practices and the potential that artworks might have to push against the dominant narratives of estate space that circulate within popular culture. In this way I conceive of estate performance as what Edward Soja, in his extension of Lefebvre's paradigm, termed a 'Thirdspace'. Drawing on Jorge Luis Borges's short story *The Aleph* (1971) in which the author presents a limitless space, unbounded by time, Soja conjures his vision for the Thirdspace:

> Thirdspace: the space where all places are one, capable of being seen from every angle, each standing clear; but also a secret and conjectured object, filled with illusions and allusions, a space that is common to all of us yet never able to be completely seen and understood, an 'unimaginable universe', or as Lefebvre would put it, 'the most general of products'.
>
> (Soja 1996: 56)

This deliberately abstruse definition invokes the complexity of spatial experience and acknowledges Soja's reading of Lefebvre's work: that any articulation of space can only be an 'approximation' of an infinitely complex and intangible thing. Soja proposes that an engagement with Thirdspace necessitates a 'praxis', a 'translation of knowledge into action in a consciously – and consciously spatial – effort to improve the world in some significant way' (1996: 22).

Performance practices that foreground site are often both inherently and explicitly political; the impetus to make work that challenges established conventions, that takes place in non-traditional spaces and includes or represents peoples marginalized in one way or another, is often related to a desire to engage in praxis: to make a difference to the world, to bring about change in the way we understand and relate to our environments. Thus, it is the 'praxical' element of Soja's model that makes it a useful tool for the analysis of performance in contested and non-traditional spaces. He provides a method with which to explore the conditions that structure the life experience of the subaltern 'other' through a close engagement with marginalized sites.

Although the use of Lefebvre's ideas about spatial production (and their extension by Soja) as an analytical model is by no means a novel approach to spatial analysis, I have taken the decision to centre this model order to position this book within an existing body of interdisciplinary theory concerned with spatiality (e.g. Rendell 2006, Holdsworth 2007, Munjee 2014). By drawing on a model widely used within the social sciences and artistic disciplines, I am able to use this study to offer insights into a range of representational practices within a performance studies context, while also allowing the work to resonate with scholars and artists beyond the discipline.

Using spatial theory as a lens through which to examine the relationship between the council estate and performance practice has enabled me to reveal how space is organized in the public imagination to produce and sustain social and political injustice. It has also enabled me to think about how performance operates in and through different types of spaces (the theatre building, the city or town where it is set or takes place, a specific estate). I have been particularly concerned with understanding how interactions between the institutional context (where and by whom the performance is produced), the social domain (in which sites and with whom the performance engages) and the material and aesthetic qualities might implicate theatre's potential to enable 'affective spatial resistance' (Holdsworth 2007: 296). In order to uncover the different kinds of interactions that exist between institutions, social domains and artworks, in what follows I examine theatrical performances from a range of practices that I broadly term mainstream, located and resident-led (see taxonomy, above). I also include a chapter on 'quotidian' performance, which considers how the estate 'performs' in mundane and sensational ways in everyday life, as well as through 'everyday' representation (television, film, newspaper press). This type of analysis *across* practices, with a focus on what I call the 'generic place' (here, the council estate), adds new potentials for understanding how representations interact with the social and political contexts of like places to produce space.

A note on 'place'

The role of space in the shaping of identity has been importantly theorized by scholars, who have differentiated the term 'space' from 'place' by suggesting that the latter constitutes 'meaningful location' (Cresswell 2004: 7). De Certeau's (1984) definition of 'place' as different from 'space' focuses on the relationship between specific places and identity; his definition suggests not only that places are created and defined by those who use them, but that the meanings attributed to places, in turn, work to create and define their inhabitants. Place is thus an important feature of spatiality. As Silvija Jestrovic notes, theatrical representations feed into the construction of spatial 'meaning', which shapes and alters the production of the 'future meaning' of spaces 'in cultural memory' (2005: 358). Jestrovic's work suggests that theatre might play a role in both the making of place and, through the reshaping of the 'collective knowledge' about places (2005: 358), feed into the creation of spatial identity that impacts on people's identity making.

Trialectics: A methodology of threes

Soja proposes that dialectical analyses are often reductive, falling victim to what he calls 'the lure of binarism' (Soja 1996: 53–60).[15] He appropriates Henri Lefebvre's central argument in *The Production of Space* (1991), suggesting that Lefebvre's triadic model usefully 'recomposes the dialectic' through a process he calls 'Thirding-as-Othering', where a 'third' element serves as an 'intrusive disruption that explicitly spatializes dialectical reasoning' (61). This 'trialectical' approach to spatiality emphasizes the ceaseless interplay between the perceived, conceived and lived elements of space which, Lefebvre argues, make up our spatial experience of the world (1991).

Soja's argument about the limitations of dialectical analysis and his emphasis on 'three' has been criticized. In a review of *Thirdspace* Andy Merrifield calls the term *trialectic* 'silly' (1999: 347). Merrifield argues that the notion of a trialectic adds unnecessary complexity to the already 'confusing' concept of dialectics (1999: 346) and that Soja's argument fudges the history of late twentieth-century scholarship, where dialectical analysis in the work of scholars such as Adorno, Benjamin, Althusser and Ollman already embraces multiplicity (Merrifield 1999: 348). Certainly, Lefebvre understood that dialectical analysis invites non-binary complexity. His criticism of Hegel's 'dialectic logic' notes that 'contradiction and even illogicality remained inside [Hegel's] system' (Lefebvre 2009: 41–45). The inherent problem with Soja's conception of the trialectic is, as Merrifield points out, that it remains, frustratingly, unapplied. That is, the trialectic remains at a theoretical distance from Soja's analysis of spaces and places in *Thirdspace*. However, despite its problems as a coherent theoretical concept, Soja's ideas have endured because an application of the trialectic – through an engagement with 'three' – offers a useful method for writing about and thinking through spatial practices. This is because looking at three things lures us away from simplistic or binary readings and encourages a complexity in the analysis (and in the readers' interpretation of that analysis) that is capable of revealing the complexity of the political structures that operate through space.

In the remainder of this book, I bring three performance or performative examples into conversation in each chapter – exploring how performances operate in their specific contexts to produce space. In this way, I offer an 'approximation' of a field of practice, while acknowledging the impossibility of a holistic account. It is intended that when read as a whole the book will offer the reader an understanding of the role of theatre and performance practice in the production of council estate space, while also enabling the reader who has limited experience of these places an opportunity to engage with an 'approximation' of estate space itself – acknowledging, of course, that analysis has its limits: applying this model to a different set of performances may well lead to different conclusions.

Structure of the book

The remainder of this book is structured in four chapters and a conclusion. The first two chapters introduce many of the themes and ideas that recur in the following chapters and so are longer. In Chapter 1 I trace 'quotidian' performances of the council estate and consider how these resonate with international discourses about economically marginalized spaces and people. Using Imogen Tyler's (2013) method of 'figuring', I examine the performance and performativity of estates in everyday life and in cultural representations that purport to depict everyday life. Using three examples of 'real' estate residents and their depiction in the media (Karen Matthews, Cheryl Cole and Mark Duggan), I illustrate how the real and the represented operate in a perpetuating cycle, creating and sustaining environments that are misunderstood and threatening to outsiders.

The following chapters each examine three examples of estate representation in theatre and performance forms (broadly conceived), using the 'trialectic' model discussed above to unpack how different forms operate to produce estate space. In Chapter 2 I explore mainstream estate representations staged in subsidized English building-based theatres (*Rita Sue and Bob Too/A State Affair* at Soho Theatre 2000, *Port* at the National Theatre 2013, *Denmarked* at Battersea Arts Centre 2017). I consider how new writing practices that operate to 'give voice' to under-represented communities nonetheless often reinforce the discourses they intend to disrupt. I suggest that this is a problem compounded by the ubiquity of social realism and by the inherent injustices produced by institutional structures.

Chapter 3 focuses on located estate works made by non-resident practitioners that invite 'outside' audiences and participants onto estate sites in one way or another (The National Youth Theatre's *SLICK* 2011, Roger Hiorn's *Seizure* 2008 and Fourthland's 'Wedding to the Bread' ceremony 2017). I explore how these practices engage in an ambivalent politics of site, thinking through how discourses of artwashing and gentrification frame the works and complicate potential readings.

Chapter 4 centres on estate residents, with a focus on how resident artists in east London have made 'theatrical use' of estate space (Jordan

McKenzie's *Monsieur Poo Pourri* film series 2010, Fugitive Image's *Estate: A Reverie* 2015 and Jane English's *21B* 2015–2017). Here I argue that such practices have potent political potential and might be considered as what Richardson and Skott-Myhre call 'hood cultural politics' (2012). I suggest that grass-roots work happening on estates is part of a connected global movement attempting to counter the neoliberal market forces that use cultural representations to create and sustain poverty. I offer three strategies used by resident artists, offering a 'way in' to understanding how hood cultural politics is articulated by residents making art practices on or about their own estates.

To conclude, I summarize insights from the case study examples in 'three thoughts', including an outline of my theory of the spatial ecology of council estate performance. I develop the term 'spatial ecology' to refer to the way that the aesthetic and political always exist in a dialectical relationship with one another. I suggest that spatial artworks rarely operate only as active forms of resistance against the status quo. Rather, they are part of a complex ecology – a system of organic and organized structures that interact to author the work. I argue that council estate representations always operate as part of this complex spatial ecology.

1

Quotidian performance of the council estate

We are constantly framing our experience of the world through representational systems. To interact with others we require a shared language, and even our visual experience involves a kind of literacy as we learn to interpret the conventions associated with photographs, cinema, paintings, street signs and so on. These systems are necessary but also dangerous. They lead us to believe that the world is a fixed and orderly place and that we occupy a privileged position of stability and coherence within it.[1]

(Kester 2004: 20)

*

My personal experience is my mum and dad. I think both of them were brought up on [an estate]. Or in one. So, they've always – until they got married really – lived in council housing. Obviously, this is years and years and years ago. So I grew up with their stories of how they were brought up. And they would paint a very lovely picture in a way: of community and everybody knowing each other and happy times, really, on the whole. But of course, media today – because we do get fed don't we, media, whether we like it or not? If you were to say 'council estate' to the Daily Mail or the papers or something [laughs] it would be a negative thing wouldn't it? Because so many of the images we get from them, or words we hear about them, aren't good. You know, they're either sink estates, or they're in need of repair, or they're being pulled down. And the people in them: there's always something wrong with them, or they're poor and they don't have many chances or opportunities, you know?

(Interview with audience member, *Off the Endz*, September 2011)

*

The first episode of *People Like Us* (BBC Three 2013) is introduced by an enthusiastic continuity announcer: 'It's been named the most deprived estate in Britain!' he tells us, almost breathless with excitement. 'And Harpurhey is the location for a new *real* reality show on BBC Three!'

The programme opens with tinny, buoyant music and a montage of moving images played in quick succession, narrated by an upbeat voice-over.

A tower block looms as the camera pans across it. Unaccompanied children roam suburban streets on bicycles. Parents sit on doorsteps drinking lager from cans as they rock their infant children in pushchairs.

'They say this area's just full of rough families', a cheerful young woman with a broad Manchester accent, immaculate make-up and thick false eyelashes says to camera. 'But I don't think it's such a bad place.'

A teenage boy falls backwards from the roof of a van onto which he is loading used mattresses. A mother and son argue aggressively with each other, sat side by side in a pair of worn brown armchairs. Someone lifts a Staffordshire bull terrier, its jaw locked around a thick rope noose, into the air and swings it in circles.

'There's a well-known local expression', an older gentleman wearing thick, plastic-rimmed spectacles and a fair-isle sweater tells us. ' "They'll steal the shit out of your arse." Not because they want it', he explains. 'Just so that you haven't got it.'

An overweight man is handcuffed and led towards a police van by a swarm of uniformed officers. A group of drunken teenagers cavort provocatively with one another at a wild house party.

'Are you the neighbour from hell?' an unseen interviewer asks a flame-haired teenage boy.

He shrugs. 'Probably, yeah.'

A youth with a skinhead haircut stands on a dilapidated street and watches a tarantula crawl across his t-shirt. A newly married couple is showered with confetti. A woman in a hospital bed cradles her newborn baby.

'Youse might think you know people like us', the same cheerful, immaculately made-up young woman says, 'but you don't know nothing yet!'

*

There is no doubt that the representation of council estates across popular news and screen media has served, in the main, to denigrate estate space and 'other' those who inhabit it – despite resistance to stigmatizing narratives from academics, journalists, online commentators and residents themselves (Allen et al. 2014, Jensen 2014: 5). As numerous scholars have shown, council estates and their residents are made regularly to perform in service of the dominant, neoliberal discourse surrounding poverty, welfare benefits, labour and capital: a discourse in which the council estate resident is positioned as pathologically lacking and morally deficient (Gidley and Rooke 2010, Tyler 2013, Shildrick 2018). But, as the above description of the opening sequence of the BBC Three reality television show *People Like Us* demonstrates, these popular estate representations, while ultimately producing negative, stigmatized discourse about estates, often operate through a paradoxical synthesis of the mundane and the sensational, producing an aesthetic in which residents' lives are depicted, at least on the surface, as both dismal and exotic, 'other' and ordinary.

People Like Us is one example of so-called 'poverty porn' (Jensen 2014) – sometimes called 'prole porn' (Adiseshiah 2016: 150): reality television programmes that expose the 'real' lives and lifestyles of Britain's poor working classes. In recent years there has been a proliferation of such shows, in which the everyday lives of 'the poor' are filmed and edited for the titillation, outrage and consumption of viewers who are assumed to live differently (and better). Such shows exploit 'the prurient fascination [with] just how badly behaved the poor have become' (McKenzie 2015: 12). Estate-focused poverty porn is a subgenre of a wider field of '[m]akeover programs, reality crime shows and observational documentaries', which serve to '[represent] the socially subordinate as shameless scroungers, overdependant, unproductive, disruptive and unmodern' (Nunn and Biressi 2010: 143). In these programmes, as in other estate representations, the estate location comes to signify the classed identity of the subjects.

A cursory glance at the titles and content of a range of estate-focused poverty porn highlights how such programmes feed into the creation of estate space in the public imagination, stigmatizing social housing residents while depicting their lives as paradoxically quotidian and sensational, mundane and salacious – an aesthetic I call 'sensational mundane':

- *Council House Crackdown* (BBC One 2015–2018), in which investigators track down and evict social housing tenants illegally subletting their homes;
- *How to Get a Council House* (Channel 4 2013–2016), in which viewers follow the complicated process by which people become social housing tenants;

- *Britain's Weirdest Council House* (Channel 4 2016), in which the 'unique' décor of a series of 'creative council tenants' is showcased;
- *My Million Pound Council House* (Channel 5 2015), in which we are shown the 'very desirable' homes of owner-occupiers (as opposed to social tenants) on a number of British estates; and
- *People Like Us* (BBC Three 2013), in which we follow the lives of young people in Manchester's Harpurhey district over the course of a summer.[2]

These ubiquitous, everyday representations influence how viewers come to understand estate spaces and, despite being televised and therefore physically removed from the estate site, nonetheless make up part of the experience of estate space at the level of the 'quotidian'.

Exploring the intersections between theatre, race and the law in America, Joshua Takano Chambers-Letson has proposed that 'overlapping and often contesting narrative and dramatic protocols akin to aesthetic forms of cultural production' operate to structure and produce 'formations such as the law, politics, history, nation, and race' (2013: 4). He argues that aesthetic practices serve as 'vessels for the mediation of legal, political, historical, national, and racial knowledge' (2013: 4). Chambers-Letson's work evidences that such knowledge production is especially important in the formation of marginalized subjectivities. Indeed, knowledge about council estates – including their legal, political, historical, national and racial formations – that is created and circulated by 'overlapping and often contesting' representational and narrative forms is central to the continued marginality and exceptionalism of estates and their residents. The 'deeply entangled' realms of 'social structures' and 'aesthetic practices' (Chambers-Letson 2013: 4) serve to foster our understandings about how the world of the estate works at the level of 'the real':[3] representations of the 'sensational mundane' estate space and social structures (such as policy and the law) operate in a perpetuating cycle, which is visited on the physical spaces of estates and has tangible impacts upon the lives of residents.

As the statement ('a *real* reality show') of the continuity announcer who introduces *People Like Us* suggests, much of the appeal of poverty porn shows lies in their supposed relationship with 'the real'. Such programmes are marketed on the basis that they offer 'authentic' access to places and people regularly alluded to in the newspaper press, depicted in television programmes, films and literature, but often marginalized and therefore hidden from mainstream culture. Although of course estate residents themselves are likely to consume poverty porn television, the rhetorical structures and content of the programmes position council estate residents as 'other' to the decent middle class who are euphemistically positioned as the viewing majority. In other words, estate poverty porn sets up a voyeuristic relationship in which – as the tongue-in-cheek title *People Like Us* infers – the estate and its residents are presented as essentially and eccentrically different from 'you', the imagined viewer.

Poverty porn television programmes are one example of a category of estate performance that I refer to in the taxonomy offered in the introduction to this book as 'quotidian'. Whereas Chambers-Letson applies the term 'quotidian performance' to make clear the distinction between 'every day acts of self-presentation' and 'aesthetic works of cultural production' (2013: 6), my use of the term is intended to encompass a range of performances that intervene at and beyond the level of the 'every day'. Unlike the other categories offered in my taxonomy, where the term 'performance' refers fairly straightforwardly to theatrical and other cultural practices, the quotidian category encompasses a messy range of self-presentation and cultural production practices. My use of the term 'quotidian' therefore embraces the 'confusion' that Chambers-Letson proposes exists between the cultural and artistic spheres (2013: 6). I consider how the behaviour of residents and its mediation might be understood 'as performance' (Schechner 2013: 9) in a variety of ways. My 'quotidian performance' category straddles Richard Schechner's continuum, in which 'both every day and specialized cultural domains' exist 'at the opposite pole[s] of everyday life', but 'with especially small gradations in between' (Pitches 2011: 4).

I am interested in the ways that representation in popular media and cultural forms distorts and often erases the boundary between the everyday and the 'culturally produced', working performatively to create estate space, producing 'that which it claims merely to represent' (Butler 1999: 5). Thus, this chapter considers how estate space and those who inhabit it are performatively represented in everyday depictions in the newspaper press, on television, in film, documentary and in literature, *and also* the means by which residents and others are called to perform in myriad ways in response to such depictions. This type of enquiry necessarily calls into question the complicated relationship between the real and the represented.

Figuring the real

Using the 'trialectic' model I presented in the introduction, I explore below quotidian performances of the council estate through an examination of the representation of three 'real' council estate residents who became notorious over the past decade or so. The residents I have selected, 'deviant mother' Karen Matthews, charged with kidnapping her own child, pop star Cheryl Cole, and Mark Duggan – the young man whose death at the hands of the police sparked the 2011 England riots – demonstrate how representations of 'the real' are leveraged to reinforce dominant understandings of the council estate: how 'real' people underpin the creation of what Tyler calls 'figures'. This is a term she uses 'to describe the ways in which specific "social types" become over-determined and are publicly imagined (are figured) in excessive, distorted and caricatured ways' (Tyler 2008: 18). Tyler draws on cultural and media examples in which working-class groups are categorized according to reductive stereotypes, thus reinforcing dominant understandings of the poor working class that circulate in contemporary culture. She describes how, for example, university students 'have been absolutely instrumental in the *fabrication* and *corporealization* of' the 'chav' figure:

> For over a decade now, Britain's students have held 'chav nites' in which they dress up as chavs. Female students carrying plastic bags from cut-price food superstores, push cushions under tight tops to feign pregnant chav bellies, and drink cider and cheap lager, enjoying the affect of being imaginary chavs.
>
> (Tyler 2013: 166)

According to Tyler, this kind of everyday cultural (re)enactment of the lives of the poor allows 'those who use, invoke or indeed perform this name [chav] to constitute themselves as "other than poor"' (Tyler 2013: 167).

Tyler's method of analysis, which I build upon below, involves 'tracking the repetition of specific figures within and across different media' in order to understand how 'representational struggles are often played out within highly condensed figurative forms' (Tyler 2008: 17). As she explains,

> we should understand mediation not only as representational (in a more structuralist sense) but as a constitutive and generative process. A figurative methodology makes it possible to describe – zoom in on – appearances of a figure within specific media and contexts, whilst also insisting that it is through the *repetition of a figure across different media* that specific figures acquire accreted form and accrue affective value in ways that have significant social and political impact.
>
> (Tyler 2008: 18–19, original emphasis)

Tyler's figuring allows us to see how 'classed figures serve as shorthand for classed discourses which have real consequences in the social world' (Gidley and Rooke 2010: 103). Tyler proposes that her 'figurative' analytical method requires a synthesis of the material and the semiotic; as she argues, 'signs and signifying practices are understood as having material effects that shape the appearance of and our experience of others' (Tyler 2008: 18).

While Tyler tends to take broader condensed 'figure' categories – the 'chav' and 'chav mum', for example (2008 and 2011) – as her point of analysis, my study reveals the way real people become figurative, forced to span the blurred lines between fiction and reality and serving to reinforce the idea that representations based on gross stereotypes are rooted without contention in 'the real' (see also Gidley and Rooke 2010). My analysis mobilizes Tyler's model by unpacking how 'real' figures become authenticating apparatus: these 'authentic figures' are used as material examples that come to signify the supposed 'truth' underpinning broader, condensed categories such as the 'chav'.

Tracey Jensen suggests in her article exploring poverty porn that the rapid production of media representation and commentary occurring in the contemporary media climate can have 'a flattening effect on public discourse' and serve to create 'doxa', which make 'the social world appear as self-evident and requiring no interpretation' (2014: 1–2). The three examples I examine in this chapter serve to demonstrate how the quotidian lives of estate residents are figured within this culture of rapid production and commentary as 'sensational mundane', creating estate doxa through the intertextual figuration of exceptional cases across media. The three examples I use highlight some of the dominant tropes of estate representation that I will revisit throughout the course of the book.

In the remainder of this chapter, then, I offer an overview of the 'real and the represented' in council estate discourse, before exploring three 'real' people's figuring across media. I demonstrate how, in estate representation, real and fictional elements operate in a perpetuating performative cycle, creating environments that are misunderstood and threatening to outsiders. I trace how these quotidian depictions connect local, global and national discourses relating to class, race, gender, poverty, welfare benefits and contested social space.

Real and represented: The problem with estate authenticity

In her book *Dramaturgy of the Real on the World Stage*, Carol Martin poses two important questions regarding the relationship between the real and the represented in contemporary culture: 'can we definitively determine where reality leaves off and representation begins? Or are reality and representation so inextricable that they have become indiscernible?' (2012: 2). These

questions encapsulate some of the key departure points for contemporary
performance studies scholarship. Performance studies as a discipline has
increasingly become fascinated with the relationship between the real and
the represented, and analyses of a wide range of practices have addressed
the complex relationship between what happens on stage and the way this
reflects, creates and affects the world beyond (see e.g. Forsyth and Megson
2009, Tomlin 2013, Sachs Olsen 2016). As Andy Lavender (2016) points
out, authenticity has become a significant means by which twenty-first-
century performance practices are conceived and understood. His concept
of 'truth-turning' suggests that the 'authentic', the 'true' and the 'real' circulate
as central, if intangible, features of contemporary performance practices –
important to artists and audiences despite the impossibility of any one 'truth'
manifesting in representation (Lavender 2016: 25).

The language of 'the real' permeates culture at many levels and is often
conflated with 'authenticity', which becomes an important official and
unofficial measure by which the quality of representations created for artistic
or entertainment purposes is judged and through which trust in public
figures and institutions is articulated. Martin suggests that the contemporary
preoccupation with 'the real' in theatre and performance practices (and
indeed scholarship) is part of a wider 'cultural obsession with capturing the
"real" for consumption even as what we understand as real is continually
revised and reinvented' (2012: 1). It is difficult, and certainly beyond the
scope of this book, to trace this contemporary concern with the 'authentic
real' in any depth. Exactly what individuals mean when they make claims
about a work's authenticity differs depending on context and is bound up
in numerous historical, philosophical and ethical conceptions of the term.
What I want to emphasize here is that it remains the case that in popular,
everyday usage the term 'authentic' suggests that the object it is applied to
has an intangible moral or aesthetic quality that includes a relationship with
'truth' and, often, by extension 'reality'.

The cultural obsession with the 'authentic real', at the level of both
representation and policy, can be seen in the language used by Arts Council
England (ACE), both formally, in reports and policy documents, and
informally, in blogs and other public relations activities surrounding their
work. The word 'authenticity' is positioned as important in understanding
the value of artistic and cultural practices. For example, a 2015 ACE report
titled *Developing Participatory Metrics*, documenting a project designed to
explore possibilities for 'a new set of standardised metrics to measure the
quality of participatory work across the arts and cultural sector' (ACE 2015),
proposed 'authenticity' (whether the work 'felt like a real artistic experience'
(ACE 2015)) as a possible quality measure. Meanwhile, in a blog post about

the merits of libraries, ACE CEO Darren Henley proposes that one of the reasons libraries should be valued is because, as trusted institutions, they 'have authenticity' (Henley 2015). 'Authenticity' in these examples is positioned as both related to 'the real' and synonymous with 'trust': an intrinsic or value-added quality, which is inherently positive and that unquestionably enhances the substance of cultural products.

Reflecting the emphasis on the 'authentic real' circulating through arts policy and more widely in contemporary culture, creators of stage, screen, visual, musical, journalistic, literary and scholarly works representing council estates often go to some lengths to make claims about the work's 'authenticity'. Very often these claims relate to the extent to which 'real' estate residents have been engaged with the work as authors, subjects or collaborators. Nunn and Biressi (2010) argue that part of the critical appeal of TV show *Shameless*, a Channel 4 drama centred around the chaotic Gallagher family and their neighbours living on the fictional Chatsworth estate in Manchester, lay in 'its authenticity as an idea conceived by Paul Abbot', the lead writer who referred to his own 'difficult, emotionally fraught, impoverished' upbringing in interviews promoting the show (149). Similarly, promotional material for the Royal Court Theatre's performance *Off the Endz* (2010) mentioned the status of the writer Bola Agbaje as an estate resident and housing officer, and often noted that members of the cast, including lead actor Ashley Walters, had lived on estates. In the resource pack for *Off the Endz*, a collection of documents about the show that the Royal Court make available online for educational purposes, director Jeremy Herrin suggests that his own lack of direct estate experience did not hamper the play's authenticity because 'most of the actors came through a very similar social situation as the characters, you know grew up on estates' (Royal Court 2010). Similar claims for first-hand experience by an author resulting in 'authenticity' circulate in relation to estate scholarship; for example, McKenzie's book documenting her ethnography of the St Ann's estate in Nottingham (2015) was praised online and in press and scholarly reviews for its 'authenticity' (see e.g. Duckworth 2015, Power 2015), a word used to highlight the fact that McKenzie was herself a resident of St Ann's.

When leveraged to validate estate representations in this way, the term 'authentic' (in addition to its association with the real) conjures at least two particular conceptions of authenticity, which I discuss in more detail below and which recur frequently throughout the examples discussed in this book. The first involves the relationship between art and authenticity, which as César Graña (1989) highlights has long been a recurring theme in the Western philosophical tradition. The second involves the relationship between authenticity, ethics and cultural exchange. I propose that these conceptions of authenticity serve to underpin each instance of council estate representation, which is always part of a 'truth-turning' exercise. This means that estate representation is inevitably subject to what has elsewhere been called a 'burden of representation'.

This burden of representation exists wherever a marginalized group is represented, because movements calling for wider representations of marginalized groups have usually resulted in individual people or groups speaking on behalf of others. Because of this,

> Representations [of marginalized people or groups] thus become allegorical; within hegemonic discourse every subaltern performer/role is seen as synecdochically summing up a vast but putatively homogenous community. Representations of dominant groups, on the other hand, are seen not as allegorical but as 'naturally' diverse, examples of the ungeneralizable variety of life itself.
>
> (Shohat and Stam 1994: 183)

In representations of council estates the burden of representation is magnified as different conceptions of authenticity crystallize to create a totalizing authentic affect.

Estates, authenticity and the burden of representation

César Graña notes that the concept of authenticity in art has long been connected with ideas of mystical revelation or of the artist as a vehicle through which 'ultimate meanings' are revealed (1989: 18).[4] He acknowledges that the philosophical concern with truth as revelation of 'ultimate meanings' is beyond the scope of a sociological enquiry, but does note that a sociological enquiry can usefully 'make the connection between the intricate circumstances of a given moment in social time and the revelation of those circumstances by the exalted manifestation of their expression' (1989: 33). As I articulate above, the circumstances of the 'given moment' of the estate in performance are bound up with a contemporary preoccupation with authenticity, where it is sometimes perceived that a (single) representation might be capable of representing the authentic totality of estate experience.

However, while the notion of authenticity as offering access to 'ultimate meanings' remains a residual feature in contemporary conceptions of art and authenticity, uses of the term today are no longer primarily connected to mystical revelation of an ultimate reality, but more closely related to ethical concerns regarding representation, ownership and authorial subjectivity. Much of this ethical concern resonates with debates regarding cultural appropriation and colonialism. Kwame Anthony Appiah (2006) has discussed the ethics of appropriation in relation to artefacts removed or displaced from their place of cultural heritage. He reminds us of the brutality to which many cultures have historically been subjected. As Emer O'Toole points out, 'the ethical dimension of [intercultural theatre] practice is a source of controversy. Material inequalities and Orientalist relationships resulting from colonial pasts inform many meetings across cultures' (2012: 1–2). Under these circumstances, where so much has been taken already, stories – those intimate narratives by which a culture comes to know itself – are perhaps even more sacred. The silencing of voices through oppressive regimes of colonialism has often led to claims of misrepresentation from those silenced groups who have featured in representations where they have not had a 'say'. Rustom Bharucha's criticism of Peter Brook's *Mahabharata* in *Theatre and the World* is a pertinent example (1993: 69–88). In a more recent example, Richard Bean's 2009 play *England People Very Nice* was criticized for gross stereotyping of almost all the groups represented. In one scene pertinent to this council estate study, a disgruntled tenant smashes up a chair in a local authority housing office. Nicholas De Jongh argued that the piece featured the kind of 'malevolent stereotypes and caricatures you find in *The Sun*' (2009) – and Bean was accused of insensitivity and the playing of stereotypes for cheap laughs.

The spatialization of the class divide in the United Kingdom has been produced via a contentious system of representation and discourse. Just as colonialism operated to appropriate and decontextualize 'other' cultures, so too – as can be seen in criticisms of poverty porn – representations of estates have served to exploit estate residents and to appropriate and decontextualize working-class experience. As a result, deeply problematic power structures and stereotypes are often reinforced by reductive representations of working-class environments offered to audiences as entertainment and social commentary. As we will see, issues relating to class, race, ethnicity and gender are often conflated in estate discourse, meaning that depictions of estates often intersect with other ethical, political and representational concerns that circulate within popular culture. The postcolonial (and feminist) discourse regarding rights to representation, which has undoubtedly filtered into a wider social consciousness, leads to audiences of estate representations becoming increasingly alert and sensitive to the power struggles that complicate what Rustom Bharucha calls the 'principles of exchange' (1993: 1).

The absorption of 'rights to representation' debates into the mainstream means that work that cannot make claims to authenticity through the experience of its creators or participants leaves itself open to controversy and criticism. However, ethical representation is complicated by the fact that the 'authentic' voice of the playwright, actor or scholar is often supposed to equate with a universal artistic 'truth', more closely aligned to the concept Graña introduces – where the representation is thought to contain the essential, 'ultimate meaning' about the places and communities who are represented. As Anna Upchurch indicates, the ability of art to foster access to love and beauty has historically been bound up with notions of a moral 'truth' in which art is understood as 'intrinsically good' (Upchurch 2016: 15) – further compounding the morality of the authentic. Thus, those who can evidence a 'real' connection to estates are often presumed to offer resistant, ethical and 'true' depiction of estate life: their work is frequently framed as unproblematically 'authentic'.

Notions of estate authenticity also have parallels with the concept of 'realness' that circulates in hip-hop culture. Jeffrey Ogbar (2007) argues that 'realness' in hip-hop refers to a tough urban black male who is intimately familiar with and willing to confront the many challenges of the 'hood'. He points out that such 'realness' is 'inexact and dynamic' (38) and 'is inextricably tied to spatial notions that are represented by class and race assumptions as well as gender and generation' (7). Claims to 'realness' operate to suggest that only the artist with first-hand experience of the violence and disorder of the 'hood' can reflect the reality of that environment. As Tricia Rose (2008) argues, this focus on authenticity in hip-hop can serve to reinforce the injustices it reveals, as corporations exploit the most sensational aspects of hip-hop narratives for profit, unfastening them from any political movement and often neutralizing their capacity for resistance.

Despite the importance of enabling marginalized groups to 'speak for themselves', a model where both the revelatory and ethical definitions of authenticity are intertwined creates a troubling slippage between notions of artistic, revelatory 'truth' and notions of authenticity fostered by 'real' experience. This slippage further compounds the 'burden of representation' by creating an illusion of absolute authenticity, which makes it difficult to question the veracity of first-hand accounts. As Wahneema Lubiano has noted, authenticity has a troubling relationship to essentialism, and claims to authenticity often operate as a 'strangle hold' for political analysis (1997: 111). It is important then to both acknowledge that estate residents need platforms through which they can speak for themselves *and also* not to totally fetishize authenticity nor allow it to erase critical analysis. As bell hooks has stated, in relation to her critiques of black feminist writing, 'I suggest that we must do more than express positive appreciation for this work, that to engage it critically in a rigorous way is more a gesture of respect than is passive acceptance' (1990: 7).

Ogbar argues that because of the commercial and institutional structures that feed into the production of hip-hop, 'to narrowly define hip hop as an oppositional art or one that inherently resists racism or oppression is an oversimplification' (39). Similarly, in analyses of estate representation we must interrogate claims to authenticity in order to erase the pervasive assumption that any relationship to 'the real' automatically positions a work as oppositional, resistant and ethically uncontentious.

Karen Matthews: Deviant motherhood on the white working-class estate

In February 2008 a nine-year-old girl named Shannon Matthews, who lived on the Moorside estate in Dewsbury Moor, a district of the town of Dewsbury, west Yorkshire, in the north of England, was reported missing after she failed to return home from a school swimming trip. News of Shannon's disappearance was reported in the local and national press, with the inference that she had been abducted by a stranger as she made her way home from school. The 'stranger abduction' inference was particularly strong because, at the time of Shannon's disappearance, there was a heightened interest in the subject of child abduction due to the high-profile ongoing case of the missing three-year-old British girl, Madeline McCann, who had been taken from her bedroom at a holiday resort in Portugal the year before (Nunn and Biressi 2010: 150). The Madeline McCann case resulted in sustained, ongoing media coverage, including multiple press conferences in which her distraught parents appealed for her return. Madeline's mother, Kate McCann, was often pictured holding Madeline's favourite soft toy 'Cuddle Cat' during coverage of the case.

In the days immediately following her disappearance, Shannon's mother, Karen Matthews, fronted a campaign for her daughter's return that bore some similarities to the McCann campaign. For example, Matthews was pictured holding aloft Shannon's favourite soft toy, a small brown teddy bear. Karen Matthews allowed news crews into her home where she was filmed curled in the arms of her partner, Craig Meehan, each of them apparently distressed, wearing white t-shirts with 'Have you seen Shannon Matthews?' printed across the front. On 3 March 2008, Karen Matthews spoke at a televised press conference in which she appealed directly to the abductor: 'If you have Shannon will you please let her go?' (BBC 2008).

Shannon's disappearance resulted in a massive search, manned by '200 local police officers and a large number of local people' (Cotterill 2010: 454). According to Janet Cotterill, the campaign for Shannon's return led to 'a police enquiry costing £3.2 million and involving some 10% of the West Yorkshire

Police's manpower' (2010: 454). On 14 March, some twenty-four days after she was first reported missing, Shannon Matthews was found alive in the base of a bed at her step-uncle's house, having been restrained with the use of ropes and tranquillizers (Cotterill 2010: 454). Karen Matthews, Craig Meehan and Michael Donnovan, the uncle, were eventually arrested: Matthews and Donnovan on suspicion of crimes related to Shannon's abduction and Meehan on suspicion of processing indecent images of children. At trial Karen Matthews and Michael Donnovan were both found guilty of kidnapping, false imprisonment and perverting the course of justice and sentenced to eight years in prison, although Matthews maintained her innocence. It was widely reported that Matthews and Donovan had sceptically plotted the kidnap, inspired by the Madeline McCann coverage, in order to claim reward money that they (correctly) expected newspapers would offer for Shannon's safe return.[5]

The media coverage of Shannon Matthews's abduction and Karen Matthews's arrest and trial demonstrates how Karen Matthews was utterly defined and constituted 'in terms of her socio-economic status and social class' (Cotterill 2010: 455). This included attention to her lifestyle, in particular her romantic and domestic arrangements.

> Matthews' seven children by five fathers, her engagement in serial relationships, her call on welfare benefits and her poor parenting skills seemed to sum up the 'chav' lifestyle already firmly established in popular journalism.
>
> (Nunn and Biressi 2010)

As Cotterill's (2010) comprehensive analysis of the newspaper coverage surrounding the Matthews case argues,[6] attention to her socio-economic status and lifestyle intensified once she was arrested. Her speech, in particular her regional, northern accent, dialectical idiosyncrasies and grammatical errors served 'to further reinforce her working-class status', while her estate 'residency became highly symbolic' (Cotterill 2010: 458) throughout the reporting of the case. Indeed, the fact that Matthews's home was located on an estate and the assumed role of estate residency in contributing to her criminality was implied in a headline in the *Sun* declaring the Moorside estate 'nastier than Beirut' (Taylor 2008).

Press coverage of the Matthews case saw frequent intertextual references, resulting in conflation between 'the real' and the fictional. Matthews was compared to well-known fictional characters based on exaggerated stereotypes, such as Waynetta Slob – a grotesque working-class mother played by actress Kathy Burke in the comic television sketch show *Harry Enfield and Chums* (BBC 1994–1998) – and to characters from *Shameless*, with some newspapers suggesting that Matthews had taken the idea for Shannon's kidnap from an episode of the Channel 4 show (Cotterill 2010, Gidley and Rooke 2010, Hancock and Mooney 2013). In January 2016, the BBC announced the cast for a two-part drama chronicling the Matthews story. The estate location played a central role in the conception of the drama, with the title *The Moorside* referencing the name of the Matthews' home. The casting of Sheridan Smith, a well-known northern, self-professed working-class actor, created further slippages between reality and representation, with her implied knowledge of working-class 'reality' imbuing the project with an additional layer of 'authenticity'. When the show was aired in February 2017, it opened with the words 'This is a true story' emblazoned across the screen.

As Cotterill points out, even the frequent use of the word 'sink estate' in describing the location of the Matthews' home had a significant 'note of intertextuality', referencing 'the gritty style of social realism ... which often depicted the domestic situations of working class Britons living in rented accommodation and spending their off-hours in grimy pubs to explore social and political issues' (2010: 458).[7] In the figuring of Matthews, then, the complexity of the relationship between reality and representation became flattened and simplified. References to fictional characters in the media coverage erased the lines between 'the real' and the fictional, operating to suggest both that Matthews was a 'typical' estate resident and that the qualities embodied by the fictional characters to whom she was compared were rooted in 'the real'. In this way, Matthews's representation evoked the 'sensational mundane' aesthetic that I mention above: her actions and the environment she inhabits are depicted as both bleak and mundane, salacious and sensational.

In terms of the subject matter of this book, the Karen Matthews case speaks to several thematic tropes of estate representation (explored in more detail below) that permeate the dominant discourse: class distinction, deviant motherhood and white trash. In each of these areas Karen Matthews becomes an authenticating mechanism for a broader figurative category. Throughout the coverage of the case she was performatively constituted as a figure through which discourse about estates and their residents might be refracted. However, while most scholarly accounts of the Matthews case have emphasized that Karen Matthews's crime was used to justify stereotypical representations of the working class, I want to suggest that both as a 'victim' and then as 'perpetrator' Matthews's media performance was subject to a burden of representation. Although her depiction in the media in the aftermath of her arrest certainly operated to authenticate negative stigmatized understandings of poor, white, working-class mothers living on estates, it is also the case that even in early, sympathetic depictions it was presumed that the Matthews case might teach us something about the authentic totality of estate experience. From her very first press conference she began to be authentically 'figured'.

Class distinction: People (un)like us

On Sunday 2 March 2008, some seven days before Shannon was discovered, the *Independent* ran an article titled 'Missing: The Contrasting Searches for Shannon and Madeline'. Reporter Cole Moreton argued that the press coverage of the Matthews case was petering out, unlike the attention on Madeline McCann and her parents. The article suggests that the reason for the declining press attention is simple: class.

> Karen Matthews is not as elegant, nor as eloquent [as Kate McCann]. Middle England may not envy her life, or identify with it. But the 32-year-old looked as lost and in pain as any other mother would when she broke down in tears outside her home.... But it seemed that almost as much attention was paid to the fact that Karen has had seven babies by five fathers. Shannon's dad Leon Rose left four years ago.
> So the family is complicated, and working-class. The people of Dewsbury Moor don't have the connections, the finances or the know-how.
>
> (Moreton 2008)

Although this is a sympathetic account of the Matthews' plight, which attempts to critique the media coverage of the family (who were, at this point, not publicly known as suspects in the disappearance of Shannon), it nonetheless draws attention to the ways the working-class Matthews are already constituted as lacking. The assumption at the end of the quotation above, for example – that the Matthews are without 'connections' or 'know-how' – projects popular understandings about estate residents' supposed intellectual and cultural capital onto the family without substantive evidence. In fact, the Matthews were fairly well-connected within the local community who launched a campaign to find Shannon – the family were also eventually supported by national newspapers, who, as I mention above, offered a reward for information leading to Shannon's safe return (Jones 2011: 13–38).

Sociologists including Beverly Skeggs (2005), Steph Lawler (2005) and Tyler (2013) have shown that middle-class identities are constructed in relation to working-class identities. They suggest that the working class, often constituted in stereotypical or figurative forms, are created – as I suggest in the introduction to this book – as an 'other' whom the middle classes can position their identities against. Moreton's article recreates a familiar 'us/ them dichotomy' (Wray 2006 134), albeit while attempting to critique that very dichotomy. The language of the article recreates a pervasive worldview where middle-class tastes and values are leveraged in opposition and superior to working-class values. This dichotomy intensified in the wake of Karen Matthews's arrest, when the class difference between the Matthews and McCanns became a means through which class disgust could be articulated:

> It was not only the clothes worn by Karen Matthews which were critiqued. Even the T-shirts used as an additional appeal method were compared between the middle-class McCann's and the working class Matthews and represented a further powerful semiotic symbol of social class difference.
>
> (Cotterill 2010: 457)

The details of Karen Matthews's private life, her clothes, accent and class were set firmly against Kate McCann in order to position Matthews, and those assumed to be 'like' her, as pathologically lacking. Matthews was not just, in and of herself, an unseemly figure, but, according to press coverage, she was able to teach the (presumably middle-class) reader something about 'people like her'. For example, in an article in the *News of the World*, journalist Carole Malone painted a picture of British council estates, which as McKenzie argues, 'found blame' for Matthews's actions in the cultures and practices of estate space (2015: 153):

> People who'd never had jobs, never wanted one, people who had expected the state to fund every illegitimate child they had – not to mention their drink, drug and smoking habits … A whole legion of people who contribute nothing to society yet believe it owes them a living – good-for-nothing scroungers who have no morals, no compassion, no sense of responsibility and who are incapable of feeling love or guilt.
>
> (Malone 2008: 15)

As Skeggs points out, class difference is rarely directly named; rather, it relies on signification through 'moral euphemism', 'relying on the process of interpretation to do the work of association' (2005: 965). The estate often serves as such a euphemism: spatializing class distinction and securing the status of the poor working class as abject. I do not mean to suggest here that it is only middle-class or upper-class people who absorb these narratives – working-class people also read newspapers and watch television, and the

stigmatizing discourses contribute to how they come to know themselves
and believe themselves to be known by others (Shildrick 2018: 785).

The repetition of classed figures, in both fictional and 'authentic' forms,
serves to create the working class as 'disgusting' (see Skeggs 2005, Lawler 2005,
Tyler 2013) and to spatialize this disgust so that the council estate becomes a
material signification of the moral, social and economic 'lack' of its residents.
Such discourses leak out beyond the popular press, impacting political rhetoric
and policy. For example, David Cameron (then leader of the opposition) argued
that the Matthews' case served as a damning indictment on 'broken Britain':

> A fragmented family held together by drink, drugs and deception. An
> estate where decency fights a losing battle against degradation and
> despair. A community whose pillars are crime, unemployment and
> addiction ... These children suffered at the very sharpest end of our
> broken society.
>
> (BBC 2008)

Representations have material effects. The damaging effects of the kinds of
stigmatizing representations of estate residents epitomized by the Karen
Matthews case are not easy to trace. Nonetheless, as the 2010 Joseph
Rowntree report into estates in Bradford, Yorkshire, notes, 'inequality and its
impact on mental health and well-being are serious obstacles to sustainable
change, rather than inadequate services and high levels of deprivation as
such. Blaming estate residents for Britain's social ills will not bring about the
changes many of them aspire to' (Pearce and Milne 2010: 4). This suggests that
the way residents are implicated, or blamed, in popular, negative conceptions
of the poor white working class impacts on the power they feel they have to
manage and bring about change in their own lives and may even exacerbate
mental illness.

Bad mothers

Karen Matthews was figured as an archetypal 'bad mother'. In 2012 the news
of her release from prison caused ITV's flagship talk show *This Morning*
to remind viewers that she had been dubbed 'the most hated woman in
Britain'. The crime of kidnapping her own daughter sealed her status as an
'evil' mother (Telegraph Reporters 2017), which had anyway already been
widely confirmed through the 'moral euphemisms' circulating about the
family's sexual, social and domestic lives – not the least of which being that
Karen Matthews had had the first of her seven children at a relatively young

age (around twenty years old, according to ages and dates given in media coverage) and that the children were fathered by different men. These two aspects of her motherhood operated further to underpin her figuring in the media and thus to authenticate ongoing discourses about working-class motherhood that circulate in popular culture.

Gilly Sharpe argues that 'a trend towards later childbearing across the western world' has resulted in a change whereby 'the dominant discourse around "problem" motherhood has shifted from extra-marital childbirth to teenage or "early" motherhood' (2015: 1). Sharpe proposes that that the moral concern with young motherhood is intimately bound up with class prejudice, wherein 'class concerns are central to constructions of young motherhood as a social problem' (Sharpe 2015: 2). Her research with female offenders reveals that despite the stigmatizing discourses about young, working-class mothers, motherhood is in fact a significant factor in curtailing women's criminal activity – but that, nonetheless, many young mothers continue to feel the effects of stigmatization 'long after they have left crime behind' (1).

Both McKenzie and Sharpe have demonstrated that working-class mothers face increased state surveillance into their activities and private lives. In an article for the *Guardian* McKenzie detailed her experience of state intrusion into women's lives as a daughter, a mother and a researcher:

> Working-class single mums claiming benefits will be asked very personal questions about what for anyone else would be private matters. They have to disclose the name of the child's father, his address, where he works, so that the Child Support Agency can chase him up. If you cannot answer these questions (without good reason) your benefits are stopped. Benefit officials may look into your garden and check your washing line doesn't have any men's clothes on it, or use credit checks to see who may or may not be living at your address.
>
> (McKenzie 2016)

Both McKenzie and Sharpe also suggest that that motherhood is a significant source of pride and self-esteem for working-class women. McKenzie demonstrates that within the value system that operates on the estate where she carried out her research, motherhood ranks highly (2015: 91). While it is, of course, the case that many women of all classes find pride in motherhood, on poor estates the limited opportunities for value-making mean that the value ascribed to mothers is often intensified. In this context, the spectre of being labelled a 'bad mother' 'became a constant fear for the women' (108) McKenzie studied. As she explains, 'when you are valued through motherhood, and you, in turn, value motherhood, it is important that you are a "good mum", and that others see you as such' (108). This fear is no doubt compounded by a cultural landscape where the figure of the 'bad' working-class mother is constantly summoned to blame poor women for society's ills.

The 'moral euphemisms' circulating in regard to Matthews's age were intensified by her relatively large number of children. The fact she had seven children is repeatedly mentioned in media coverage in a way that works to suggest her 'sexual excess' (Adiseshiah 2016: 160), calling upon versions of the archetypal working-class woman as sexually deviant and immodest (see Skeggs 2001, Gidley and Rooke 2010). Tyler contends that the 'chav mum', the archetypal figure of the 'bad' working-class (often single) mother, has become such a prominent feature of contemporary culture that it 'marks a new outpouring of sexist class disgust' (2008: 26). She points to the fictional character Vicky Pollard, the fifteen-year-old single mother with 'more than 12' children (Fandom N.D), a comic creation for the popular *Little Britain* television series, as a significant method through which class disgust in the United Kingdom is articulated. She shows how Vicky Pollard, a 'subliterate, sexually promiscuous female chavette', became a cultural touchstone, used as a 'shorthand within "serious" debates about the decline of social and educational standards' (Tyler 2008: 28).

These popular derogatory conceptions of council estate women have real consequences for those women who live on estates. Cunningham and Cunningham state that pervasive stereotypes have the potential to influence the practices of public sector workers, such as social work teams, who come into contact with young mothers and other welfare recipients (2012: 127). Indeed, Karen Matthews's 'authentic badness' was leveraged by Conservative party councillor John Ward to vilify working-class mothers more widely. In a 2008 speech Ward stated, '[t]here is an increasingly strong case for compulsory sterilization of all those who have had a second child – or third, or whatever – while living off state benefits' (McKenzie 2009: 17).

My intention here is not to argue that Matthews was not a 'bad mother' – the moralistic binary of good/bad is entirely unhelpful in understanding this case or the wider context in which it has been situated – rather it is to draw attention to the way a familiar trope of estate discourse was leveraged within the coverage of a unique and unprecedented case to present Matthews as evidence for wider delinquency and deviance in estate mothering, and by extension the working class at large. The sensational nature of her crime is rewritten onto the mundane landscape of Britain's council estates and operated to legitimize derogatory discourse about working-class women (that they should be sterilized, that Matthews is an indictment of 'broken Britain' rather than an anomaly). In this way the estate is produced as 'sensational mundane', as the visibility of rare 'spectacular events' (Richardson and Skott-Myhre 2012: 19) subsumes the mundane and becomes a lens through which the everyday practice of estates is refracted and understood.

White trash: A global discourse

It is not only white working-class women who are represented as authentic figures of sexual excess, immorality and disgust. White men too are frequently positioned as lacking, deviant and disgusting in the mainstream media, as was exemplified by the case of Keith MacDonald, a young estate resident who had allegedly fathered up to fifteen children by fourteen different women. Like Matthews, MacDonald was positioned as an 'authentic' working-class figure, with newspapers calling on moral euphemisms that positioned him as feckless and shameful, implicating the working class in general. Ed West of the *Telegraph* used MacDonald to legitimize his view that estate residents are not only immoral but also uncivilized and primitive in their behaviour. He expressed concern at what he called 'state-funded inner-city polygamy' and argued that the welfare state 'has recreated the conditions of the savanna on British council estates' (West 2010), a statement that manages to be both classist and racist. Both Matthews and MacDonald might be understood as examples of archetypal 'white trash'.

The phrase 'white trash', while originating in the United States, has become pervasive on both sides of the English-speaking Atlantic to describe the stigmatized white working class. As Tyler points out, there are parallels between British invocations of the 'chav' and global conceptions of economically marginalized groups who are othered by the discourse of the local and national cultures in which they live. She suggests that '[w]hat characterizes neoliberal states is the creation of "wasted humans" within and at the borders of sovereign territories' (Tyler 2013: 7). These 'wasted humans', she suggests, are figured as socially abject, and that abjection creates 'classes of people who are, paradoxically, classless, a section of the population that has been omitted "from the processes of representation to the point where it can no longer think of itself as a class"' (Tyler 2013: 19).

The popular website, 'urban dictionary', which offers definitions for slang and colloquial phrases, describes 'white trash' as a

> term for white people that usually live in a trailer park. With low incomes that spend their tax returns on things like big screen TV's [*sic*] instead of clothes for their kids. These people tend to be mouthy and

fight frequently. Generally these people are uneducated and have little concern for personal hygiene.

(Urbandictionary.com)

This definition reveals how 'white trash' as an identity category creates an intersectional 'boundary' identity (Wray 2006: 134), which encompasses racial, spatial, economic, bodily, moral and social aspects to secure a group of people as utterly abject. As an identity category, 'white trash', with its focus on whiteness, allows us to see how the intersections between the 'big four' 'modal categories' of race, class, gender and sexuality feed into a 'larger process of social differentiation' (Wray 2006: 5). Lawler argues that, in England, attention to whiteness in media and fictional representations has increasingly focused on the 'problems' of the white working class, stripping the concept of whiteness from middle-class identities. In media conceptions of English whiteness, Lawler proposes, 'white-working class people have become cast as the bearers of a problematic and unreflexive whiteness that has come to be located in the past' (2012: 420). English white working-class identities are created around stories that position 'the white working class as racist, bewildered, threatened and unhappy, at the sharp end of multiculturalism' (422).

As Wray states,

> *White trash* and its related slurs exhibit the general features shared by symbolic markers of stigma and dishonor. Primary among these features are effects of symbolic distancing and social exclusion through moral disapproval, resulting in 'us/them' dichotomies that both enable and enact different forms of inequality, prejudice, and discrimination.
>
> (Wray 2006: 134)

Although the phrase 'white trash' is intimately and specifically woven into the fabric of US history (see Wray 2006), its adoption beyond the United States and its parallels with British conceptions of the white working class remind us that class and the inequalities it produces are of global concern. The Marxist argument that 'the history of European thought is premised on the foreclosure of the poor through practices of naming (class-making)' (Tyler 2013: 173) allows us to understand how seemingly local figurings are part of a global neoliberal project, predicated on 'naturalizing poverty in ways that legitimize the social abjection of the most socially and economically disadvantaged citizens within the state' (Tyler 2013: 171). Karen Matthews offers us a British example of a global discourse that has local articulations and consequences. Attention to these micro-articulations of global categories can help us to understand the nuanced processes by which people and places are marginalized and think through how local performance and other artistic practices operate in dialogue with global discourses that visit structural violence upon their victims.

Cheryl Cole: Working-class pride, escape from the estate and middle-class identity making

One week after Karen Matthews's conviction, the *Times* newspaper published an article titled 'Sink Estate Superstar'.[8] Journalist Giles Hattersley described a visit to Cresswell Street in Walker, a district of the northern English city of Newcastle-Upon-Tyne. Hattersley had taken this trip in an attempt to understand how pop star and 'national treasure' Cheryl Cole had managed to transcend her council-estate beginnings to achieve mainstream success in the music industry and the adoration of the British public. Hattersley's description of Cole's childhood neighbourhood reproduces some of the common signifiers of estateness, which we have already seen repeated in representations throughout this chapter. These signifiers contribute to an ongoing feedback loop that sustains the concept of the estate as 'dreadful enclosure'. He paints a picture of a bleak, morally desolate landscape in which residents are either terrified of their neighbours or are themselves the threatening, potentially violent criminals who are rightly feared.

> 'This is just a terrible place to live', sighed a pensioner, hunching her back against the cold. 'Drunk or drugged-up yobs roam the streets at night terrorising families. Law-abiding people are terrified to leave their homes after dark – and its only getting worse.'
>
> Others had defiant pride for these tatty streets, yet astonishment remained: how could one of their own have done such a thing?
>
> Perhaps you are thinking Cresswell Street was the home to Karen Matthews, the 33-year-old mother who was convicted last week of staging her daughter's kidnapping.
>
> Wrong. This terrace in Walker, one of Newcastle-Upon-Tyne's toughest neighbourhoods, was the childhood home of Cheryl Cole, 25, an extraordinarily pretty pop star and Wag[9] who is fast becoming the nation's favourite celebrity.
>
> (Hattersley 2008: 14)

Hattersley's article is an example of how the working-class credentials of actors, musicians and other prominent public figures are frequently used to frame stories of bravery, overcoming adversity and to signal the authenticity that is used to sell the products they create or are affiliated with. Cocker et al. indicate how celebrity class identities intersect with commercial and corporate interests and are often 'unsettled', enabling 'celebrity brands' to 'occupy multiple, contradictory identities' (2015: 503). Indeed, the implicit and explicit references to the working-class roots of famous people that circulate in popular culture are often contradictory, wrapped in ostensibly positive nostalgic conceptions of working-class pride, while, at the same time, repeating and sustaining reductive depictions of working-class communities and suggesting that success and public acceptance require 'escape'.

Throughout her time in the public eye, Cole's working-class identity has regularly featured in interviews, documentaries and commentaries on her life. Her council-estate upbringing is used to both contextualize and excuse her less-favourable behaviour (such as her 2003 assault on a nightclub toilet attendant) and to suggest that her success is exceptional, especially 'remarkable'. Cole herself also publicly references her council-estate background, usually in order to signal her 'realness' and to express pride in her roots and upbringing. While these expressions likely do reveal a genuine, deeply held sense of identity rooted in her working-class background that might be understood to resist the dominant discourse, the mediation of her identity barely allows for a resistant reading. Rather her 'pride' is politically neutralized through its unthreatening and often banal mediation, which inevitably positions Cole as nostalgic, a-political and unintellectual.

Attention to Cole's career and to the stories about her that circulate through popular culture again reveals significant tropes of estate representation and illustrates again how popular understandings of the council estate are performatively constituted through authentic figurings. Below, I examine how Cole's depictions across media forms operate to create her as an 'authentic' figure, reinforcing dominant ideas about community and nostalgia, escape from the estate and middle-class identities – which produce estate space in the public psyche.

Nostalgia and 'community': Working-class pride

The pop star best known as Cheryl Cole[10] came to prominence as a contestant on the 2002 reality television show *Popstars: The Rivals*. In the finale of the series Cole (then Cheryl Tweedy) was selected to form a girl group with four other contestants, resulting in the phenomenally successful pop group, Girls

Aloud. Her subsequent marriage to England footballer Ashley Cole, and their divorce following his infidelities, led to Cole becoming staple fodder for the British tabloid press: her marriage and many personal struggles, including apparently contracting malaria after a safari in Tanzania, were reported in forensic detail. In 2008, Cole became a judge on the popular *X-Factor* reality television show, which escalated the press interest in her life and activities and later saw her move to America for a short stint on the US version of the programme. A subsequent marriage and divorce, and her relationship with pop star Liam Payne, of the popular boy band One Direction, some ten years her junior, have continued tabloid and celebrity magazine gossip surrounding her life.

In her media appearances and the PR and merchandizing used to market her career, Cole's working-class background is often directly or indirectly referenced. During an episode of the UK *X-Factor* that first aired in 2010, for example, Cole confronted a contestant who had made derogatory remarks about her council estate upbringing. 'I believe you've made some comments this week about me being from a council estate', she said. 'You are absolutely right: I'm very proud of my roots and I'm very, very lucky' (LovesTweedyX 2010). This confrontation was much reported in the press (see e.g. Jeffries 2010, Johnson 2010), where it served to generate excitement about the show and to further reinforce Cole as a 'real' working-class figure.

Her 2012 autobiography expresses similar sentiments about 'pride':

> I feel very grateful to my Mam and Dad for giving me such happy memories, especially as I know now that it wasn't easy for them. The 'massive house' I remember was in fact a tiny, box-like council-house that must have been really cramped with seven of us under the one roof. There wasn't a lot of money, but as a little girl I never remember feeling poor ... Pride is a massive thing for Geordies and Mam made sure that, one way or another, we always looked presentable and we never went without.
>
> (Cole 2012: 2–3)

The colloquial language ('Mam', 'under the one roof') and conversational syntax in the extract above act as a nod to Cole's class identity, although in this context they are positively presented – unlike in the Matthews case where accent and vocal mannerisms were used to symbolize Matthews's moral and intellectual inferiority. As in the *X-Factor* example, Cole's words here have the potential to be read as resisting dominant representations of working-class estate life. However, both the everyday and the sensational, extreme events of Cole's life are delivered in a fluffy, prosaic, cliché-ridden voice throughout the autobiography – producing a work which is banal in the extreme, despite its spectacular 'Cinderella' narrative. In the figuring of Cole, the 'sensational mundane' is leveraged through banality, and that banality, being utterly unthreatening, operates to politically neutralize the resistance that a working-class 'pride' might imply.

It is important to remember that Cole's autobiography is ghost-written (by Rachel Murphy), that her words on television shows are co-opted by the press to boost viewing figures and act as 'clickbait' – attracting online readers to access articles about her life. As such Cole's public 'voice' is primarily a product that serves as a promotional tool for her music and television appearances and as a way to create merchandise – it is a means to generate profit from her fame. Its purpose is to reinforce Cole's marketability by creating the pop star as a 'brand': projecting her as a likeable, 'salt of the earth', authentic figure who poses no threat to the dominant order. For example, her references to economic inequality are politically neutralized by her assertion that childhood poverty did not negatively influence her life, but rather contributed to a cosy, stable 'down-to-earth' upbringing. On the one hand, this figure is a 'real' person, but she is equally a media construction and therefore it becomes difficult to disentangle the fictional aspects of her public persona from any underlying 'truths' about her life experiences.

Cole's expressions of pride in her working-class origins can be read through the frames of nostalgia and community. These two terms are frequently invoked in both scholarly literature and public discourse on estates. In the case of Cole they operate, on the one hand, to reinforce her as a fetishized, 'authentic', working-class figure while, on the other, feeding into wider conceptions of estate space and working-class identity that circulate in relation to council estates and their residents in the popular imagination.

Council estates are often subject to narratives of community, which reference a fantasy idyll of working-class life where sociality and collective identity are associated with safety, stability and mutual support (see e.g. Ravetz 2001: 140–149, Beswick 2016b). Zygmunt Bauman (2001) has proposed that notions of community can be dangerous; he suggests that negative perceptions held by outsiders have often operated to fracture and marginalize already marginalized groups further, as individuals accept external labels and form voluntary ghettos. Bauman's notion of community as a dangerous form of othering is useful in drawing attention to the way that Cole's representation across media creates nostalgic, ostensibly positive conceptions of working-class 'community' while, at the same time, positioning estate residents as a homogenous 'other'.

As scholar and writer Richard Seymour discusses, the white working class have often provoked 'a form of sentimental nostalgia and patronizing endearment' (Seymour 2017). In the figuring of Cole, the narrative of working-class pride constructs a sentimental, politically unthreatening figure whose authenticity is a commodity through which her music is marketed. The invocation of her estate heritage authenticates reductive narratives through which 'real' working-class nostalgia – and by extension the white working class at large – is depicted as sentimental, backward-looking, and politically redundant.

Although the flavour of nostalgia produced in the figuring of Cole serves to perpetuate caricatures of the working-class 'girl done good' which pose no threat to the dominant order, nostalgia is not in and of itself politically redundant (as I will expand later in this book). This is to suggest that there are perhaps ways of understanding Cole as a resistant figure, even if the media framing of her makes that difficult. Svetlana Boym (2001) illustrates how nostalgia is nuanced and complex and functions in distinct forms under different circumstances.[11] Boym highlights the various ways nostalgia may be leveraged critically. In doing so, she offers a model of two kinds of nostalgia: 'reflective nostalgia' and 'restorative nostalgia'. For Boym, 'restorative nostalgia does not think of itself as nostalgia, but rather as truth and tradition', while '[r]eflective nostalgia dwells on the ambivalences of human longing and belonging and does not shy away from the conditions of modernity' (xviii). Although Boym appears to suggest that it is reflective nostalgia that is most critically useful (342), I propose that it is within the dialectical exchange between the two types of nostalgia that there is potentially space for criticality. As Boym argues, '[r]estorative nostalgia protects the absolute truth, while reflective nostalgia calls it into doubt' (xviii). In an exploration of the character 'White Dee' in the poverty porn series *Benefit Street*, Kim Allen et al. (2014) indicate the ways that nostalgic readings of seemingly reductive working-class figures can resist shaming discourses of otherness. Similarly, Ben Jones critiques the negative discourse surrounding nostalgia. He uses the 'QueenSpark', an initiative created by working-class residents in Brighton, which included a newspaper and exists as an archive of writing and history, as a case study to argue that nuanced nostalgia allowed residents a means of critiquing the 'stigmatizing representations of working class neighbourhoods in the wider culture' (2010: 367). Jeanette Edwards too argues that pejorative conceptions of nostalgia are often reductive in explaining the complex ways that individuals express how they are connected to their environments (Edwards 1998: 148).

Escape from the estate

The concept of so-called 'social mobility', of 'escape' from the estate environment, recurs frequently in both 'real' and fictional stories about estate residents. For example, in the play *Off the Endz* (Royal Court 2010), the idea of escape frames the drama as Kojo and Sharon, an aspirational working-class couple, attempt to improve their financial circumstances through hard work so that they can move 'off the endz' (away from the estate). The criminal behaviour of their old acquaintance David and the temptations of easy money through crime eventually thwart their attempts at social mobility. The play was widely understood by critics as a 'morality' tale (a perspective reinforced by writer Agbaje's own estate residency) cautioning (black) estate residents against the easy criminal lifestyle presumably available to them. Similarly, an article on the BBC website written by poet Byron Vincent reflects on his trajectory into the middle classes, arguing that his successful social mobility enabled him to escape the culture of crime that blighted his teenage and young adult life (Vincent 2014).

The 'moral euphemisms' that circulate about working-class estate residents become less euphemistic when the question of social mobility or class escape comes into play. Here deterministic discourses (see Beswick 2011b: 427–430) that suggest estate space and working-class culture produce 'antisocial' morality are often in full view. Of course, as Vincent (2014) outlines in his account of his youth, the 'ghettoization and isolation' of impoverished communities do often work to produce criminal and so-called antisocial behaviour. However, the dominant narratives that circulate about estate criminality do not tend to draw attention to the fact that economic inequality produced by government policy and systemic disadvantage produce conditions for crime, but rather blame the poor working classes and the architecture of their environments for their circumstances. Even where there is an acknowledgement that policy and social structures do produce crime and violence, the idea that getting 'off' the estate is both possible and desirable underpins much of the moral discourse about estate spaces and is distinctly tied to the notion that working-class identity is shameful, lacking and undesirable. The concept that working-class people have their own system of values, indeed their own historical and intellectual culture, which has been suppressed, stilted and appropriated (see e.g. Winlow et al. 2016) by the dominant middle-class culture, and from which they have no desire to 'escape', is rarely if ever, articulated in popular discourse.

As I indicate above, Cole's estate residency is often alluded to in order to mark her 'exceptionality'. This exceptionality serves to reinforce the bounded nature of estate residency in two paradoxical ways: as an 'escapee' she authenticates the notion that escape is possible and desirable and that those who don't 'get out' have failed – while at the same time her 'exceptionality' does not erase her working-class identity. The fact that she is 'still' working class despite her economic achievements reinforces the idea that estate residents will never be fully embraced as members of the middle classes – especially not when they continue to express pride in their heritage. The idea that middle-class culture might need to change to accommodate working-class experience is entirely absent in exceptionality narratives, which focus on the escapee's will and ability to change. In this way, the exceptionality discourse surrounding Cole resonates with the social inclusion discourse that has impacted social policies (including arts policy) since the adoption of social inclusion as a key policy agenda under New Labour from 1997 onwards.[12]

The term 'social inclusion' is part of the 'social exclusion' agenda that developed out of debates surrounding inequality in France from about the 1970s.[13] Initially, these debates viewed exclusion as the 'breakdown of the structural, cultural, and moral ties which bind a society' and eventually as a way to define 'groups who had become marginalised, economically, socially or culturally' (McKenzie 2009: 27). It was absorbed into the popular British consciousness during the New Labour period (1997–2010), when social exclusion became central to emerging policies that sought to find ways to fight the structural causes of inequality (McKenzie 2009: 31–32). Thus, social *ex*clusion is the social phenomenon used to describe certain conditions produced by inequality, while social *in*clusion refers to the policy objectives concerned with addressing conditions of inequality. For example, 'social inclusion' is a core equality and diversity agenda emerging from the Equalities Act 2010 (Hyder and Tissot 2013).

As McKenzie (2009) has argued, the term 'social inclusion' operates as a part of a 'discourse of social exclusion', which works to identify injustice and also – because it operates from within existing structures of inequality – to create and maintain disadvantage.[14] As Michael Etherton and Tim Prentki's work indicates, social inclusion agendas often result in superficial measures which are primarily concerned with 'whether an excluded group now considers itself to be included' (2006: 148) and where 'it is much rarer for any assessment to be made about whether the marginal group has made any impact upon attitudes or behaviour in so-called mainstream society' (148–149). Cole's 'authentic' working-class identity is tolerable because she exists in the narrow gap between the kinds of mainstream success acceptable to the dominant political order and the stereotypical depictions of a politically redundant, backward-looking working class who pose no threat to the prevailing culture. In other words, she is able to be an exception precisely because she is unthreatening.

Middle-class identity making

In the Karen Matthews section above, I identified that authentic figures
operate to position middle- and working-class identities in opposition –
thus sustaining discourses of 'lack'. Here, I want to point out that even the
ostensible social mobility evidenced by working-class celebrity figures is
undermined by the ways they continue to be utterly bounded by their class
identity in media representations. Tyler and Bennet point to the importance
of the figure of the 'celebrity chav' in the creation of moral euphemisms that
'contribute to wider processes of social stigmatization and marginalization'.
They emphasize the performative elements of working-class celebrity culture,
contending that

> Celebrity is a form of improvisatory, excessive public theatre.
> It is class pantomime and the 'chav', a vicious and grotesque
> representation of the undeserving poor, is a stock character. Despite
> its apparent unpredictability (through regular exposés, scandals and
> embarrassments), celebrity culture has a highly formal structure with
> coherent, bounded narratives that permit and contain extemporization
> by a cast of recognizable social types.
>
> (Tyler and Bennet 2010: 380)

In an interview about her life, conducted by journalist and media
personality Piers Morgan, televised as part of a series called *Piers Morgan's
Life Stories* (2010), shown at prime time on the popular British network
ITV, Cheryl Cole appears at pains to emphasize the 'ordinariness' of her
day-to-day life. Explaining how she is far from the 'style icon' portrayed
by the newspapers, Cole tells Morgan: 'Sometimes I just wanna rock out
in me scruffs and me uggs you know?'[15] Morgan pulls a confused face in
response. 'Your scruffs and your uggs?' he says, laughing and imitating
her voice with a mock-Newcastle accent: 'What ... what are scruffs?'
(GirlsAloudFan79 2014).

This seemingly banal exchange characterizes his attitude to her throughout
the interview; while he is respectful of her 'nation's sweetheart' status,
Morgan – a former tabloid newspaper editor who speaks in the clipped RP
tones of the middle classes – goes to some lengths to illustrate the difference
in their backgrounds and behaviour using a mixture of faux-bafflement
and condescension. These exchanges serve to euphemistically underpin the
class difference between them and to remind the audience that, unlike Piers
Morgan, Cheryl Cole – despite her successes – is working-class and therefore
cannot entirely shake off the gauche and vulgar traits associated with her

class identity. At one point, for example, he asks about rumours that she spends excessive sums of money on clothes. 'I read that you spend a quarter of a million pounds a year on clothing', he says. And then, after a pause, 'And I note no immediate denial' (GirlsAloudFan79 2014).

As McKenzie (2015: 103–145) demonstrates, the fascination with how working-class people spend their money has increasingly featured in morally outraged coverage of estate residents and welfare-benefit claimants, who are often positioned as wasteful and economically ignorant, incapable of organizing their financial affairs. Morgan's question about Cole's spending habits – although denied by Cole – again serves to remind the audience of Cole's estateness and to authenticate narratives about estates and the working class that circulate in the public imagination. They also point (again) to the fact that working-class women's private lives are placed under scrutiny regardless of the wealth, achievements or personal circumstances in which they live.

If the interview with Piers Morgan serves to remind the audience that this nation's sweetheart is still a chav, an identity from which there can be no escape, then other much repeated 'facts' about Cole's life similarly operate as moral euphemisms that authenticate stigmatizing narratives about the white working class. For example, that Cole assaulted a black nightclub attendant in 2003 is repeated in newspaper articles and television coverage (see e.g. Singh 2011, Ellen 2012), while attention is frequently drawn to her tattoos (*The Graham Norton Show* 2014, Farmer 2016) and 'bad-taste' clothing (Fitzmaurice 2012, Mullen 2014). While such representations don't always explicitly name the ways in which Cole is morally objectionable, they feed into a received understanding of working-class women as 'repositories of negative value, bad taste' (Skeggs 2001: 298). So too they serve to authenticate existing white working-class identity narratives, in which working-class people are violent, prejudiced and reactionary.

As Tyler and Bennet (2010) and Tyler (2013) indicate, these kinds of narratives about working-class celebrity identity, and by extension the identity and character of the working class at large, are repeated in formal and informal ways on social media and blogs, securing the legitimacy of such identity narratives in public discourse. For example, in a thread about the nightclub assault on the social media platform Reddit, many of the 124 comments position Cole's behaviour as 'typical' of working-class estate residents:

I'm confused. When did being a racist, violent chav make you a celebrity?
    Shes [*sic*] a girl from a rough family from a rough estate got very lucky, can't change that upbringing.

> Nasty, conceited Geordie charver that somehow got "discovered" by
> a bargain basement (even for 2003) music show. If Pop Idol[16] had never
> run she would probably be hanging around Byker going why aye pet.[17]
>
> (Reddit 2015)

The stories that circulate about celebrities are significant. Like all stories, they inevitably shape the way we see and come to know the world. Narratives 'are important in working-class lives. It is how we explain ourselves, how we understand the world around us, and how we situate ourselves in a wider context' (McKenzie 2015: 6). Understanding and unpacking how persistent stories about working-class people are circulated and gain legitimacy can, as Tyler and Bennet point out, enable identification of and the challenge to social classification (2010: 390). Stories also serve as a means of resistance with which performance makers and artists can 'speak back' to official and dominant discourses that structure and produce spatial and classed inequalities, as we will see in later chapters.

Mark Duggan: Race, black masculinity and resistance on the council estate as hood

On 4 August 2011, Mark Duggan, a 29-year-old mixed-race father of four, was shot dead by police in Tottenham, London, following an attempted arrest by officers. In the days that followed his killing, friends and family gathered outside Tottenham police station seeking information about his death. By Saturday 6 August, a large group had gathered near the station. At about 9 pm violence erupted as tensions between police and those representing the Duggan family escalated, resulting in arson, looting and fights along Tottenham High Road and the surrounding areas. Rioting spread to neighbouring London boroughs and intensified. Over five days, as news of the so-called 'London riots' circulated in the press and on the popular 'BlackBerry Messenger' mobile phone service, parallel riots erupted in cities across England including Birmingham, Liverpool, Manchester and Nottingham. Images of young, often black and mixed-race, men and boys wearing hooded sweatshirts and engaged in acts of theft and violence were circulated across the news media as the riots took hold. There were five deaths nationally and numerous injuries to police officers, rioters and members of the public not involved in rioting. Many buildings were damaged and destroyed, and it was widely reported that the looting of consumer goods had been a significant feature of the riots in all the cities where they had taken place (LSE/Guardian 2011).

In the immediate aftermath of the 2011 riots politicians argued that the violence was the result of a 'feral', criminal underclass with no political motivation (Solomos 2011: 3). Prime Minister David Cameron announced that '[g]angs were at the heart of the protests and have been behind the co-ordinated attacks' – a statement later proven false by studies that demonstrated how gang members involved in violence acted as individuals and that the riots effectively served as an informal ceasefire between gangs (LSE/Guardian 2011: 21). In the mainstream newspaper press Mark Duggan was initially described as a violent 'gangster' with a criminal past. It was reported that he had been involved in serious crime, investigated for murder and that he had taken part in a shoot-out with police officers in the lead-up to his killing. Duggan was positioned as a figurehead for gangs of criminal, black men (although he was mixed-race it was his blackness that was euphemistically invoked in media coverage) who had unleashed a frenzy of lawlessness in the wake of his killing. In his initial figuring, then, Duggan served to authenticate ideas about dangerous black masculinity and inner-city estate violence. He was a vicious, drug-dealing career criminal, born and raised on the notorious Broadwater Farm estate (a site of riots that erupted as a result of tensions between residents and police in 1985, see Power 1999: 195–218) and as such his killing was euphemistically justified in the interests of order and public safety.

As in the figuring of Matthews and Cole, Duggan's initial representation in the mainstream media and beyond speaks to quotidian, stigmatizing ideas about the council estate and its residents that circulate in the wider culture. Namely, he authenticates the notion (discussed in more detail below) that inner-city estates are populated by violent gangs of (predominately non-white) disreputable men and boys who pose a threat to their communities. However, while the figuring of Matthews and Cole operate fairly straightforwardly to authenticate dominant, reductive narratives about estates – and by extension the poor working classes at large – the figuring of Duggan is more complicated. In the wake of his death, activism orchestrated by his friends and family and publicly supported by prominent activists (such as the racial equality consultant Stafford Scott) and racial justice groups (such as the Institute of Race Relations) led to a counter-narrative emerging in which Duggan's initial figuring was called into question. Although an inquest into his shooting found that Duggan had been 'lawfully' killed, the public discourse leading up to it and the eventual ruling complicated the official narrative – finding that Duggan had not been in possession of a gun at the moment he was shot and was therefore effectively unarmed. Duggan's 'resistant' figuring has served to underpin emerging, oppositional narratives about police brutality and institutional racism that circulate globally. He has become a cultural touchstone in discussions surrounding police race relations in the United Kingdom. This resistant figuring demonstrates how grass-roots movements can build on emerging global discourses to co-opt reductive representations for resistant political purposes.

In what follows, I trace how Duggan's figurings operate to authenticate ideas about the estate. First, I explore the relationship between race and class, and examine how Duggan's initial representation worked to validate reductive tropes about dangerous black masculinity. I then argue that his 'resistant' figuring demonstrates how the estate connects to global sites of inequality. I propose that by framing the resistant estate space as 'hood' marginalized communities can 'speak back' to official, reductive discourses as part of an international cultural political movement that imbues marginalized spaces and identities with resistant potential.

Race and class

The issue of race and the 'generic' council estate is complicated by geographical inflections. Race is a central, if contested feature of estate identity, nationally shaping how residents are understood and represented in one way or another. I indicate in the Karen Matthews section, above, how raced images of 'white trash' 'chavs' shape public perceptions of council estates and working-class residents. Lynsey Hanley argues that the current political discourse surrounding the 'white working class' operates divisively to fix working-class identities – 'whether or not they bear any resemblance to the messy reality' – as white (Hanley 2017a). As we have seen in this chapter, the white working class is often constructed as backward-looking, racist and 'lacking'. This divisive race politics operates to suggest that the white working class is a homogenous group, cut off from the daily realities of living side-by-side with people of all races.

Rogaly and Taylor (2011: 4–5) similarly argue that representations of the British working class are dominated by depictions of whiteness, while ethnic minorities are defined solely by their ethnicity, with class rarely operating as a significant identity marker. However, as the figuring of Mark Duggan illustrates, contemporary representations of the council estate do engage with the multi-ethnic reality of these spaces, in which the classed identity of ethnic minority groups is central. This 'multicultural' depiction of the estate, however, is geographically bound, with estates in London and other large cities (e.g. Birmingham, Bradford, Nottingham) often depicted as 'multicultural working class', while rural, suburban and post-industrial regions are frequently understood as 'white working class'. Fictional representations in television and film especially tend to separate 'multicultural' and white residents in geographical terms – with multicultural casts often used to depict the inner city, but focusing on issues relating to stereotypes of black subculture, particularly gangs (see e.g. *Kidulthood* 2006, *Sugarhouse* 2007, *Top Boy* 2011 and 2013), and majority white casts used to depict run-down suburbs and northern towns (*This Is England* 2006, *Fish Tank* 2009, *Shameless* 2004–2014).

As Anne Power proposes, there is a common perception that race is a 'root cause and explanation of social problems' on inner-city estates (Power 1999: 5). Les Back asserts that the racial discourse of the city effectively 'maps' urban areas and structures feelings of belonging or not-belonging to a particular place. He argues that 'racism draws a map, it creates places in the process of narrating them' (Back 2005: 19). Reay and Lucey (2000) meanwhile point out that young estate residents are often tainted by the media evocation of gang culture. The fear of a 'black crime wave' (Reay and Lucey 2000: 411) on the (generic) inner-city estate is one way that these spaces are created as 'dreadful enclosures'.

The complicated racial politics of council estates was demonstrated by the political and media coverage of the 2011 riots, some of which suggested that black gang crime on estates was central to the rioting (see Castella and McClatchey 2011). Fernando Duarte's (2011) description of council estates as 'pockets of apartheid' during his interview with Bauman on the causes of the rioting points not only to the spatial segregation of estates, but also to the increasing alignment of inner-city council estates with racial diversity and tension.

In an article published in the *Daily Mail* following the inquest into his death, Duggan's race and class were both euphemistically leveraged in order to position him as unquestionably 'bad'. The reader was reminded that he grew up on the Broadwater Farm estate and that he was raised 'largely by his mother'. Both of these facts suggest a classed identity and act as moral signifiers (with single mothers frequently blamed for social problems presumed to result from the disintegration of family values), which suggest his class already constitutes him as 'lacking'. In the images accompanying the online version of this article, Duggan is pictured with his arms around two black men who the newspaper describe as 'dangerous criminals'. The *Daily Mail* drew euphemistically on racial stereotypes to accuse the Duggan family of misleading the public about the identity of their son.

> His family and supporters continue to insist Mark Duggan was a 'peaceful' family man who abhorred violence.
>   But this photograph suggests his links with the criminal underworld were far deeper than first thought. Staring menacingly into the camera, the gangster poses with his arms around two dangerous criminals who

are each serving long sentences for murder and attempted murder. As
one police source said: 'He lived by the gun.'

(Martin 2014)

The figuring of Duggan as a violent criminal with links to organized crime serves
to authenticate the racist and classist notion that working-class black men are
dangerous and disrespectable. Stuart Hall has illustrated how representations
of race, ethnicity, class and gender are important, because they constitute 'an
essential part of the process by which meaning is produced and exchanged
between members of a culture' (1997a: 15). The perpetual representation
of members of a group using 'a few simple, vivid, memorable, easily grasped
and widely recognized characteristics' (Hall 1997b: 258) creates stereotypes,
which serve to reduce everything about a person or group of people to these
characteristics and 'fix them without change or development to eternity' (Hall
1997b: 258). Stereotypes form part of our experience of the world and influence
the ways we understand and relate to each other. In this way, stereotypes can
operate performatively to construct our identities. They have the potential to
form one of the 'structuring structures' (Swartz 1997: 100–103) that create
'habitus' – a term developed by sociologist Pierre Bourdieu (1977: 82), which
refers to the ways that learned behaviour shapes cultural behaviour and
structures life chances. As Richardson and Skott-Myhre propose, habitus
operates to make certain behaviours 'appear natural' (2012: 11). In other words,
repeatedly representing young black men as drug dealers and gangsters on stage,
on screen and in the newspaper press can serve to suggest that young black men
are 'naturally' inclined towards crime and violence. These representations, when
perpetuated, can influence the creation of social structures and the operation of
institutions (schools, the police, universities, theatres), producing conditions
under which certain young black men might, eventually, become more likely to
commit crime and violence than they otherwise would have been – not because
it is a 'natural' inclination, but because our experiences and opportunities
(including the representations that shape how we see and understand ourselves)
inform how we act. Which is not, for the avoidance of doubt, to say that Duggan
was unquestionably a violent criminal, but rather to point out the layered nature
of racial injustice and the damage that representations such as those in the *Daily
Mail* article I describe above can visit on communities.

Black masculinity on the estate

In the years and months leading up to Duggan's death, there was an increased
concern in the mainstream UK media and beyond with the relationship

between gangs and violent crime. In 2008, a sequence of fatal stabbings of young people in Greater London – including the high-profile murder of the sixteen-year-old white boy Ben Kinsella, brother of television actress Brooke Kinsella, by a group of black men – meant that the issue of knife crime, often represented as an issue emerging from the black community, was prominent in the news media and in popular cultural representations. In March 2008, debbie tucker green's critically acclaimed play *random*, which follows a black family for twenty-four hours in the lead-up to their son's murder, premiered at the Royal Court. That same month a documentary titled *Why Kids Kill*, exploring gangs in London and Glasgow, was shown as part of Channel 4's 'Dispatches' series. In March 2011, *Pigeon English* (by Stephen Kelman), a novel set on a South London estate and closely echoing details of the high-profile death of Damilola Taylor – a ten-year-old black boy killed on the North Peckham estate in 2000 – was published. The book was shortlisted for the Man Booker Prize. In September 2011 Arinze Kene's *Estate Walls*, a play exploring the threat of knife crime and its affect on black boys on a London estate, was staged at the Ovalhouse. Although these representations are not all, by any means, reductive depictions of black masculinity, they point to the cultural preoccupation with the relationship between gangs, race, class, estates and violence.

Discussing the 2011 riots on BBC's *Newsnight* programme, historian David Starkey drew on the public perception of a link between black masculinity and gang violence, invoking stereotypes of black men as 'naturally' violent criminals to argue that England had been polluted by a 'destructive, nihilistic gangster culture', in which 'the whites have become black' (*Newsnight* 2011). The England riots preceded a wave of filmic and television representations of young black men involved in gangs and violence in one way or another, often set on estates (e.g. *Top Boy* 2011 and 2013, *Sket* 2011, *Attack the Block* 2011).

Just as gender intersects with discourses of class in representations of working-class mothers to produce authentic 'deviant mother' figures, race discourse intersects with class and gender to create the working-class black male as an authentic figure of disrespectability. And, as fictional and 'real' examples of deviant motherhood operate to authenticate the notion that estate mothers are 'bad', so too the ubiquitous fictional and real representations of black men as criminal and violent circulate to secure the identities of black men in reductive, stigmatizing terms. The depiction of inner-city estates as populated by black men who are criminal gangsters, for which Duggan serves as an 'authentic' figure, is a divisive, racist trope. It operates not only to produce the estate space as dangerous and unseemly, but also to create and foster racial tensions on and around estates as the hypermasculine, criminal black male becomes a figure against which working-class white males can construct an oppositional 'respectable' identity.

This concept of 'respectable' white identity (see e.g. Nayak 2006, Rhodes 2011) serves to fuel racism and to 'other' black men further in the dominant estate discourse. Black women are mostly missing from the discourse entirely, especially in the news media – in films, plays and television programmes they mostly feature in a supporting capacity as accomplices in gang crime, bereaved wives and mothers, or judgmental bystanders (although there is a growing body of vibrant estate performance authored by and often starring black women that goes someway towards rectifying this lacuna, including Michaela Coel's play *Chewing Gum Dreams* (National Theatre 2014) and its television series adaptation *Chewing Gum* (2015–present), Jancie Okoh's *Three Birds* and Agbaje's plays including *Gone Too Far*, which was adapted into a film in 2013).

In popular representations then working-class black males are frequently aligned with gang violence, family dysfunction, criminality and drug use (particularly drug dealing) and have become synonymous with disrespectful council estate practice through media portrayals of black gangs. But it is this very divisive racial politics that produces the conditions for resistance. For it is through the repeated portrayal of disrespectable, dysfunctional, black culture that the council estate becomes 'hood' – embodying the danger, energy and political potential of the American inner city.

Council estate as hood

Despite its association with North America, Richardson and Skott-Myhre (2012) define the hood (slang for a marginalized inner city neighbourhood, usually populated by black and Hispanic people) as a multiple, shifting, global site of marginality.[18] They propose that, because of the appropriation of North American hood culture globally, the 'global hood' has become a conceptual space, which comprises multiple sites of struggle and resistance in a variety of low-income urban areas. This conception of a shifting, global site of urban struggle resonates with Walter's notion of 'the dreadful enclosure' (see Introduction).

Unlike Walter, however, who suggests that the 'dreadful enclosure' is a limiting fantasy, Richardson and Skott-Myhre argue that the hood is a space that 'can be both liberating and limiting'. They argue that in its global incarnation the hood is defined by its residents' 'activism, art, personal experience and day-to-day living' and can serve as a site of 'liberation and revolution' as well as one of marginalization (2012: 19). Richardson and

Skott-Myhre propose that the 'creative works within the hood and outside of it (re)present a cultural politics' (2012: 22).

The creative activity of the hood can be positioned as political because it is usually concerned with challenging existing systems of power and control in a specific spatial context – thus meeting Collini's definition of politics as 'the important, inescapable, and difficult attempt to determine relations of power in a given space' (Collini in Kelleher 2009: 3). The resistant potential of the hood's cultural politics hinges upon residents engaging in the production of creative works and activist movements – through which they challenge their marginalized position and survive in a culture weighted against them. The cultural politics of the hood can therefore be defined as a resistance 'against the forces of control and domination', where 'networks of self-production [are] no longer constrained by the axiomatic discipline of the dominant media, the state, or the market'. Importantly, these acts of resistance are produced 'within the bounded space of the hood itself' (Richardson and Skott-Myhre 2012: 19). According to Richardson and Skott-Myhre, it is from the located hood environment that residents are most effectively able to resist the dominant narratives produced about them by those outside of that environment.

They highlight Nas's album *Illmatic* (1994) and the movies *Boyz in the Hood* (1991) and *Menace II Society* (1993) as defining examples of hood representation. These commercially successful examples illustrate how hood practices are almost always created by (or with) artists who might be positioned as 'authentically hood'. For example, Nas grew up in the Queensbridge Houses Project, a public housing development in Long Island City, Queens; *Menace II Society* was directed by the Hughes Brothers, half Armenian, half African-American twins who were raised by a single mother in Los Angeles and have suggested that the movie worked within a paradigm of 'art-imitating-life or life-imitating-art' (Takako 2014); and *Boyz in the Hood* stars rapper Ice Cube, who grew up in south central Los Angeles, an area that was synonymous with gang violence and racial tension during the latter part of the twentieth century.

In addition to negative depictions of estates that we have explored so far, so too the 'spirit' of 'liberation and revolution' that Richardson and Skott-Myhre describe as a central feature of the cultural production of the hood has become an important feature of estate representation. One area in which this is particularly evident is British hip-hop music, which draws upon a conventional hood genre to politicize council estate space, celebrate estate culture and resist oppressive mainstream representations of estate spaces. Ostensibly autobiographical narratives of resistance in the face of poverty and struggle are significant features of British hip-hop music. Artists regularly refer to their personal experiences of living on council estates in their lyrics to suggest that such spaces, like the American hood, are identity-making spaces 'of creative force' that are 'built on a certain kind of survivorship and mutual suffering' (Richardson and Skott-Myhre 2012: 19).

For example, British rapper Skinnyman's single and music video 'Council Estate of Mind' (2004) draws on the conventions of hood culture to politicize the experience of living on a council estate. The music video for this track comprises intimate shots of the interior and exterior of a council estate from a first-person perspective. Affiliation with the American hood is suggested through shots of posters on the walls of the homes within the estate depicting the emblematic American rapper Tupac. The lyrics are darkly humorous and undercut with a sense of hopelessness. Like Tupac's music they can be read as a cry of despair, echoing out from the margins, calling for political intervention (Richardson 2012: 198): 'I live amongst smashed syringes / squatters' doors hanging off their hinges / hookers looking money for Bobby / shotting their minges.' However, the lyrics also portray a sense of collective experience, of survivorship in the face of desolation: 'So these lyrics are for my people / living on the streets who / know there ain't nothing else to retreat to' (Skinnyman 2004).

The history of the British adoption of hood culture, by both estate residents and outsiders, is undoubtedly tied up with the globalization and commercialization of hood identity, which has occurred through the successful marketing and distribution of the forms of cultural production mentioned above. Music corporations and commercial brands have cynically and exploitatively appropriated the generic conventions of the hood and the youthful, energetic 'spirit' it embodies over a number of decades. Hip-hop artists are regularly included in global marketing and advertising campaigns, with prominent brands such as Adidas receiving endorsement from hip-hop artists such as Run-DMC. There are certainly ethical questions to be posed regarding this globalization of hood culture, such as who profits from the appropriation and how such profits are distributed. Kitossa (2012) proposes that narratives of the hood are seductive and potentially dangerous; we must be mindful that urban marginality differs from place to place (Waquant 2008). The British appropriation of hood culture, particularly via hip-hop music, has been subject to accusations of fuelling American-style gang violence. However, rather than focus on these negative aspects of hood appropriation, already well-established in popular discourse (see Rose 2008), I am interested in how the global hood might have the potential to work as a resistant political space. This relies on understanding that the council estate is in fact a global expression of the marginalized hood and that hood culture has the capability of facilitating productive transnational exchange.

There is plenty of scholarly support for the idea that marginalized inner cities in both the United States and the United Kingdom have long been in dialogue. Indeed, the image of the criminal 'sink' council estate is bound up with ideas that emerged from the debates that arose out of Oscar Newman's (1972) *Defensible Space* study of public housing projects in New York (Minton 2017: 62–63). So the very discourse that creates estates as 'dreadful' might be understood as 'transnational' in its conception. As Andy Wood (2009) argues, although hip-hop's UK appropriation took on a specific and dynamic localized identity, it nonetheless enabled conversation and solidarity to emerge between local and global conditions for the black urban diaspora on both sides of the Atlantic.

The resistance to Mark Duggan's initial figuring in the press can be understood as operating within a cultural politics of the global hood. His resistant figuring demonstrates how he has been positioned to act as a 'voice' for those marginalized from mainstream politics and subject to stigmatizing representations. By using Duggan as a figure with which to 'speak back' to oppressive power structures, his family and supporters authenticate the wider struggles of marginalized black working classes and connect their plight to a global system of inequality that visits violence on the poorest members of a society.

Duggan's resistant figuring is encapsulated by the documentary *The Hard Stop* (2015), which explores the events leading up to Duggan's death and the effects of his killing on his friends. The documentary challenges the veracity of the official accounts of Duggan's shooting, relying on familiar 'hood' conventions (particularly the use of hip-hop music and fashion and the adoption of Americanized language such as 'hood' and 'feds') to position Duggan's murder and the subsequent struggle for justice within a framework of the global struggle for justice fought by poor, racially and economically marginalized communities all over the world. Duggan's friends, who appear in the film, celebrate their position as 'others' and readily admit they have been involved in crime and violence. However, the film, like many of the 'archetypal' hood movies described above, does not depict these acts of crime and violence as unquestionably 'bad'. Rather it reveals that the neoliberal system operates to produce conditions in which whole communities are angry, disenfranchised and eager for change.

The Broadwater Farm estate features significantly in *The Hard Stop*. It is positioned as a place of ongoing struggle for the community who live there: the estate is the site from which Duggan's supporters leverage their resistance. His cousin, Marcus, tells the viewer that he feels safe on

Broadwater and describes his and Duggan's childhood years living on the estate. He dispels the received understanding of Broadwater Farm as a 'dreadful enclosure'. Duggan's murder is placed within a history of ongoing tensions between police and residents. Invoking the 1985 Broadwater Farm riots, in which a police officer was killed after a black woman died during a police search of her home, the documentary suggests that Duggan's death was part of a trajectory of oppressive, divisive, state-sanctioned tactics in which young black estate residents are made to pay the price for the attempted resistance of their forebears. The aggressive policing methods that resulted in the death of a young father are at the centre of the film – the words 'the hard stop' reference a tactic whereby suspects are apprehended with no warning.

By drawing attention to the ongoing tensions between the police and the black estate community, and by using familiar hood conventions, *The Hard Stop* depicts Duggan's death as both a local, highly specific case of injustice and an event connected to international injustices. For example, as the Duggan family's struggle for justice was gaining significant public attention in the United Kingdom, the Black Lives Matter movement, campaigning for an end to systemic violence and injustice against black people, was gaining global traction. This movement grew out of a number of cases of police killings of black people in the United States and has been adopted globally by those who see the systemic racial profiling of black communities as an example of structural violence that sustains and perpetuates racism.

Of course, I emphasize again that despite the parallels between the North American hood and the contemporary British council estate, as Wacquant (2008) and Kitossa (2012) warn, direct comparisons between urban spaces 'run short of apprehending the distinctiveness of each of them' (Kitossa 2012: 127). While some of the appropriations of hood culture by British artists are undoubtedly rooted in local identification with global forms of resistance, there are marked differences between UK and US contexts. Therefore, we must be mindful that the notion of the hood has the potential to work as a potentially reductive, homogenizing fetishization.

However, understanding the council estate as an incarnation of a conceptual, global space, despite the problems with this approach, allows for an international contextualization of the activities that take place there. These located, ostensibly local activities are part of a network of global, grass-roots practices that exist alongside the structures that create the conditions that necessitate their existence. This grass-roots, global movement reveals how artists and activists, acting locally, can draw on international networks of support to build and enact resistance and signal working-class solidarity that crosses international borders.

The role of artistic performance practice?

The tropes of estate discourse we have seen revealed in the figurings of Matthews, Cole and Duggan demonstrate how everyday representations are constitutive in ideas about council estates. Residents are overwhelmingly implicated in council-estate discourse, particularly in news media and screen representations. This implication has significant effects – both in developing the habitus of individual residents and in creating a culture whereby the 'spectacular' elements of council estate practice become highly visible and create a totalizing narrative from which it is hard to escape. The term 'council estate' is often used as a stigmatizing shorthand, an ideological spatial container where social, economic and political contentions are contained and concealed. Despite the obviously devastating affects of this shorthand, it nonetheless means that estate spaces are fertile sites for fostering the conditions that might create the will to resist. As we will see, theatre and performance makers have used the estate as a site through which to explore the social conditions that structure and produce systemic inequalities. However, it is too easy to suggest that artworks will necessarily transform discourses or bring about change in a way that other media cannot. After all, they also operate *within* the systems that produce disadvantage. As Jen Harvie notes in her exploration of socially engaged art practices, 'broader social and material contexts' shape 'opportunities for qualitative experiences' of and participation in artworks (2013: 10). The ideas produced and sustained by quotidian performances of the council estate circulate through arts practices in various ways, providing a social context which structures possibilities for the reception of artworks. Any consideration of the role of arts practices in producing space must therefore consider the dynamic spatial context from which they emerge – reflecting on how the institutional, aesthetic and social conditions of works operate as overarching structures that produce meaning. The following chapters will, therefore, take the relationship between institutions, aesthetics and social contexts as a starting point for analysis.

2

Class and the council estate in mainstream theatre

I know [the writer] has got first-hand experience, so at least it's coming from a point of view where he can say: 'No actually, I've seen that, so why not put it in?' But it's different being like, 'it's being realistic and reflecting reality', because you can argue that but at the same time, I think, you could write about anything so be careful what you're writing about. It's not necessarily good enough to say you're reflecting reality, because you're also, you're choosing to write a play: you're saying something.

(Interview with youth theatre participant, 2011)

*

When I was young – younger – I think I was about 20, I discovered Samuel Beckett. And I was fucking blown away. I could not believe that towards the end of his life he gave up on English, started only writing in French. He gave up on French and was writing in silence. He was writing plays with no words. For TV. For ITV, broadcasting Samuel Beckett on a fucking Saturday night. I was blown away by him. I started reading everything I could get of his; stuff I didn't understand I would force myself to read it again and again. I found out there was a play on called End Game, *in town. And I'd been out gigging the night before, I'd got absolutely hammered – me and my drummer had nicked a bottle of rum from behind the bar – because we weren't getting paid anything, so we got really smashed on the way home. So, I'd woken up late and I had tickets for a matinee that I'd booked. And I was really hung over, and, I shouldn't say this in an interview, but I'd vomited the night before and it was on my shoes, and I was like 'fuck it, I've got to go and see this play.' So I ran, ran across town, arrived kind of sweating, feeling really uncomfortable, it was in a really big theatre in town, like one of the big West End ones, and I ran in, turned my phone off, and there was like, this middle aged very wealthy couple in front of me. I was just in time and I was turning my phone off and she turned around – the woman – and she hit me. She*

hit my leg. And I was so shocked, I was so shocked, that [had happened]
in this environment. But I didn't know that she wasn't allowed to do
that to me. Because everything was – nothing was comfortable. So I sat
there and thought 'I don't belong here. Everything, everybody's telling
me I don't belong here.' So I put my phone away, was like 'oh, sorry', you
know? And I watched the play and like: it was fucking, it was for me. He
wrote that play for me. . . . I think what happened was I sneezed, and she
hit me again halfway through. But I think because I felt so unwelcome
anyway there. Everything about it made me feel like I didn't belong, but
the artwork itself.

(My interview with Kate Tempest, September 2016)

*

June 2006: My mother and I are at the National Theatre waiting to watch
David Eldridge's *Market Boy*, which is being shown on the Olivier Stage.
I am a Drama graduate and have almost finished an MA in Acting at a well-
known drama school. As a family, we have often visited the theatre – we
have a tradition of seeing a big West End show or major London theatre
production every Christmas. But we speak with 'working-class' accents
(my mum's is Essex inflected and mine broad south east London), we are
loud and our sentences (mine mainly) are peppered with swear words.
Usually, I don't feel out of place in a theatre foyer, but tonight there is
a stuffy air at the National Theatre bar: I am hyper-aware of the other
audience members, dressed in expensive clothes and speaking in braying
voices with their clipped, polished RP accents. I carry two large glasses of
wine back from the bar and a woman looks me up and down – I imagine
I'm dressed in jeans and Doc Martens, but I can't quite recall – and tuts
loudly. I feel brash and uncouth – exposed and uncomfortable, as if I am
vulgar and don't really belong.

In the queue for the toilets just before the play starts my mum and I are
chatting excitedly, this is a rare night out together and we have been looking
forward to it – partly because the show we're about to see is set in 1980s
Essex, in the working-class world of market stalls and single mothers,
white stilettos and struggling to survive under Thatcherite politics. My
mum, having been raised by a single mother in a council house in Essex
during the 1970s, is excited about seeing the world of her youth depicted on
stage. As we laugh in the toilet queue, wedged in the small, tiled partition
between doors that serves as both entrance and exit, a haughty middle-
aged, middle-class woman in a black fur coat leaves the toilets and shoves
my mother out of the way. She's dismissive and superior, annoyed that we
were so engrossed in our conversation we didn't see her trying to get past

us. 'Will you learn how to behave in the theatre!' She admonishes. My mother is about to apologize but I step between them, angrily explaining to the woman that just because the toilets are badly designed, and she feels ownership over the theatre space, she does not get to speak to my mother that way. Perhaps my language is not that measured. Perhaps I block the door so the woman can't get out. Perhaps I push her against the wall and say she can't leave until she has apologized to my mum.

My mother and I enjoy the show, but there are parts of it that don't ring true in terms of our experience – we think the 'Mum' character, played as frumpy, meek and unassuming, doesn't have the hard, solid edges of the single mothers we know. As we leave the auditorium I overhear a posh-sounding woman praising the show's authenticity. 'And the thing is', she says to her husband. 'That's just what it was like. The playwright lived through this you know.'

*

Until very recently, class politics has sat euphemistically beneath many of the public, academic and policy-driven discussions surrounding theatre practices. A reluctance to name class directly has contributed to the ambivalent class relations that operate within the mainstream theatre space, and that will be the focus of this chapter. When theatres launch programmes aimed at attracting 'socially disadvantaged' groups, when ACE reports mention engaging 'lower socio-economic' and 'community' audiences, the implications are that those groups are, at least in part, comprised of working-class people (who are also often non-white) who will be improved or have their lives improved by engaging with events at theatre venues and who need different kinds of events to attract them to the theatre. The anxieties evident in arts policy and academic literature are symptomatic of far deeper anxieties that result from the systematic and structural devaluing of the working class in the wider culture, discussed in the previous chapter.

Class-naming

ACE's avoidance of directly naming class inequality was especially visible in their 2011 report *Arts and Audiences: Insight*, in which they used a 'segmentation' method that enabled them to categorize the population in class-based terms, without ever explicitly mentioning class. For example, members of the population considered 'non-engaged' in the arts were organized into groups with euphemistic titles including 'limited means, nothing fancy' and 'a quiet pint with the match'. ACE's description of the latter group, quoted below, points to participation in so-called 'low' culture and local pastimes, revealing how it is possible to mark a segment of the population as working class without actually saying so: summoning stereotypical, commonly accepted understandings of working-class people as parochial, closed minded and unsophisticated.

> This group spend a lot of their free time at home, and there they tend to watch TV or play computer games. Aside from this they go out to the pub for a drink fairly regularly.
>
> Watching TV is their main pastime, but they may also be found participating in team sports such as rugby or 5-a-side football or going fishing to relax. A small proportion plays the pools, bingo and poker regularly.
>
> They are fairly conservative in their outlook, have little interest in other cultures and are not environmentally minded. As the majority struggle for money they place most value on material gains as a sign of success.
>
> (ACE 2011: 50)

This excerpt reveals how *Arts and Audiences* positioned working-class groups in negative terms (i.e. as lacking) by their 'non'-engagement with the arts, despite the ready acknowledgement of a rich engagement with 'low' cultural activities. By 2017, ACE had changed their segmentation terminology: 'limited means nothing fancy' and 'a quiet pint with a match' were replaced by a category called 'up our street' – a group identified by their 'modest habits and means' and engagement with 'popular culture' (The Audience Agency 2017).

The attitude towards the working class evident in the *Arts and Audiences* reports bears the residue of ideas that Upchurch explores in her book about the formation of the arts council movement, where intellectuals and philanthropists understood providing access to the arts as their moral duty and a means to address social problems. The enhancement of arts practices (along with 'love, beauty … and nature'), in this model, was understood to constitute 'the "sole criterion of social progress"' (Upchurch 2016: 15). This moral position, rooted in the values perpetuated by an 'intellectual aristocracy' (Upchurch 2016: 50), ultimately risks elitism – as we see in the way that cultural pursuits are classified in euphemistically moral terms (those attending poker games, fishing or playing football are 'not engaged', while those attending exhibitions, gardens and cultural festivals are 'engaged'). As Linda Strudwick, Development Director of Heads Together, a grassroots arts organization based in Leeds, Yorkshire, suggested in a blog post written after ACE's 2017 round of National Portfolio Organisation funding was announced, the Arts Council's terminology operates to justify their continued funding of 'high' arts practices – thereby further distancing the working class from access to the means of cultural production. She argues that 'the ACE model to fund organisations to produce "great art" and then try to force those same organisations to widen participation hasn't worked' (Strudwick 2017).

By avoiding explicit class-naming, ACE participates in a wider phenomenon, which Tyler draws attention to in *Revolting Subjects*: the erosion of class analysis, which fuels the neoliberal myth that class inequalities have dissolved in contemporary culture (see Tyler 2013: 156–159). This myth has impacted the possibilities for a politics of effective resistance to the global order based in class identification (Winlow et al. 2016). In other words, by ensuring class remains unnamed it becomes impossible to address the macro- and micro-injustices that permeate neoliberal culture and result in class inequality where structural violence is visited on the poor in large and small ways. These injustices filter into the inequalities evident in the creation and dissemination of arts practices, including theatre, and contribute to the marginalization of working-class people – and by extension working-class culture – in all spheres of cultural production (see Oakley and O'Brien 2016) and reception. The Acting Up Inquiry, an initiative led by the Labour Party seeking to explore the barriers facing working class and ethnic minority workers in the performing arts, has evidenced that 'snobbery, stereotyping and racism' work alongside structural and institutional barriers to produce 'a diversity crisis on our stage and screens' (Brabin et al. 2017). This inquiry marks a recent turning point, where issues of class in the arts appear to be gaining explicit acknowledgement in the mainstream cultural sphere – with a spate of newspaper articles (see e.g. Gardner 2018, Love 2018), performances (see e.g. Common Wealth's *CLASS: The Elephant in the Room* 2017, Ellie Harrison's *Power & Privilege* 2018, Scottee's *Working-class Dinner Party* 2018) and scholarly works (see e.g. Murphy 2012, Barrett 2016, Friedman and O'Brien 2017) naming and addressing the issue of class in arts and culture.

As Paul Murphy (2012) points out, a reluctance to address issues of class also characterized theatre scholarship in the first decade of the twenty-first century as global capitalism intensified class-based inequality and issues of identity politics solidified around race and gender. While attention to class in theatre scholarship has increased since (and in part as a result of) the publication of Murphy's article, focus on class is often either concentrated on the textual analysis of plays in relation to the sociopolitical context in which they are performed (Murphy 2012, Adiseshiah 2016) or on the practices of theatre institutions themselves (Bell 2014a, Brigden and Milner 2015) in attracting or excluding working-class audiences and artists. Scholarship has more rarely (although not never, see e.g. Barrett 2016) offered detailed consideration of the ways in which class politics are embedded in theatre-going on both micro- and macro-levels and solidified through the dynamic and sometimes ambivalent interplay between the institutional, social and aesthetic dimensions of performance works.

Theatre: A matter of class

It is usually presumed that theatre is predominately attended by (mostly white) middle-class people; certainly the fact that theatre audiences 'tend to come from more affluent social groups' (Barrett 2016: 17) is borne out by a number of empirical studies (Chan et al. 2008, Bennett et al. 2009, Neelands et al. 2015). Working-class people, however, are not necessarily absent from theatre audiences – indeed, accurate measures of working-class theatre attendance are difficult to capture through the sometimes-blunt instruments often used to measure class (such as occupation, income, education, postcode analysis), the limits of which have been acknowledged by social scientists (Savage 2015). Additionally, detailed information is rarely gathered from actual theatre audiences as part of longitudinal studies, with data from national surveys like *Taking Part* (Department for Digital, Culture, Media and Sport 2016), which relies on randomly selected participants recruited through Post Office data, often used as key sources in empirical studies. The difficulty of measuring the class dimension of theatre audiences is exacerbated by the fact that 'class' as a category is complex and inexact, constituted by myriad factors including, but not limited to, income, inherited wealth, identity, taste, education, values, opportunity, leisure pursuits, occupation, location of (family) home, upbringing and accent.[1] How one perceives one's own class does not necessarily equate with how one's class is perceived by others. Nor does the received understanding that theatre audiences tend to be middle class justify the way in which addressing working-class marginalization is so often reduced to a concern with increasing participation through outreach programmes separated from core activities (such as the Royal Court's problematic 'Theatre Local' initiative, discussed below, or the Royal Opera House's 'Welcome Performances', staged exclusively for families who haven't attended opera before), a 'social inclusion' approach that tends to reinforce existing social divisions.

The invisibility of working-class audiences has for a long time been compounded by the invisibility of working-class criticism, especially in mainstream newspapers, where critics are overwhelmingly white, middle class and male – although this is changing, especially with the advent of online criticism throughout the 2000s opening up space for 'other' voices (Dolan 2016, Haydon 2016) and the establishment of initiatives such as Critics of Colour (Snow 2018).[2] This means that the interpretation of cultural products is often transmitted through a middle-class lens, further shoring up inequalities in cultural production and consumption and concealing working-class perspectives from view. This is important, because representations may be understood differently by different audience members depending on their upbringing, life experiences and relationship to the material on stage. Richardson and Skott-Myhre connect this propensity to read representations differently to habitus, arguing that the collective experiences of classed (and raced, geographically bounded) groups inevitably lead to different readings of artworks by those different groups, because habitus structures how we understand the world. They use the example of O-Dog in the film *Menace II Society*, where he is described as 'America's nightmare: young, black and didn't give a fuck', to argue that perceptions of representations change according to our classed and raced experiences. They propose that, '[t]o an affluent, white member of Beverly Hills this description might provoke fear', while '[t]o O-Dog's friends, this description may be flattering' (11–12), to illustrate how those from 'outside' of a culture might interpret representations differently from those who are 'inside'.

The anecdotes I offer at the start of this chapter, one from an interview with poet, novelist and playwright Kate Tempest and one from my own theatre-going experience – which I include because it was in many ways the catalyst for my thinking deeply about class relations within the theatre – are not objective, scientific data. Although they are 'true' in the sense that they recall events that really happened from the subjective point of view of the teller, they are, like the representations discussed throughout the book, single stories that cannot represent the totality of class politics as they play out in the theatre space. They are stories that have been mediated and selected to speak to the material in this chapter in a particular way. Nonetheless they point to the fact that class relations are complex, nuanced and enacted and experienced in myriad ways both within and beyond theatre auditoria. These anecdotes also feature instances of violence, which point to how structures of class power are enacted and resisted violently in the everyday, and filter, often imperceptibly, into the 'elite' cultural sphere.

They also point to how individuals read and receive artworks differently depending on their learned experiences. Attendance at the theatre is a matter of class, and the invisibility of working-class people as both audience members and cultural producers forms part of the ecology of theatre spaces, shaping received understandings of performances and their social contexts that filter into the wider culture.

Spatial euphemisms: The estate as class metaphor

In arts practices, inequalities are often addressed through spatial means: notably by taking artworks to spaces beyond 'traditional' building-based institutions such as the theatre or the gallery. In his influential book *Conversation Pieces*, Grant Kester describes how this turn towards spatiality was often enacted through what he calls 'dialogic' art practices, which sought to foster diversity through facilitating conversation with and between excluded groups (Kester 2004: 1).

In the theatre, examples of space-based approaches that might be understood as dialogic include the work of SPID (Social Political Innovative Direct) Theatre Company, a community-based charity that seeks to 'empower neighbourhoods'. It signals its dedication to overcoming class inequality by working 'with people on West London council estates' (SPID 2017) to create theatre works often performed or set on estates, to a diverse audience base including estate residents, residents from the affluent surrounding west London area and across London.

SPID is permanently located on the Kensal Rise estate in Ladbroke Grove, London, a space where estateness becomes a class euphemism, used to justify, sustain and maintain funding for the company, as evident in the 2009 corporate planning document.

> [Our projects with youth residents] are our way of honouring architect Maxwell Fry's vision of the community rooms as a place where residents recognise their potential to help and entertain each other. Situated in St Charles Ward, which is amongst the top 10% of deprived wards nationally, the residents are a transient group including a high proportion of refugees and a diverse ethnic mix; drug use violence and unemployment are rife. Using theatre as our tool, we see ourselves as catalysts for the regeneration of the community rooms and the estate itself.
>
> (SPID 2009: 8)

Attempts to 'engage' working-class audiences through located practices in this way are usually well intentioned (and in many ways SPID's work has been highly effective; see Beswick 2011, 2016a, 2016b); however, they are not without their own risks of problematic class politics. For example, as housing activists (see e.g. Harling 2017) and scholars (see Pritchard 2017) have pointed out, and as I will explore further in the next chapter, site-focussed practices taking place on council estates have often operated as a way to 'artwash' gentrification, by using artworks to distract from the so-called social cleansing that often happens when neighbourhoods undergo regeneration and working-class residents are forcibly removed to make way for middle-class residents willing and able to pay high prices for homes on developed sites.

Mainstream theatre, which remains the focus of this chapter, has also addressed class inequality through spatial means, although not always in ways that fit Kester's dialogic model. In the twentieth century many theatres were established in working-class districts, particularly in London, in an ostensible attempt to engage local communities who might not traditionally be considered to include a large theatre-going demographic. Examples include the Deptford Albany and the Ovalhouse – with the latter's artistic policy stating that it represents 'anti-heroes and underdogs' (Ovalhouse 2012). The Theatre Royal Stratford East (TRSE) is another example of a London theatre that has used its location to engage with social concerns. The well-documented history of TRSE includes its use as a permanent base for Joan Littlewood's Theatre Workshop between 1953 and 1979. The Theatre Workshop's ambition to create 'people's theatre' for the local community was reflected in TRSE's 2012 mission statement, which asserted that the theatre sought to 'produce new work which draws from and reflects the talent, concerns and dreams of its local communities'. In addition to these socially engaged theatres, there has also been a proliferation of community-focused arts centres, such as The Space in London's Docklands, a converted church that produces plays in-house, hosts touring productions and offers community outreach and discounted tickets to local residents. Additionally, prominent mainstream theatres have changed their practice of space, working beyond their established building-based locations to engage with a wider audience demographic. For example, the Royal Court Theatre, based in Sloane Square, an expensive and exclusive area of London, has established a programme called 'Beyond the Court' (previously 'Theatre Local'). This programme was piloted in 2008 and revived in 2010, 2011, 2012 and 2013, when it took selected performances to 'alternative' areas of London. These include the predominantly working-class locations of Peckham and Elephant and Castle (both in the London Borough of Southwark). Theatre Local, despite its claims to locality, in fact operated to make the area 'navigable' to unfamiliar visitors, leveraging 'cultural production for an incoming, and touristic, "creative class" ' (Bell 2014a: 203). From 2014 to 2017 Beyond the Court attempted to address criticisms aimed at Theatre Local by working with communities in London's Tottenham and Pimlico to develop work by and for local people. Of course, as Gay McAuley points out, just because a theatre is located in a working-class area there is no guarantee that it will attract a working-class audience, 'but the location nevertheless makes some kind of statement about who is expected or encouraged to participate and who might feel discouraged from attempting to do so' (McAuley 1999: 45).

It does not always require moving beyond the theatre space or even into a working-class district to 'make a statement' about who the play is for or to signpost class politics. Very often, instead, the council estate operates as a spatial euphemism, allowing theatres to address class in one way or another (and often, as we shall see, ambivalently). Particularly in new writing works, the estate is referenced in order both to appeal to new audiences and to reflect on the 'state of the nation' (Sierz 2011), exploring social issues that are often presumed to be bound up with class (such as race, crime, housing conditions and domestic violence), bringing the 'reality' of working-class life to a core middle-class audience.

In new writing concerning working-class characters, the council estate often serves as the 'fictional place' (McAuley 1999: 29) where the play is set or where working-class characters live – but the estate is also often referenced in subtler ways including through set design, marketing (posters, trailers), the first-hand experience of the playwright (or sometimes the actors) made explicit in promotional interviews and in the dialogue or backstory of a play's characters.

In what follows, I analyse three productions staged at English theatres, thinking through the ways that their social, aesthetic and institutional contexts contribute to what Lefebvre would understand as the 'production' of estate space. In order to do so, I take specific productions of the plays in question (rather than treat the written play text as the object of analysis). The productions I look at are the 2000 revival of Andrea Dunbar's *Rita, Sue and Bob Too* performed as a double bill with Robin Soans's verbatim work, *A State Affair*; the 2013 revival of Simon Stephens's *Port*; and the Battersea Arts Centre's (BAC) 2017 production of Conrad Murray's *DenMarked*. While the first production of a play is often considered the most culturally significant, and has been used to define new writing as a distinct genre (Bolton 2012), I revisit significant revivals of the first two plays to reveal the ways in which enduring representations of estates speak across decades – pointing to the 'fixity' of estate representation discussed in the introduction to this book.

My analysis interrogates how the council estate serves as a metaphor for class inequalities, highlighting the ambivalent and paradoxical ways that estate representations operate within the social space of the theatre.

Rita, Sue and Bob Too/A State Affair: Andrea Dunbar and the 'authentic voice'

Rita, Sue and Bob Too was writer Andrea Dunbar's second play. It was first staged at the Royal Court Theatre in 1982, where it was directed by the Court's then Artistic Director, Max Stafford-Clark. It followed Dunbar's successful debut *The Arbor* (1980), which she famously began writing as a schoolgirl, aged 15, and which debuted at the Royal Court Theatre's Theatre Upstairs during the Young Writer's Festival 1980, before transferring to the Downstairs, main stage venue. In 1981, Dunbar won the George Devine Award for Most Promising Playwright; *The Arbor* transferred to New York the following year (Stripe 2016: 3). Her third and final play *Shirley* (1986) also premiered at the Royal Court. In 1987 a film adaptation of Dunbar's first two plays, *Rita, Sue and Bob Too!* was released. Marketed with the strapline 'Thatcher's Britain with Her Knickers Down' it was an upbeat, rowdy interpretation of Dunbar's work, with a light-hearted ending that eschewed the pessimism that characterized her play texts. The film became a popular cult classic, with the British Film Institute re-releasing it on Blu-ray and DVD in May 2017. The year 2017 also saw a revival of *Rita, Sue and Bob Too* as a collaboration between Out of Joint, Octagon Theatre Bolton and The Royal Court.

Like *The Arbor*, *Rita, Sue and Bob Too* was critically acclaimed at its debut. Both plays were also widely understood as largely autobiographical and set on the Buttershaw estate in Bradford, West Yorkshire, a post-industrial city in the north of England – the estate where Dunbar was born, raised and lived for most of her short life (she died of a brain haemorrhage at the age of 29). The term 'New Brutalism', coined to describe Dunbar's style of writing, indicates how her work was linked more widely with the (generic) estate in the public imagination. Dunbar's writing came to symbolize the 'concrete high rise aesthetic of post-war Britain' (Stripe 2016: 6). Her themes and storylines not only resonate with familiar depictions of the white working class I explored in the previous chapter but also acknowledge the mixed-race reality of life in Bradford, with the 'Girl' in *The Arbor* dating a Pakistani boyfriend (indeed this too is autobiographically inflected; Andrea's eldest daughter, Lorraine, is mixed-race, with a Pakistani father).

Rita, Sue and Bob Too centres on an affair between two teenage girls (Rita and Sue) and a married father (Bob). In the opening scene Bob has sex with the girls in the front seat of his car after driving them home from babysitting his children, while his wife, Michelle, waits at home. As the girls navigate their affair with Bob – each conducting a side-affair with him, alone, unbeknownst to the other – the audience are offered glimpses into their home-lives, characterized by arguments, violence and abusive language.

Scene Two

*When **Sue** comes home her **Dad** is sitting there waiting.*

Dad Where do you think you've fucking been?
Sue Baby-sitting.
Dad What? Till two a fucking clock in the morning? Don't lie to me lass.
Sue I'm not. You ask my mum, she knows I was.
Dad Your mother's a fucking lying bastard as well. You better tell me where you've been or I'll go in that kitchen and get that brush and wrap it around your bastard neck.
Sue I've told you, I've been baby-sitting.
Dad (*hitting her across head*) You lying little cunt!

(Dunbar 2000: 26)

At the end of scene six, after taking Rita and Sue into the countryside for a day, where he rails against the injustices of unemployment and instability visited on his life in the wake of the Thatcher government, Bob fails to get an erection as the trio attempt to have sex. It is difficult to view this moment as anything other than a ribald metaphor for the threat to traditional male roles posed by deindustrialization and the onset of rampant neoliberalism. Despite this, however, the play is notably apolitical in its depiction of poverty and offers no coherent moral stance on the facts of the underage sex, child grooming or extramarital affair it depicts. As Adelle Stripe has noted, Dunbar's work is characterized by an 'uneasy and contradictory' (2016: 6) version of estate life, with the humour, wit and self-possession of the characters sitting against a backdrop of abject poverty and decline that critics have found difficult to reconcile. A review of the 2017 revival noted that the play's lack of 'judgement' over the actions and lifestyles of its characters makes the world depicted in the play 'all the more appalling' (Love 2017). In interviews, Dunbar argued that she was presenting her own experience of the world.

'This is life', Andrea Dunbar told the Yorkshire Post in 1987 defending the film version of her play Rita, Sue and Bob Too. 'The facts are there.'

Dunbar was adamant about telling the truth in her work, insisting 'you write what's said, you don't lie.'

(Love 2017)

Dunbar was clear that her work was comedy, rather than any kind of politically inflected social critique (Peirse 2016: 8). Nonetheless, Stafford-Clark, who acted as a mentor for Dunbar throughout her writing career, positioned her authenticity as a political act in and of itself; as 'an articulate record of life in the lower depths ... recorded not, for once, by an outsider but by someone still passionately involved in that life themselves' (Roberts and Stafford-Clark 2007: 113).

Certainly, Dunbar's refusal to package the play in a way that offers a convenient moral coherence for the theatre-going elite operates as a resistance to the dominant narratives that tend to frame estate dramas. In particular, the promiscuity of the teenage girls, who are depicted as willing and autonomous (if naïve and damaged) participants in the affair, exemplifies a phenomenon Siân Adiseshiah has identified in other dramas centred on working-class experience: an articulation of 'working-class modes of personhood in forms that resist assimilation to already classed ways of knowing' (2016: 151). The energy and tone of Dunbar's work – and the enduring recognition of her plays within and beyond her community – exemplifies McKenzie's argument that allowing working-class people to tell their own stories results in artworks that can appeal to working-class audiences 'who want to see themselves represented through their lens' (RT.com 2017).

At the end of the play fifteen-year-old Rita falls pregnant with Bob's baby and sets up home with him, promising to maintain her friendship with Sue. The final scene sees Sue, Sue's mother and Michelle (Bob's now ex-wife) meet in a local pub. Bob has stopped making financial contributions to the family he had with Michelle and has had to sell his car. When Sue leaves, Mum and Michelle agree that the affair was Rita's fault, and that men are mostly no good, anyway ('All fellas do the dirty on you sometime or other'). They decide to stay at the pub for a final drink, although they know there are families waiting for them at home.

Some ten years after Dunbar's death, writer Robin Soans returned to the Buttershaw. He interviewed some of the estate's residents, including Dunbar's eldest daughter, Lorraine, about their experiences of living on the estate in the years since *Rita, Sue and Bob Too* was written. Using their testimonies to create a verbatim piece called *A State Affair*, Soans documented the estate's decline in the years since Dunbar's death, as the deindustrialization of the north of England continued, and many of the Buttershaw's residents succumbed to heroin addiction. *A State Affair* creates a desolate picture of a struggling community, who narrate in graphic detail the devastation heroin and alcohol addiction have wrought on their lives.

In 2000 *Rita, Sue and Bob Too* was revived in a double bill with *A State Affair*, directed by Stafford-Clark and with a single cast playing roles across each production. This touring production was realized as a collaboration between Stafford-Clark's company Out of Joint, the Soho Theatre and the Liverpool Everyman and Playhouse. It premiered at the Liverpool Everyman in October 2000, before transferring to the Soho in December 2000. In 2001/2 the production toured across the United Kingdom, in theatres including the Soho Theatre, the West Yorkshire Playhouse in Leeds, the Traverse Theatre in Edinburgh and to Ireland and New Zealand.

As Elaine Aston and Janelle Reinelt note, in a review of *Rita, Sue and Bob Too/A State Affair* staged at Soho, Out of Joint's policy of staging 'a classic drama with a linked piece of new writing' means that the plays worked to comment upon one another, 'in the interests of mutual interrogation or illumination' (2001: 286). In this way, *Rita, Sue and Bob Too* operated to suggest the inevitability of the estate's decline, as the 'harsh realities' (Stripe 2016: 1) of teenage sexual grooming, domestic violence and rampant unemployment set the scene for the physical and psychological decline of a struggling community. The estate setting serves, in this way, as a physical and metaphorical site of ruin (Beswick 2015). Evoked by graffitied walls and the heavy, grey geometric shapes of reinforced concrete that serve as a set, dominant narratives of social decline and decay on the generic council estate underpin the miserable inevitability of the double bill's conclusion.

Performed in tandem with *A State Affair*, the 2000 revival of *Rita, Sue and Bob Too* served to secure Dunbar's place as an 'authentic' voice.[3] I use this term to refer to how Dunbar has been created as an authentic, classed figure in the popular imagination and to point to how her work exemplifies a new writing trope where the life experiences of the playwright become authenticating mechanisms for stage representations. The authentic voice can be seen in a number of genres, but is especially common in socially realist works.

Samantha Lay defines social realism as texts in which 'there is a high degree of verisimilitude, placing an emphasis on ensemble casts in social situations which suggest a direct link between person and place' (2002: 20). Socially realist dramas also tend to emphasize realism's tendency towards class politics – usually featuring issues that highlight structural inequalities related to class (Williams 1977a: 63). Laing (1986) highlights how concepts of 'authenticity' have characterized social realist representations of working-class environments almost from their inception. For example, he notes that in Shelagh Delaney's *A Taste of Honey*

(Theatre Royal Stratford East 1958) the 'double guarantee of authenticity' was created by the author's personal knowledge and close observation of the world depicted on stage (89–90).

Social realism's emphasis on the link between person and place is heightened in 'authentic voice' depictions of council estates. The notion of authorial authenticity, especially when aimed at audiences unfamiliar with the estate environment, can result in authentic voice plays being framed as unproblematically 'real'. This imbues the work with an added burden of representation, as the stage depiction operates to solidify existing understandings about estates and is often read as reflecting the authentic totality of estate experience.

The revival of *Rita, Sue and Bob Too* in the context of its double bill with a verbatim play raises questions about the role of theatre in representing estate 'reality', as well as questions about the ways in which issues of class are presented and received on the mainstream stage. Both Adiseshiah and Anna Harpin have argued, in relation to Jez Butterworth's *Jerusalem*, that working-class representations can flirt 'dangerously with a kind of class porn' (Harpin 2011: 70) in the mainstream theatre where, 'the differently classed spaces of stage and auditorium accentuate the lack of shared habitus among characters and audience' (Adiseshiah 2016: 158). Under these conditions what are the potentials and the limits of theatre in facilitating class analysis and in challenging and sustaining popular understandings of estate space?

The real and represented: Aesthetic potentials of mediality

At an aesthetic level *Rita, Sue and Bob Too/A State Affair* offered a potentially powerful intervention into estate discourse. The act of allowing a working-class woman to speak for herself, even from beyond the grave, is, as Stafford-Clark argues, a political act in its own right. Nor did the production enable only easy readings of the stage representation within the dominant discourse. It provided moments where the power of the authentic voice was punctured – enabling reflection on the mediated nature of the plays. In particular the scenographic elements of the performance worked against the formal social realism of the play texts to draw attention to the constructed nature of the stage representation.

While the estate itself was symbolically evoked, as mentioned above, through graffiti and grey, concrete-like slabs, the domestic and interior car scenes were played out on the main stage space – with the positions of furniture marked out in coloured tape across the black floor. A set of blue car seats were manoeuvred around the stage to become different locations – the car interior, Bob and Michelle's living room, the pub. The tape-marked spaces collided and overlapped, resulting in a chaotic, unreadable map of the plays' fictional world, present throughout both performances. Meanwhile an ironing board, used by both Michelle and Rita in their respective homes (its space on stage marked out boldly in tape on the floor), served to introduce a note of intertextuality for those audience members with the theatrical vocabulary to read it – referencing the iconic ironing board from the Royal Court's *Look Back in Anger*. Ashton and Reinelt propose (albeit with a perhaps reductive view of the working-class psychology on display in the play) that the ironing board worked as a gendered critique in which

> Dunbar's girls (and women) are differently positioned to Osborne's middle-class Alison within his misogynist framing. By contrast, her young women will fight for whatever they can in the face of acute social deprivation, and without lamentation for lost causes, or lives desired to be lived differently.
>
> (2001: 287)

Ten television monitors, set into and around the grey pillars that framed the stage space, drew attention to the episodic nature of *Rita, Sue and Bob Too* – which, with its short, high-stakes scenes, is reminiscent of a television soap opera. So too, they suggested the constructed nature of the dramatic representation. Aston and Reinelt propose that 'the presence of the monitors seemed to mark the interpenetration of media into real life and private experience, constantly reminding us that a new subjectivity is created in relation to the constant recourse to television' (2001: 286–287). This statement suggests the ways in which the 'meta-commentary' (Aston and Reinelt 2001: 287) offered by the television sets afforded the possibility for critical reflection – wherein a consideration of the blurred reciprocal relationship between fictional representations and real life becomes possible within the frame of the play.

However, it is 'the juxtapositions of the second play' (Aston and Reinelt 2001: 289) through which the authenticity of the first is most clearly called into question. The complicated space between fiction and reality is confronted by Andrea's daughter Lorraine in *A State Affair* when she reflects on the role her mother's plays take in representing the estate and its residents to the outside world. In direct address Lorraine tells the audience that her mother made herself 'look a right tart' (Soans 2000: 134) and questions the works' negative portrayal of estate life, suggesting that a more balanced view of life on the Buttershaw might provide moments where the residents' hope and strength were visible:

If I wrote a play I'd do it about the Buttershaw [e]state. It'd show some people getting their lives together with a lot of courage and determination. But it would also show others going up a steep hill, into a big black hole.

(Soans 2000: 134)

This moment draws attention, again, to the fictional nature of the stage representation, opening up a space where the audience are invited to consider how far the stage reality reflects the reality of life on the Buttershaw. It points to the subjective nature of *Rita, Sue and Bob Too* and reminds us that there are other subjective experiences, invisible within the context of the drama.

Institutional context: A complicating frame

The 2000 production of *Rita, Sue and Bob Too/A State Affair* was a multi-institutional work. Not only because it was produced as a collaboration between a number of institutions, but also because it toured a range of venues. It inevitably retained institutional ties to the Royal Court, both because *Rita, Sue and Bob Too* was first produced there and because the Royal Court was, in many ways, Dunbar's ongoing theatre 'home' for the duration of her career.

Out of Joint, Liverpool Everyman and the Royal Court all have reputations for producing groundbreaking new work and make explicit claims to (broadly progressive) politics. The official, institutional histories, narrated online on their respective websites, signpost ongoing concerns with the political in their work and practices. The Everyman, for example, highlights its original location 'in an area of Liverpool noted for its bohemian environment and political edge' (Everyman N.D.), while Out of Joint claims to make '[i]nquisitive, epic, authentic and original' work 'that broadens horizons and investigates our times' (Out of Joint N.D.). The Royal Court, meanwhile, has long had a reputation for producing 'state of the nation' plays, which reflect and comment upon pertinent social issues, and which often include the representation of working-class social environments (see e.g. Little and McLaughlin 2007, Stripe 2016: 4–5). In a section of their website titled 'Our Story' the Court states that it is an institution 'at the forefront of creating restless, alert, provocative theatre about now. We open our doors to the unheard voices and free thinkers that, through their writing, change our way of seeing' (Royal Court 2017).

Despite these institutional claims to more or less progressive ideals the theatre industry remains in an ambivalent and complex relationship with progressive politics. For example, the 'unheard voices' the Court claims to amplify are almost always positioned as an 'other' – a means by which the theatre-going (presumably middle-class) elite can further enrich their understanding of the world (suggested in the sentence 'change *our* way of seeing', emphasis added). Indeed, *Rita, Sue and Bob Too/A State Affair* was a production conceived for a middle-class audience, whom Stafford-Clark felt needed 'information about that [council estate] world' (Logan in Aston and Reinelt 2001: 292). The newly built Soho theatre provided the perfect setting in which to bring the working-class experience into middle-class consciousness:

> Both upscale and seedy, Soho has a history and association with strip-shows, drugs and youth culture, but more in evidence now are 'tasteful restaurants' and 'chic shops'. However, Soho still remains a crossroads of artistic and bohemian life, especially for twenty-something white-collar workers.
>
> (Aston and Reinelt 2001: 286)

Both the Royal Court and the Soho Theatre are positioned within the theatre industry as pioneering new writing venues. They run writing programmes aimed at nurturing new and emerging talent, and the Royal Court has run a number of programmes (such as Critical Mass and Unheard Voices) that specifically target economically disadvantaged and minority ethnic communities. These programmes often ask participants to use their own experiences of a particular context as a basis for storytelling (Bell and Beswick 2014). This emphasis on the writer's first-hand experience, and the influence of these theatres on the new writing landscape across the United Kingdom, has led to a proliferation of plays written in the authentic voice.

As playwright Arinze Kene (*Estate Walls*; *God's Property*) proposed in a 2013 interview with the *Guardian*,

> A lot of writers like myself – young, from London – write ourselves into a corner. We write what is expected of us, and often what's expected is knife-crime stories.... . I can speak from experience and say that it's easier to be listened to, to get your work on stage, if you depict the same old shit.
>
> (Costa 2013)

Kene's comment suggests that, rather than offering a platform from which playwrights from disadvantaged and minority communities can write their own stories, the mainstream theatre industry structures opportunities for writers in ways that coerce them into producing works that reinforce dominant conceptions of inner-city life. His words indicate how institutions and institutional structures act as gatekeepers, dictating the form and content of dramatic works in ways that often shore up the status quo. That is to say that the kinds of working-class stories offered a platform are usually those stories that are understood to be the most palatable, marketable and entertaining to the presumed (middle-class educated) theatre-going audience who finance ticket sales. Or, conversely, to those working-class groups identified as 'non-engaged' by ACE.

This is not to suggest that there aren't significant ethical reasons for the evolution of authentic voice narratives. As I discussed in Chapter 1, the focus on authenticity in theatre and in the wider culture has emerged in part to address issues of the silencing and cultural appropriation of marginalized and disenfranchised groups. Rather, I want to make the point that within theatre, as elsewhere, those with the most power – such as the producers who commission work, the directors who cast roles and the newspaper critics whose views circulate beyond the space of the theatre – will likely have their values more clearly visible within the 'public square' (McCracken 2007: 90, see also Beswick 2014) in which a performance operates and where, unlike in Jürgen Habermas's 'public sphere', inequalities in power are always pre-existent and will always shape the conversation in one way or another.

Indeed, the power imbalances that exist within and without the theatre came into sharp focus during the writing of this chapter, when it was revealed that Max Stafford-Clark had been asked to step down as Artistic Director of Out of Joint due to accusations of sexual harassment against young women who worked for him – including writers (although there is at the time of writing no evidence he harassed or behaved inappropriately with Dunbar). The Royal Court performance run of the 2017/18 production of *Rita, Sue and Bob Too* was cancelled, and then reinstated, as a public debate emerged about whether the play's ambivalent sexual politics were an uncomfortable reminder of Stafford-Clark's impropriety or a representation of the authentic experience of Dunbar as a working-class woman (Coatman 2017).

Stafford-Clark's exit from Out of Joint emerged in the wake of the scandal over allegations that Hollywood producer Harvey Weinstein had raped, assaulted and harassed female actors and staff over a period of decades. That these men had been able to harass and assault women points to how the absolute power of individuals in the creative industries is secured (and easily exploited) through an unequal system where 'making it' relies on receiving the favour or support of those with access to the means of production.

The power imbalance that exists in the public square resulted in the 2000 production of *Rita, Sue and Bob Too* enacting an ambivalent class politics. On the one hand, it undoubtedly revived a work that had resonated across the class divide (especially due to the film adaptation) and offered an ongoing platform from which a working-class voice might speak – with a depiction of working-class life that might resonate with working-class theatre-goers. On the other hand, the narrative thrust of the drama and the characterizations, which include archetypal working-class 'types' – including promiscuous young women who fall pregnant before they have left school, violent and abusive husbands, sexual predators – might (and were) easily read as securing already existing dominant discourses about estates and their residents. The lack of any coherent class analysis within the play itself did challenge the status quo, but it also enabled these dominant depictions to operate as authenticating mechanisms for existing understandings of estate life. Understandings that were then circulated and disseminated beyond the theatre by newspaper reviews of the productions, which overwhelmingly focused on the 'reality' and 'authenticity' of the works and the bleakness of the worlds they depicted. The humour, wit and spirit of survival demonstrated by the characters, if mentioned at all, were secondary to the emphasis on decline and despair.

Writing for the *Telegraph*, for example, critic Charles Spencer invoked familiar conceptions of the feckless working-class in his interpretation of the play:

> Thatcher is conveniently figured as the villain of the piece in Rita, but in A State Affair everyone seems beyond seeking either political blame or political solutions. Life is merely a dismal, irredeemable mess.
>
> Yet while one feels compassion watching this play, there is a terrifying ducking of personal responsibility. The women move from one ghastly boyfriend to the next, while their fatherless, undisciplined kids drift into addiction and thieving.
>
> (Spencer 2001)

Meanwhile, the *Guardian* critic Phil Daus reports that the double-bill depicts a world that sees

> [T]eenage girls fucking around and fucking up; the misogynist men who manipulated them; and their violent drunken parents. Two innocently vulgar 15-year-olds who share the shifty 27-year-old man for whom they babysit, then fall out when one gets pregnant and his marriage collapses.
>
> (Daus 2000)

It is clear that, for Daus, the 'verbatim' nature of *A State Affair* operated to further authenticate the depiction of estate life offered in *Rita, Sue and Bob Too*, so that, taken together, the production was understood to offer a representation that reflected an 'authentic' version of estate experience.

In the words of Dunbar's daughter, as quoted in the new work, 'It was horrible before, but there was a sense of community ... If my mum wrote the play now, Rita and Sue would be smackheads and working in the red-light district. Bob would probably be injecting heroin.' So much for progress, and for the millions spent on regenerating the estate.

(Daus 2000)

Much of the mainstream critical response to *Rita, Sue and Bob Too/A State Affair* echoes this emphasis on the hopeless 'reality' depicted by the production, overlooking the fact that, as Stripe argues 'in many respects verbatim is no more "authentic" than a work of fiction' (2016: 27). The focus on Dunbar's authenticity served to neutralize the political potential of her play, which did not, in the context of being targeted at a middle-class audience, provoke any lasting outrage that might transform into political action. In the mainstream, institutional context in which the 2000 revival operated, the work did not call for audiences to reflexively engage with the ways in which their own lives and lifestyles might contribute to the poverty and pain evidenced on stage. Rather, they served to underpin the estate as 'other' narrative that, as we saw in the previous chapter, contributes to the ongoing divisions between social classes that create inequality.

These class divisions are further reinforced by Dunbar's position as an 'exceptional' talent, bolstered by coverage in the popular press during and after her life. In almost all the writing about Dunbar's life and work the fact of her estate residency is evoked (alongside words such as 'genius') to suggest either directly or through euphemism that her talent was *especially* unusual because of her working-class identity. Reviewers and critics have mined the landscape of her life, patronizingly incredulous that talent might develop from such unlikely roots. A BBC Arena arts programme filmed in 1980 shows her parents and sisters, holding babies in their arms, gathered on the doorstep of their estate home, as a reporter asks her father, 'Where do you think she gets the writing from?' It is difficult to imagine a middle-class playwright's family interviewed on similar terms.

As I argued in the previous chapter, exceptionality is a means by which dominant estate discourses are maintained and authenticated, solidifying and justifying class inequality in the wider culture. In the cultural industries, ideas of exceptionality operate to reinforce dominant ideas about meritocracy that further reproduce existing injustices in terms of access to the means of production. Meritocracy is the prevailing belief that individuals are able to rise to positions of power and influence on the basis of merit, regardless of discrimination. Sociologists Mark Taylor and Dave O'Brien have evidenced that, despite the cultural industries' reputation for 'openness and anti-discrimination' (2017: 2), there are well-evidenced barriers to access for working-class people attempting to enter the arts professions. Furthermore, they found that those with the 'strongest belief in meritocracy' are overwhelmingly those 'in the most privileged positions' (2017: 1). By emphasizing Dunbar as an 'exceptional talent', then, the media coverage surrounding her work leverages Dunbar as an authenticating figure for dominant beliefs about talent and reward: if you are good enough, you will make it – ensuring that her exceptionality cannot effectively lead to any change in the way the theatre industry operates.

Buttershaw beyond the stage

My criticisms above indicate how the institutional and social contexts in which an artwork is produced can complicate and compromise its politics. This is not to suggest that *Rita, Sue and Bob Too/A State Affair* operates only to reinforce dominant stereotypes. Indeed, the blurring of fiction and reality that the production enacted has influenced the representation of the Buttershaw in the years since it was produced, inflecting more recent representations of that estate with an unusual nuance.

There have been two significant creative works produced subsequent to the production of *Rita, Sue and Bob Too/A State Affair* that have used the relationship between the real and the represented to examine Dunbar's life and legacy: Clio Barnard's 2010 documentary *The Arbor* and Adelle Stripe's 2017 non-fiction novel *Black Teeth and a Brilliant Smile*.

In *The Arbor*, Barnard uses audio-recordings of interviews with Dunbar's friends and family, centralizing their voices as actors lip-sync precisely to the words. Collaged with documentary footage of Dunbar and her family, and scenes from Dunbar's *The Arbor* filmed on the contemporary Buttershaw estate as residents look on, the film explores the dialectical relationship between fiction and reality in the playwright's life and work. Lib Taylor calls the aesthetic affect of the archival documentary footage of Dunbar and her parents, juxtaposed with scenes from the play in which they all feature as characters, 'doubling'. This doubling, she proposes, 'makes apparent the artifice of both theatre performance and documentary performance of self' (2013: 375).

Like *Rita, Sue and Bob Too*, the aesthetic and moral complexity of the film evades easy interpretation within existing estate discourse. Indeed, the film's aesthetic strategy was criticized in the *Guardian* for the fact that the actors' bodies drew attention to the artifice of the representation.

The archive clips of grizzled and raddled unfortunates highlight the gap between them and the posh, smooth-skinned performers goldfishing the speech of their contemporary counterparts. The effect is to diminish credibility rather than enhance it.

(Cox 2010)

This criticism indicates the discomfort experienced by those in the mainstream cultural sphere when representations require nuanced reading and cannot be conveniently framed as unproblematically 'authentic' to reinforce dominant discourses.

Black Teeth and A Brilliant Smile similarly layers real events with fictional ones, using real and imagined characters to offer a fictional biography of Dunbar's life – one that again is predicated on the understanding that the representation is not (or not only) 'real'. 'By using poetic licence and fictional devices it is, importantly, a *portrait*, as opposed to a factual account which uses Dunbar's own autobiographical scenes as inspiration' (Stripe 2016: 34, original emphasis). As Stripe suggests, both her method and Barnard's draw on and extend the techniques pioneered in Robin Soans's verbatim work. Her novel works deliberately to mythologize the subject (2016: 33), acknowledging that biography operates as a form wherein 'fact and fiction collide', resulting in 'an unstable alchemy, one which is difficult to define precisely' (2016: 35).

The aesthetic devices of *Rita, Sue and Bob Too/A State Affair* similarly create an 'unstable alchemy'. Removed from its institutional frame, therefore, the performance offers a potential interruption into narratives of the 'authentic real' that produces council estate space in the contemporary culture. To paraphrase Kate Tempest's words in the quotation at the start of this chapter, it is the 'artwork itself' that offers possibilities for seeing estates differently: possibilities that are made difficult, if not impossible, to realize within the structural mechanisms of the theatre industry as it currently operates, where authenticity becomes a primary means of reading estate artworks.

Port: Working-class exceptionality and the estate as ruin

Port is an epic work by playwright Simon Stephens that maps thirteen years in the life of Racheal Keats, a fictional girl from Stockport, as she grows from a child into a young woman. First shown at the Manchester Royal

Exchange in 2002, the play was revived for the National Theatre's 890-seat Lyttelton space in 2013, where it was directed by Marianne Elliott, who had also directed the original production. *Port* was awarded the Pearson Award for best play in 2001, and was subsequently staged (in German) at Graz, in Austria and Gothenburg (Stephens 2013: 1) before its 2013 UK revival, the first professional UK revival since the original production.

Stephens is a prolific playwright, whose professional debut *Bluebird* was staged as part of the Royal Court's Young Writers' Festival in 1998. He has averaged a play a year since 2000, has had his works staged in many of the United Kingdom's leading theatre venues, across Europe and in North America, has worked as playwright in residence at both the National Theatre and the Royal Exchange, acted as writer's tutor for the Royal Court's Young Writers' programme and had his plays translated into at least fourteen languages (Bolton 2013: 102). Prior to commencing full-time work as a playwright, Stephens was educated at the University of York and worked as a teacher. Unlike Dunbar, whose personal life is almost always irrevocably entwined with her writing in analyses of her work, Stephens's plays tend to be scrutinized for their formal and literary innovations. Particularly, scholars have been interested in exploring adaptations of his work in Germany and its influence there (see Barnett 2016, Love 2016).

Set in Stephens's (and Elliott's) native Stockport, a northern English town located in Greater Manchester, *Port* comprises eight scenes, set at two yearly intervals (scenes seven and eight both take place in 2002). Although the play is not entirely set on a council estate – scenes take place in various locations including a hospital canteen and a pub garden – the *idea* of the council estate frames the play. Both the opening and closing scenes are set in a car parked outside a looming concrete façade, described in the play-script as 'the flats on Lancashire Hill' – presumably referring to the tower block development in Lancashire Hill, Stockport, built in the 1960s as council housing. The landscape of poverty, domestic violence, crime and longing for escape that the play depicts resonates with dominant estate tropes, invoking the estate without explicitly mentioning it. So, too, the trailer for the 2013 production (discussed below) foregrounds the estate location, marking this as a 'working-class' drama.

In the opening scene (set in 1988), an eleven-year-old Racheal takes refuge from her violent father with her mother and younger brother, Billy. Sat in a car with the estate's block visible in the background behind, an articulate and lively Racheal narrates her every thought as her mother studiously attempts to ignore her.

Racheal   What you thinking? Mum? Mum what are you thinking?
                Tell us.
Christine   Has he put a light on?
Racheal   You gonna tell us or what.
Christine   Has he Rache? Is that our flat?
Racheal   I don't know. I can't tell.

(Stephens 2013: 15)

The central theme of entrapment and escape emerges as Racheal predicts her mother's imminent departure and sets the tone of longing and disappointment that recurs throughout the production.

> **Racheal** I think you were thinking all about Dad and all about this and how mental it is and about us and about how you want to kill him and about how much you love him and about whether you're going to leave him and about whether you're going to leave us and about how old Billy is and about how old I am and about whether you're going to go and I think that you think that you're going to. That's what I think. Am I right?

(Stephens 2013: 16)

In subsequent scenes we see Racheal, now motherless, navigate her grandfather's death, teenage friendships, her brother's arrest, lost love and an abusive relationship. Throughout the play Racheal tries to leave Stockport, and in scene seven (2002) we learn that she has recently divorced her violent husband and spent a short time in another city before returning home. She reminiscences with an old boyfriend and asks whether he might leave his new girlfriend and child for a life with her (he refuses). The final scene mirrors the first as Racheal and Billy – who has recently been released from prison – again sit in a parked car outside the flats, illuminated by the yellow street lamps, Racheal, this time, planning her own escape. The play ends with Racheal looking out into the distance as the sun rises over hills, bathing her face in a soft orange light.

In the original production, staged at the height of the New Labour government's success, when the dominant rhetoric of a classless society made possible by inclusion through social mobility seemed like a possibility, Racheal's dreams of a better life elsewhere could predict an optimistic social future. Adiseshiah argues that the play's ending exemplifies what Dan Rebellato identifies as Stephens's 'ability to situate us within and without the everyday, locating us firmly in what *is* but offering us an ethical sense of what *might be*' (Rebellato 1995 in Adiseshiah 2016: 161).

This movement between the quotidian *now* and the utopian *not yet*, a structure of feeling that infuses the play from its inception, also makes space for moments of what Markels calls the 'groping on unfamiliar terrain for [Raymond] Williams's "emergent" culture of classlessness', a glimmer of which manifests non-verbally in the final image of the play.

(Adiseshiah 2016: 161–162)

By 2013, however, the political reality of a widening gap between the rich and poor, the bite of austerity politics, successive housing crises and the failed promises of New Labour inflect the work with a pessimism that makes it difficult to believe, even optimistically, that Racheal will realize her dreams of escape. This elegiac closing, for which the estate serves as a backdrop, pierces the ending with a poignant sense of hope whose cathartic potential is undercut with the possibility that this planned escape, like Racheal's others, is doomed to failure. The 'structure of feeling' offered by the utopian '*not yet*' of the 2002 production is lost in the 2013 revival, as the 'not yet' has passed, and with it the optimistic impossibility of a better future.

Class at the National Theatre

By staging a play about the working-class landscape of the late-twentieth-century north of England in the nation's capital, more than a decade after the millennium, the National Theatre places issues of class centre stage. But what does it mean to stage a play at the National Theatre? Marvin Carlson indicates that, despite their differences, all national theatres are rooted in ideas of nation (2008: 21). It is through its national theatres that nations shape and reflect their cultural and political landscapes, offering stories that intervene in and at times dictate national discourses. Unsurprisingly, the British preoccupation with class has been embedded in the National Theatre from its embryonic stages, as indicated in the narrative history of the theatre offered on its webpages (2017), where, like the theatres mentioned in the previous section, the National draws attention to its roots in a progressive politics. In a quotation from the (1904) preface to *A National Theatre: Scheme and Estimates* by William Archer and Harley Granville Barker, displayed on the 'History' section of its website, the National frames itself as historically concerned with appealing across class barriers (although I am aware there are different interpretations of this history).

It must not ever have the air of appealing to a specially literate and cultured class. It must be visibly and unmistakably a popular institution, making a large appeal to the whole community.

(National Theatre 2017)

In this context, *Port*'s revival might be understood as a predictable attempt to appeal to the 'whole community' in the wake of ACE's emphasis on widening audience participation (the NT receives significant funding from ACE), as well as solidifying the National Theatre's own institutional vision – a means through which the theatre suggests its commitment to diverse access.

Nonetheless, in many ways, the revival of *Port* at the National Theatre, some eleven years after its debut, was a curious programming choice. Although it had been a successful, award-winning production it had not achieved the cult status of, for example, *Rita, Sue and Bob Too*, nor entered a contemporary canon that might explain its revisiting. Looking at the National Theatre's 2012/13 programme (see theartsdesk.com 2012), *Port* sits uneasily alongside a contemporary version of Carl Zuckmayer's 1931 German satire *The Captain of Köpenick* (adapted into English by Ron Hutchinson) and the Christmas production of the fairytale Hansel and Gretel (directed by Katie Mitchell). It is perhaps easiest to understand the decision to programme the play in the context of the runaway success of Stephens's adaptation of Mark Haddon's novel *The Curious Incident of a Dog in the Night Time* (2012). Also directed by Marianne Elliott, the sell-out production received rave reviews and transferred to the West End's Apollo Theatre in spring 2013,[4] before touring extensively across the United Kingdom. However, it is highly unlikely that the success of *The Curious Incident* would have been evident when the 2013 season was first conceived. Rather, it seems that either *Port* was a late programming decision through which the National decided to recognize Stephens's and Elliott's *Curious* success or else Nicholas Hytner, the then artistic director, had already made a decision to invest in Elliott and Stephens as a creative team on the basis of their previous work and respective reputations within the theatre industry. Either option points to the operation of the theatre as a public square, revealing how institutions have the power to elevate and amplify voices based on the taste, reputation and commercial aspirations of their directors.

An email exchange between me, Simon Stephens and Deputy Artistic Director Ben Power offers further insight into the rationale for the revival – confirming that *Port* was indeed intended as a platform for Stephens and Elliott:

The decision to revive PORT for the NT's Lyttelton Theatre in 2013 was taken for a number of reasons. The National wanted to recognise Simon Stephens' astonishing play as a contemporary classic and one which charted and celebrated a Northern working-class narrative. The production continued Simon's long relationship with NT Associate Director Marianne Elliottt and created a major opportunity for an actress to chart Racheal's journey. It was an opportunity that Kate O'Flynn seized and the production lovingly and authentically placed a world and a voice rarely seen or heard in front of the National's London audience.

(email correspondence from Ben Power, 2017)

The brief email offers a glimpse into the ambivalent class and gender politics at play in the programming. *Port* offered a female actor the chance to play a substantial leading role, and the working-class world of the play provided an opportunity for a (presumably educated middle-class) London audience to experience an 'authentic' version of the impoverished north. Here we see again how the language of authenticity operates to facilitate a class politics where the stories and experiences of the 'authentic' working class are offered up as entertainment and education for an audience to whom they are 'other'.

Whatever the reasons for its staging, the production of a decade-old play, with realist attention to historical detail, invites comparisons between *then* and *now*. The nostalgic texture of 1980s and 1990s scenes, which would have been evident in the original production, is heightened in the revival where all the scenes depict the past. Thus the whole production becomes a comment upon the relationship between the past and present, inflected with a politics of inclusion – as the protagonist struggles to find her place in the world beyond Stockport, the estate and the working-class culture that surrounds her.

Realism and ruin aesthetics

The online trailer for the 2013 production of *Port* opens with a brief shot of a residential tower block from below, as if the viewer is craning their neck to see the top of the building. The external shots are intercut with internal shots: the estate is viewed from the window as a child draws onto the steamed-up pane with its finger; a family settles for breakfast – their class marked by the objects visible on the table: cigarettes discarded in a plastic ashtray, a full English breakfast, tea served in a plain white ceramic mug, the bag discarded next to it on a teaspoon, a copy of the tabloid newspaper the *Sun*. A young girl dressed in a fluorescent pink tracksuit top, wearing large hooped earrings, blows cigarette smoke at the camera. She runs from the estate with a young man – he is also wearing a tracksuit – their backs to the screen. The camera pans across the aisles of a corner shop; a pub table; the spinning drums of mid-cycle washing machines in a launderette. Someone is putting on tights and high-heeled shoes, painting their nails. The camera moves backwards to reveal Kate O'Flynn (the actor who played Racheal) applying make up in the mirror of a dressing table.

The images collaged in this trailer recall the images from the poverty porn reality television programmes described at the beginning of the previous chapter and also other popular images steeped in 'white trash' and 'chav' stereotypes – the derogatory chav character Vicky Pollard (see previous chapter), for example, wears a pink tracksuit. Although the trailer ends with an element of mystery, as the 'reveal' of the protagonist suggests an unexpected story will emerge, familiar and stereotypical images of working-class life, presented in a realist style, are used, with the estate as a backdrop, to situate the play within a classed frame. The trailer, intended as a promotional tool for the production, marks this as a realist estate drama.

Realism, as I mentioned in the previous section, is a form that has long been used to depict class inequality. In contemporary culture, however, the oppositional or resistant possibilities of social realism, which has the potential to draw attention to the machinations of the world so that they might be acted upon, have been diluted. This is partly as a result of the prevalence of the 'authentic real' in contemporary culture. Andrew Higson notes that realism demands a 'novelistic attention to detail', which can often translate into a 'fetishistic' surface concern with 'iconographic detailism': he calls this 'the spectacle of the real' (Higson 1984: 4), while Christopher Innes has argued that the use of realist conventions can troublingly imply that work is valid, factual and objective; as he notes, the term 'realism' is often used to refer 'an objective portrayal of daily life that appears true to the spectator['s] ... actual experience' (2000: 4). This conflation between realism and the realistic is compounded by the proliferation of reality television shows, documentaries and realist dramas that make up much of the popular television schedule, resulting in a landscape of 'realistic' representation. Thus, in some respects, realism (often conflated with naturalism) is no longer recognizable as a distinct form, but has come to dominate popular representation to the extent that it is likely to be the standard form with which many television, cinema and theatre audiences are acquainted (Innes 2000: 1). In a contemporary theatre environment, audiences will arrive well-used to seeing a variety of protagonists depicted in 'realistic' representations in film and on television. In this context the nostalgic aesthetic of *Port* risks a troubling politics, in which the inevitability of the character's miserable trajectory is authenticated by the 'realism' of the social environment depicted on stage.

As I have argued elsewhere (see Beswick 2015), council estates are often used in contemporary theatre and visual artworks as generic symbols of social ruin and decay. Using an estate as the realist backdrop for a working-class drama creates a 'ruin aesthetic', in which discourses of ruination associated with the fixed identity of estates in the popular imagination influence our interpretations of the play and its characters. Higson has claimed that, in cinema, shots of the outside space work as a 'pull between narrative and spectacle' (1984: 3). He argues that 'the emphasis on *place* in – or against – the narrative historicizes the narrative, shifting it away from the particular, to a more general level of concern' (1984: 8). I similarly propose that in *Port* the views of the outside space in both the trailer and the play itself shift the narrative in from the 'particular to the general', facilitating a dialectical interplay between *this* fictional site and other estates, elsewhere.

In this way, the ruin aesthetic operates to position Racheal within, and against, a fixed understanding of the 'real' working-class estate resident – creating a narrative of exceptionality that still positions the estate and its residents in fixed terms, despite the nuance with which Racheal herself is depicted. As Adiseshiah argues,

> the danger in *Port* – with its strikingly resilient, compassionate, dynamic and intelligent protagonist, Racheal – is the ease with which the play re-narrates part of the structure of the working-class-made-good Billy Elliott story, a story that inadvertently exceptionalises a working-class individual, leaving the dominant paradigm of a stagnant, wilfully ignorant, feckless working-class normative subjectivity in tact.
>
> (2016: 160)

Indeed, *Port* is riddled with a middle-class morality that is at pains to highlight Racheal's exceptional 'goodness' through her subscription to middle-class modes of respectability. Most strikingly, this is implied through Racheal's relationship with sex and sexual pleasure. Despite being accused of loose morals ('You fucking tart' (2013: 6)) and promiscuity ('You and Chris? Did yer do it with him? Yer did didn't yer? I knew it!' (49)) throughout her childhood and adolescence, the play implies that Racheal is unusually chaste. We never see her engaged in sex or pleasurable, intimate physical contact with a man, beyond fleeting touches, and during scene six we discover that, despite spending the first romantic night with her boyfriend Danny, Racheal hasn't had sex with him ('Does it bother you that we didn't have sex last night?' (65)). The only significant physical contact with a love interest we do see Racheal engaged in is as a victim of domestic violence, when her husband, Kevin, grabs her by the hair and throws her across a hotel room.

If Rita and Sue express a rejection of middle-class morality through their embrace of immoral sexual practices and refusal to act as victims to the violence that surrounds them, then Racheal signals her moral personhood through a rejection of sexual pleasure and victim status. To align chastity and victimhood with middle-class values is not to suggest that working-class women are universally promiscuous or willing objects of violence – rather it is to point out that references to Racheal's chastity operate here to signify her exceptional personhood within the working-class environment. It is through a rejection of stereotypical working-class attributes (sexually available, criminal etc.) that Racheal is presented as 'resilient, compassionate, dynamic and intelligent'. This paradoxically serves to reinforce dominant understandings that working-class women's private sexual experiences are a means through which they can be morally categorized.

Authentic voice?

The marketing for *Port*, like the marketing for many estate plays, highlighted Stephens's personal connection to the subject matter and, as we see in the email exchange above, served to secure a narrative about the play's authenticity. However, Stephens was clear in interviews that the work was not autobiographical:

> I interviewed a lot of women who had lived in Stockport all their lives. That helped. But in retrospect I don't think writing Racheal was any different to writing any other character I've written. Her gender is one of the many things that define her that I don't share and so had to imagine. I've also never lived in the part of Stockport she lived in. My Mum never left home. My brother never got into trouble with the law. I didn't see my Granddad after he'd died. I think writing characters requires a lot of empathy and a lot of imagination and that is absolutely the bloody fun of the thing.
>
> (Antoniou 2013)

As is evident in the reception of his works by both critics and scholars, and the broad span of his writing in terms of themes and subject matter, Stephens does not meet the definition of an 'authentic voice' playwright. In other words, Stephens's works are understood in both scholarship and the wider culture as fictional representations, replete with poetic licence, and are not therefore subject to the same burden of representation that exists in authentic voice works. Nor do the power imbalances that permeate the public square in 'authentic voice' work necessarily transfer here in the same way – Stephens is an established playwright, with a significant industry profile, who writes – and is commissioned to write – about a variety of subjects.

Certainly, despite the claims to local knowledge made by both the playwright and the director, *Port* was not received as convincingly authentic by many of the newspaper critics who reviewed it. Indeed, mainstream newspaper critics are far clearer about the representational failings and potentially damaging stereotypes offered in *Port* than tends to be the case in authentic voice works, where the critical reception often positions the representations as 'true' – even where similar criticisms might be levelled. Writing in the *Daily Telegraph*, for example, critic Dominic Cavendish criticizes the lack of 'truthfulness' in many of the play's performers and points to the clichéd nature of the stereotypical depictions of working-class life as one of the play's failings:

> Writing about his home town, Stockport, Stephens strives for a pointed realism that can be so studied it tips into heavy-going soap-operatics. In its depiction early on of unruly children and mildly delinquent teenagers, the evening teeters on the edge of cliché.
>
> (Cavendish 2013)

The *Daily Mail*'s Quentin Letts (2013) similarly suggests that the play falls into cliché, in a one-star review in which he argues the play shows nothing of the 'decent and admirable' Stockport Letts has visited.

Meanwhile, despite her praise of the play's 'demon precision', the *Observer* critic Susannah Clapp notes,

> In summary, the plot reads like a social worker's manual: not only wife-beating but flashing, not only smash-and-grab but granny-bashing. Some of the laconic flatness, the almost tape recorder-like veracity, could do with a tuck.
>
> (Clapp 2013)

Unlike *Rita, Sue and Bob Too/A State Affair* then, *Port* is not positioned as an accurate, totalizing portrayal of estate life. This is, in part, perhaps, because the vitality and 'realness' that characterize Dunbar's writing are missing from *Port*: which is to say that *Port* suffers from its lack of authenticity, despite also being subject to a reduced burden of representation because of it.

Of course, even as I write the criticisms above I am aware that my perception of the writers' respective class and gender positions flavours my readings of their work. This is to bring us back to one of the many problems of authenticity, which is that it is difficult to deduce how far perceptions of authenticity colour both academic and mainstream critical readings: when you watch a play your knowledge, assumptions or understandings about the playwright's relationship to the subject matter – along with your own perspective on the representational world – inevitably inflect the viewing experience.

To suggest that Stephens is not an authentic voice is not to suggest that *Port*'s burden of representation was entirely removed. Although his position as creative writer (as opposed to an 'authentic voice') means that the play is at a critical distance from 'the real', the aesthetic elements of the production – particularly the close attention to nostalgic detail in the stage design and regional vernacular – offer less possibility for glimpses into the ambiguous space between the real and the represented than is the case in *Rita/A State Affair*. The realist form of the production, the claims to (albeit removed) authorial experience of the subject matter and the National Theatre context ultimately operate to reproduce, circulate and fix dominant ideas about estates and their residents in the public imagination – there is little room for reimagining estate spaces within *Port*'s frame.

DenMarked: Beyond realism – hip-hop, the hood and council estate rage

DenMarked is an autobiographical one-man 'confessional' performance in which writer and performer Conrad Murray combines *Hamlet* and hip-hop to narrate his experience of growing up on a council estate in Mitcham, south west London. It was evolved through a commission from the BAC, after Murray performed a five-minute monologue as part of the London Stories festival (BAC 2013), where Londoners were invited to develop and perform short one-to-one performances detailing their experiences of living in the city. *DenMarked* was shown at the BAC in 2016, 2017 and 2018, and toured across the United Kingdom as part of the BAC's Collaborative Touring Network; it was also performed at the Camden People's Theatre in 2017.

Unlike the other two plays in this chapter *DenMarked* is not part of any version of the contemporary canon. Its core creative team – including directors Ria Parry and Laura Keefe – are still 'emerging' artists, in that, at the time of writing, their reputations haven't been secured within the national mainstream theatre establishment. The BAC, despite its location in London, is a fringe venue that does not have the status of establishment venues such as the Royal Court and National Theatre. Nonetheless, *DenMarked* is a useful example of council estate performance practice that meets the definition of 'mainstream' I offered in the introduction – that is, it is a scripted piece of theatre, primarily performed in subsidized building-based theatre venues. The play demonstrates how emergent forms of cultural production can speak back to dominant estate narratives, fostering a cultural politics that feels engaged at the grass roots. It articulates an authenticity that does not primarily seek, either at the level of creation or institutionally, to facilitate the consumption of 'real' poverty narratives for the middle classes. It is also an example of how the hood, as presented through hip-hop forms, can connect profoundly local concerns to global conditions of urban poverty.

Murray is a musician, performer, writer and beatboxer who has a long-term relationship with the BAC. He was a member of its 'Homegrown' youth initiative, which offers those aged between 12 and 29 opportunities to create original performance working alongside professionals. He now runs the BAC's Beat Box Academy, a 'beginner collective of beatboxers, singers, poets and MCs' (BAC 2017) who develop performances during weekly 'jam' sessions held at the BAC (including the critically acclaimed 2018 adaptation of *Frankenstein*). Educated at the University of Kingston, where he completed a degree in Drama, Murray is committed to exploring class injustice in his practice. In 2015 he established the theatre company Beats & Elements with collaborator Paul Cree, piloting his 'hip-hop theatre' form in *No Milk for the Foxes*, in which the duo attempted to bring what they called 'council estate rage' to the theatre (Trueman 2015).

DenMarked develops Murray's experiments with hip-hop theatre and the council estate rage aesthetic. Delivered in direct address to the audience, the play is organized into titled sections, arranged like chapters that deliver an unfolding story. The piece juxtaposes storytelling, rap, song, beatboxing and Shakespeare, moving between past and present to explore how Murray's council estate upbringing continues to inflect his life. *Hamlet* serves a dual purpose in the play: in terms of the story it is a text gifted to Murray by a beloved teacher, one he returns to again and again, a metaphor for the power of education to transform lives. It is also a formal construct, a means through which he explores his identity, particularly his relationship with his violent father. The repeated refrain, 'there is nothing either good or bad, but thinking makes it so', epitomizes Murray's drive to overcome an abusive, tumultuous childhood and find meaning and nuance in his past and future. The title is both a play on 'Denmark' (as in Hamlet, Prince of Denmark) and a reflection on the extent to which his past continues to shape his present – that is, how he has been 'marked' by his 'den' (slang for home).

The piece opens with Murray, spot-lit on a bare stage, dressed in a 'New Era' brand baseball cap, black t-shirt and jeans. In the first section, 'Interview', he narrates his experience of arriving for a job interview as a secondary school drama teacher. He recounts how, arriving at the school, holding a cup of takeaway coffee, his sense of inferiority, shaped by the stigmas associated with growing up as a poor, working-class, mixed race, council estate resident, interrupts the interview process, causing him to feel perpetually 'not good enough' for a professional job. He worries because he hasn't read *King Lear*, tells us that he feels uncomfortable in his new suit – that he wishes he had worn his signature New Era cap and come as himself instead of attempting middle-class respectability.

I start convincing myself that I'm not going to get this job because of this coffee cup. They are going to know exactly what kind of lowlife I am all because of this cardboard coffee cup. I don't deserve to be here. I'm a piece of shit. How can the agency not have seen this? How? Why am I here? What the fuck am I thinking? I can't talk properly, I have bad handwriting, I haven't read King Lear, and I call myself a drama teacher?!
    What have you, my good friends, deserved at the hands of Fortune that she sends you to prison hither?
    Is that *Hamlet* or *Lear*. Fuck I can't remember!
    Prison my lord ... We think not so.
    To me it is a prison.

(Murray N.D.)

Subsequent scenes, told in working-class London vernacular, recall significant people and events in Murray's past, including his father's arrest and imprisonment; his experience as a victim of race violence ('Paki bashing'); his social worker, Julie; his mother; and influential friends and teachers. Periodically, scenes are interspersed with original songs, for which Murray beatboxes as he performs, laying down the beats live and playing them back on a recorded loop as he raps over this vocal backing track.

In a section titled 'Dawn' Murray recounts how stereotypical narratives of council estate girls as promiscuous and sexually excessive played out on his estate. He describes how he befriended a local girl called Dawn, who was rumoured to have 'had sex in the graveyard'. When she tried to kiss him, after they climbed a tree together, he tells us, he became scared and ran away. They never spoke again. The direct address mode of delivery allows him to explore the conditions that produced Dawn's behaviour, presenting her as complex and human, and adds nuance to his own reaction to her advances.

It was a shame, because no one liked her, and she was kinda abused by the other boys. She went to a special needs school. I think she was quite vulnerable. People called her a hoe and a sket, and although I liked her, I wasn't really ready for sexual contact.
    I felt really guilty, but I couldn't handle th[o]se kind of feelings at the time. I'm not sure I've ever been able to deal with them properly.

(Murray N.D.)

The direct address method of performance also ensures that the interpretation of Dawn's behaviour is not left up to the audience. Rather than present an 'authentic' scene and allow the audience's own perception of the story to frame the reading, Murray intervenes to illustrate how the trope of 'promiscuous working-class girl' conceals the textured experience of the human being living that stereotype. In doing so he reveals how girls 'like' Dawn are produced by an unequal social environment, closing the gap in understanding through which audiences might 'read' her as morally deficient.

At the closing section, we return to the interview, where Murray describes how he was offered the drama teaching job he had applied for. The interviewer asks if he's read *King Lear* and he pauses ('Fuck!'), before she corrects herself, she's got it wrong, she says, it's *Hamlet* they're doing.

'Yeah', he tells her, 'Yeah, I know that one' (Murray N.D.).

Council estate rage

In an interview I conducted with Murray in preparation for this book, we discussed the state of class politics in the theatre industry. Murray argued that class is still a more or less invisible issue and told me that he found producers at the BAC far more receptive to the race politics evident in his work than the injustices of class that it draws attention to (my interview May 2017). For this reason, this analysis focuses on the class rather than dealing also with race politics of the work. Discussing the state of contemporary class representations in the theatre more widely, Murray pointed out the ways that working-class culture is often made palatable for middle-class audiences. In particular, he noted how rap and hip-hop have been reframed as 'spoken word poetry' to make the forms appear more literary and remove them from the politically inflected global context of hip-hop.

Murray told me that the missing element in most contemporary mainstream representations of the working class was what he called 'council estate rage'. This statement resonated with me as I recalled the incident at *Market Boy* with my mother that I relay at the start of this chapter, remembering how the 'Mum' character was missing something we understood as fundamental about the character of single mothers in our circle of working-class culture.

So-called working-class anger has received significant attention in the wake of the vote to leave the European Union in June 2016 – a result widely understood to have been connected to a large proportion of working-class voters opting to 'leave' (although the extent to which working-class voters influenced the leave vote is highly contested, see e.g. Iyer et al. 2018). McKenzie shows that the articulation of working-class anger through the leave vote is often misrecognized – attributed to ignorance, stupidity and a lack of understanding about economic and political realities. In her ethnographic work in Nottingham and east London, McKenzie argues that she found, in fact, that those working-class people who did vote for the United Kingdom to leave the European Union did so to articulate the simmering anger they felt, pushed to the margins of society, systematically 'left out' and ignored by the political classes: an anger rooted in 'absolute fear of the future that appears overwhelming and unbearable'.

> For a brief moment in 2016 the apathy of the British working-class electorate subsided and gave way to a howl of anger despite being 'invisibly visible', being seen only when policy needed to draw upon their 'bad culture' to explain a deepening and widening unequal Britain.
>
> (McKenzie 2017: 208)

Under these conditions, the leave vote might be viewed as a message from those at the margins: 'they just couldn't stand it being the same' (2017: 208).

What McKenzie's work indicates, and what is evident in Murray's practice, is that working-class anger at the social and political status quo, or 'council estate rage', is not inarticulate, uncontrollable fury. A working-class rage aesthetic, then, is not the representation of working-class people behaving 'badly' or exhibiting furious, incomprehensible violence – rather it is an insider perspective, where a presentation of what might seem 'antisocial' by middle-class moral standards is revealed as a glass shield that barely conceals the core of discontentment, fear and pain that often characterizes the working-class lived experience. Paradoxically, 'rage' also makes room for humour, optimism and celebration of the culture that creates it. In this way, Murray's 'council estate rage' is much like the spirit of survival and resistance that Richardson and Scott-Myre argue epitomize the global hood that often expresses its solidarity through hip-hop.

Hip-hop, the hood and the possibilities of authenticity

Scholar Murray Forman details how hip-hop offers a unique means for youths from disparate marginalized contexts to give voice to the paradoxically painful and optimistic aspects of their experiences. He reminds us that 'conditions of despair and desperation are often matched by more promising conditions steeped in optimism, charity, and creativity' and that hip-hop provides a unique form to express the 'contradictory tensions' produced by urban marginality (Forman 2002: 8).

In *DenMarked* the use of hip-hop conventions, including beatboxing, 'street' vernacular and fashion (the 'New Era' cap and hooded sweatshirt Murray wears in the trailer, for example), signals an affiliation with the global hood, while hip-hop forms such as rap are the means through which he articulates his rage. In the closing number 'Cotchin',[5] for example, Murray nostalgically narrates how it feels to be 'left out' of mainstream capitalist culture:

> Cotchin'
> I remember cotchin
> People living their lives
> I was sitting watching
> Barely taking it in
> My adviser taking the piss
> You should go look for a job
> But all the jobs are shit

(Murray N.D.)

In a line that echoes McKenzie's ethnographic findings, Murray speaks back to the culture that views him as worthless and invisible: 'they say we're chavs, council housed and violent / I just hate being denigrated and silent'.

As Bakari Kitwana explains, and as I explored briefly in the previous chapter, hip-hop has transcended its roots in the poor inner-city African American communities where it originated. It is adopted by young people worldwide who 'adapt it to their local needs, responding to the crises of our time', equipping them with a 'culture that corporate and political elites can't control' (2005: 11). It is especially appealing to poor urban youths both because it remains connected to the streets where it was created and because its basic tools are free (as evidenced by, e.g., beatboxing as 'an approximation of back beats with the vocal chords alone' (Huq 2006: 155)).

Writing about his experiences of using hip-hop in prisons, Scottish rapper and writer Darren McGarvey (aka Loki) illustrates how this global grass-roots form operates in practice to enable working-class culture to be seen and valued. He describes how he introduces himself at prison-based workshops using a track called 'Jump', which recalls painful aspects of his childhood.

> The lyrics are autobiographical and detail my school years and the sudden death of my mother. But the song is also deliberately laden with the imagery and language of lower class communities with references to alcohol products like MD 20/20 and Buckfast, and rap artists like

Tupac Shakur. Themes of family breakdown, abandonment, alcoholism and bereavement, as well as playful jibes at the middle class and law enforcement, not only reflect their own experiences back at them but, crucially, recognise the validity of those experiences. The song, like much of the culture they engage with, regarded as coarse, offensive or lacking sophistication, appeals to them because it reveals the richness of their own experience; the poetry in what is often regarded by wider society as the dereliction and vulgarity of their lives.

(McGarvey 2017: 26)

Hip-hop similarly offers Murray a means to articulate his rage in a form that, despite being very much part of mainstream music culture, evades total co-option by the dominant forces of the media, the state and the market, appealing beyond traditional theatre audiences. Erin Walcon, director of Doorstep Arts, an arts education organization, described to me how, when Murray toured *DenMarked* to Torbay, Devon, a coastal town in the south west of England, the local working-class young men who had previously been reluctant to engage with Doorstep's outreach programme joined in with Murray's beatboxing workshops, able to express themselves in a form they could relate to.

Part of hip-hop's appeal resides in its adherence to a very specific aesthetic of authenticity, distinct from, although related to, the 'authentic real' that dominates realist dramas. While, as I outline in the previous chapter, hip-hop realness also risks authenticating damaging stereotypes, as Rupa Huq argues, authenticity or 'realness' in hip-hop is not so much about absolute truth, or fetishistic adherence to the 'realistic', but rather about evidencing a grass-roots connection to the subject matter and a drive to produce art that isn't, or isn't only, motivated by commercial success (Huq 2006: 113). As Huq implies, hip-hop's 'cut and paste' aesthetic rejects the realist form that has dominated popular culture and problematizes authenticity through its intertextuality, referentiality and fragmentation (Huq 2006: 115).

I want to suggest that hip-hop realness, in legitimizing marginalized voices in a sphere somewhat out of the control of the theatrical elite, offered Murray the possibility of intervening in dominant discourse – positioning his story as part of a global picture of urban marginality, rather than only a personal, local struggle. Hip-hop also serves in this example to appeal directly to young working-class audiences – using contexts, settings and vernacular that are familiar to them. Unlike the plays discussed in the previous sections, *DenMarked* makes no attempt to attract a middle-class audience interested in consuming narratives of the 'other' (although of course middle-class people also came to see the play and also see and consume hip-hop; this is not a binary). This insider perspective, however, meant that the play was mostly ignored by critics in mainstream publications, a state of affairs that both limits the longevity and cultural impact of the performance and artistic team – pointing to the role that newspaper reviewers play in creating the 'theatre establishment' – and allows it to stand on its own merit.

Form and innovation at the Battersea Arts Centre

As I have suggested above, the institutional contexts in which works are produced and performed, especially the operation of power within a 'public square', shapes their final form, their interpretation by audiences and their reception by critics. Like the theatre institutions explored above, the BAC articulates a commitment to more or less progressive politics and to engaging with a diverse audience base (BAC 2017a). Unlike the Royal Court, Soho Theatre, Out of Joint and the National Theatre, however, the BAC does not emphasize traditional 'plays' in its programming. Rather it positions itself as a 'development house' (2017b), committed to facilitating artists to experiment with form and space. In its 'How we programme' document, available online, the BAC states that it tends not to produce work that involves a 'fourth wall' separating performers and audience and that it is especially interested in political ideas that facilitate connections between people.

Murray, like all artists who work with the BAC, was assigned a producer (Liz Moreton), who worked to help him shape and refine his initial five-minute monologue into a scripted, full-length show. *DenMarked* also underwent the BAC's signature 'Scratch' process, where works in progress are periodically shown to small audiences and developed using iterative feedback sessions. The BAC privileges the artist–producer relationship and tends to offer individual artists and companies an unusual amount of freedom to develop the 'whole play'. That is, it is very often artists and companies who are commissioned and developed, rather than already existing works or proposals for single works. Although there is clearly a balance of power held by the BAC in this model, the institutional structure is not strictly hierarchical, meaning that productions themselves do not reproduce the hierarchies evident in the other productions we have seen – with the director or artistic director given more or less absolute creative control of the text once the writer hands it over. Working-class stories are not, therefore, mediated through the interpretative lens of a director. Directors (where they are used) instead act as an outside eye, often working under the creative control of the writer/performer, rather than the other way around. This results in a diversity of output in terms of innovation with form and means that the diverse and marginalized voices sometimes given a platform at the BAC are not held at a distance from the creative process. Work produced at the BAC, therefore, often feels raw and vitally connected to both the performers and the audience – no doubt compounded by the 'no fourth wall' policy. For example, poet Kate Tempest's 2012 work *Brand New Ancients*, an epic spoken poem about working-class south east Londoners, developed at BAC and performed with a live five-piece band, was awarded the Ted Hughes Prize for innovation poetry and praised for connecting the audience with the emotional core of the subject matter – binding audience and performer 'together in a different world' (McConnell 2014). Nonetheless, the marketing for *Brand New Ancients*, where a poem that very clearly drew from hip-hop forms was billed as 'spoken word', illustrates Murray's concern with the decontextualization of rap from its hip-hop context. The BAC, like all cultural institutions, exists within a public square in which class inequality operates and is perpetuated, despite a will to resist and a commitment to progressive modes of creating and disseminating theatre.

Indeed, despite its articulation of a politically potent estate rage, *DenMarked*, as a classed representation, did at times adhere to dominant ways of understanding the estate. Particularly in the online trailer, in which Murray, sitting on a bench in front of a council estate, dressed in a hooded sweatshirt and baseball cap, uses his authentic estateness to sell the production. The trailer evokes a gritty urban realism and does not draw on hip-hop forms of intertexuality to subvert or complicate the narrative. Nor is the hip-hop form, now itself part of the dominant 'mainstream' without its own inherent tensions: I mentioned in the previous chapter that hip-hop is regularly subject to accusations of fuelling crime and gang violence and has been appropriated by corporations fuelling negative depictions of black inner city life (Rose 2008). This means for those 'outside' of or already opposed to the culture, Murray's representation – merely by its hip-hop form – may reinforce their worst prejudices about non-white estate residents.

Despite this, *DenMarked* does indicate how under-represented voices can overcome some of the problems posed by the authentic real when they move away from realism – and how institutional structures, including long-term investment in local talent, can facilitate formal innovations. Feminists including Sue-Ellen Case have illustrated how 'the hierarchical organising-principles of traditional form … served to elide women from discourse' (Case 2008: 129); these structures similarly elide working-class people – maintaining the middle-class lens as the status quo, even where working-class voices are foregrounded. Institutional contexts that prioritize experiments with form, and particularly those that enable artists to move away from conventional theatre hierarchies, might pose the most powerful means for working-class people to produce work about their own lives, on their own terms.

Dominant, residual emergent

The analysis I have offered above reveals how estate plays performed in mainstream theatre venues manifest a complex, ambivalent politics – this politics might be best understood within Raymond Williams's model of the dominant, residual and emergent (Williams 1977b: 121–127). Williams's model illustrates how the interaction between the residual and emergent elements of a culture creates the 'character of the dominant' (125). In other words, the dominant is produced by interactions between the residual and emergent, which opens up the possibility that the dominant might eventually give way to emergent ways of seeing and being.

The dominant, fetishized 'dreadful' conception of estate space and its residents is produced by existing structures of power, from which working-class people are marginalized. The dominant conception of estates is rooted in residual understandings of working classes and their home spaces as pathological – such as those discourses prevalent in the 1970s in relation to the relationship between architecture and psychology (see Beswick 2011) and those historical narratives of the pathological working classes, characterized by the Charity Organisation Society's 1869 distinction between the 'deserving' and 'undeserving' poor (Rose 1972: 25). The dominant council estate discourse, however, also contains elements of emergent council estate discourse. Emergent forms of discourse offer resistance and can be found in, for example, the kind of spatialized resistance offered by the located cultural politics of the hood, which is also often appropriated and fetishized as part of a global market of hood representation.

Existing structures of power are perpetuated and reproduced in the theatre, particularly through realist forms. In mainstream performance practice, as we have seen, institutions often produce work that attempts to articulate resistance as part of the emergent culture, with varying degrees of success. There is an ostensibly utopian agenda within representations of working-class lives – particularly those that offer 'voices' to disenfranchized groups. Nonetheless, this utopian agenda is compromised by the prevalence of the residual cultures in the structures that author the work. The interplay between the institutional context, the material and social conditions of a production, the artists involved in creating the performances, the aesthetic form and the audience is rarely straightforward. The desire to engage with, or contribute to, a socially progressive emergent culture is complicated by the deep residue of determinism that permeates conceptions of the council estate – therefore estate dramas can easily become part of the dominant discourse in which the ideological gap between estate residents and non-estate residents is fixed, despite the presence of emergent culture driven by those with a will to resist. This means that institutions that produce estate dramas negotiate a complex set of relations, where work that attempts to challenge existing structures is nonetheless authored, to some extent, by those structures. In the next chapter we will see how works that move beyond the walls of 'mainstream' institutions are also compromised by an ambivalent politics, where the existing power dynamics at play in social space are reproduced within artworks, even when artists attempt to overcome them.

Located on the estate

September 2011: Following directions I've downloaded to my mobile phone, I climb the steps set into the slope that leads from the back of Sheffield train station up to Park Hill. Performers are positioned along the route and as I pass them they point to the estate at the top of the hill. I arrive and dozens of actors are milling about the courtyard. There is an air of celebration, as we, the audience, are separated into groups. We learn that, in the fictional world of the play, we are on a 'gap year' between school and university and that the estate's buildings, shadowy and imposing in the near-distance, are a ship on which we will travel to a far-away island known as Utopia: a land mass constructed entirely from plastics removed from the seas.

In 'real life' the Park Hill estate is undergoing redevelopment by a company called Urban Splash, and as we enter the 'ship', the real and fictional spaces of the performance site collide. Huge, beautiful structures made from plastic bottles line the walkways, a scenographic intervention that hints at the play's environmental themes and illuminates the dusk with a silvery, otherworldly light. At one point, I find myself overwhelmed by the beauty of the vast urban landscape that is the view from the top of Park Hill's north block, as a plastic sheet flips backwards and reveals the panorama to me.

I make my way through the estate/ship, finding stowaways hidden in the cracks of the building work. They warn me that all is not as it seems in Utopia. Pale, sickly figures whisper terrible secrets: previous volunteers are concealed on the ship, dying – poisoned by the chemicals released from rotting plastic. Throughout my journey, the world of the performance is interrupted by Urban Splash signage and the visible signs of construction, such as scaffolding, and partially built interior walls.

We leave the estate/ship and arrive at 'Utopia', sited on a grass verge lined by the estate's blocks. The performance culminates in a spectacular aerial display as the island's residents revolt against the corporation exploiting them. As the sun sets, dancers abseil down the huge façade of the block we have just travelled through. Hundreds of performers move in a breath-taking, synchronized choreography.

I turn to leave and the lights of the city gleam below the hill. I think that this would be an amazing place to live. Someone from the performance approaches and hands me a canvas bag stuffed with promotional leaflets and sales brochures, detailing how I can register my interest in buying a property on the redeveloped estate.

*

February 2014: At the Yorkshire Sculpture Park, I sit with my cousin and her girlfriend on a bench beside a large, square, concrete structure, surrounded by bald winter trees. The women at the entrance tell us that we won't have to wait too long. They hand us thin blue-and-white plastic slippers, like elasticated carrier bags, which we must wear to cover our shoes. We fumble to put them on, holding our gloves in our mouths as we pull them up over our boots.

Inside it is almost exactly as it looks in the pictures I've seen in the press. The walls are lined with sparking crystals, cobalt blue, poking out everywhere, sharp and dazzling. The claustrophobic smallness of the flat surprises me – the way it has been reduced by the crystals – as does the cold. The crystal crust has enveloped the space so that it feels less like an apartment and more like a cave, or a grotto.

We move slowly. I run my hands along the freezing, spiky walls. My cousin pokes her head out from behind an arch that I assume was once a doorway, and I jump. We leave the space laughing.

*

October 2017: I stand at a makeshift altar in the garden of the Wenlock Barn estate in east London. A table laden with bread sits directly in front of me. Plants and shrubbery conceal the scene from the street. The smell of wet grass and lavender, and some other fragrant herb that I don't recognize, moves through the damp air. I am wearing a colourful cape – it is *appliqué* and adorned with dozens of tiny, mirrored sequins – and brandishing a large ostrich feather.

I open the ceremony with a short speech offering a brief history of the evolution of British council estates, drawing attention to their origins in ideas of community, connectivity, security and togetherness. I say, 'We are gathered here today to celebrate this marriage to the bread.'

I feel extremely silly. My cheeks flush with pins and needles as I garble my speech. I wonder what they think of me, the residents watching a university lecturer they have never met conducting this strange ceremony on their territory.

After I have finished speaking, children from the estate approach the table, marching slowly, holding out loaves of bread adorned with ribbons. They carefully place them on the bread table at the altar.

We move into a circle, offering gestures that sum up our positive feelings about the community on the estate where this ceremony is taking place. Someone makes a circle with their hands, and we all join in, reciting a promise of commitment to the bread as we make and repeat the gestures.

Knives are handed out and residents from the estate approach the table, breaking the bread with the knives and their hands. We feast on the bread and on food that residents and Fourthland, the artists' collective who have organized the event, have prepared.

In small groups we're ushered to a shed that has been fashioned into a cinema. A black-and-white movie, featuring the estates' residents conducting elaborate ceremonies in the garden where we have just 'married the bread', begins to play.

*

In November 2017 I was added to a private group on the social media platform Facebook that had been created in response to news that the Victoria and Albert (V&A) Museum had acquired a three-storey section of a block on the soon-to-be demolished Robin Hood Gardens estate, in Poplar, east London. The group included housing activists, academics and estate residents. The members shared feelings of anger and unease at the idea that a section of this once vibrant estate had been saved for museum preservation and display, at great expense, while the estate's residents were forced to move from their homes after years of campaigning to save the estate from demolition.

The wider context in which the acquisition sat needs to be taken into account in order to understand the strength of the anger that it raised in some quarters. Since at least the turn of the twenty-first century, on estates across England, but especially in London – including the Aylesbury, Carpenters, Cressingham Gardens, Ferrier and Sweets Way estates – residents have campaigned, with varying degrees of success, to stop the demolition of their homes. In campaigns that include direct action, legal challenges, alternative proposals and occupation, residents have fought against the so-called 'social cleansing' agenda – where social housing is demolished and replaced, usually by mixed tenure buildings, with reduced or zero capacity for social housing, and often with huge numbers of luxury flats for private sale, marketed at inflated prices to overseas investors.[1] In this model, residents removed from their homes are often unable to return, or to afford alternative accommodation locally, and face the prospect of having to move to other parts of the country where homes are cheaper, but where they have not chosen to live, and where they are often removed from jobs, networks, schools and family.

Meanwhile, in June 2017, just five months before the V&A announcement, a fire broke out at tower block in west London called Grenfell Tower, killing at least seventy-two people living in or visiting the block at the time. The building had recently been refurbished, with cladding fixed on the outside of the concrete block to make it look more attractive within its surroundings. This cladding was unsuitable for such a high building and exacerbated the spread of fire (see e.g. Booth 2018). Residents had repeatedly expressed concerns, in complaints to the Kensington and Chelsea Tenant Management Organisation (TMO) who managed the block and in a public blog (Grenfell Action Group 2016), that the building conditions constituted a fire hazard. Their warnings were ignored.

Many people, myself included, saw the Grenfell Tower disaster as connected to the wider phenomenon of social cleansing in London and beyond – a direct result of a broken housing system in which those who are perceived to rely on state-subsidized housing are consistently overlooked and completely devalued (see e.g. Tucker 2017, Shildrick 2018). We felt that Grenfell Tower was a clear example of structural violence, wherein the negligence of institutions acting on behalf of the state (in this case the Kensington and Chelsea TMO) wrought material harm on those relying on its services. Importantly, we felt that this violence happened because the residents were not seen as fully human – a result of the devaluing of the working class, compounded by racism, that I discussed in Chapter 1.

In this context then, the V&A's acquisition of a portion of a demolished housing block for display in a museum appeared extremely insensitive and ill-considered, not least because, as I evidenced in the previous chapter, participation in cultural activities, including museum-going, is predominately understood as a middle-class pursuit (notwithstanding that working-class people do of course attend museums and other 'elite' cultural institutions). One member of the Facebook group I mention above designed a satirical poster in response to the possibility of a V&A exhibition of the Robin Hood Gardens building, expressing his anger that working-class homes had been acquired for the entertainment of the middle classes. On a pastel-pink background it depicted a section of tower block and the silhouette of a hooded, baseball-cap-wearing figure (a stereotypical working-class youth, see Bell 2013), both behind bars. It read:

> The last working class person left in London is to be displayed in a reconstruction of its natural environment in this exciting new immersive exhibition by the Victoria and Albert Museum: Prole Zoo, Opens May 2018.

This poster was conceived as a public artwork and was displayed on underground trains and sites in London in May 2018 as protests erupted in response to the display of the preserved section of Robin Hood Gardens at the 2018 Venice Biennial (see Hunt 2018). The poster and protests illustrate a binary that frequently emerges in debates surrounding site-based artworks and estates. This binary operates between understandings of estate-based artworks as either socially engaged activism or as instruments of artwashing. In the latter, the artists and institutions who create the works are understood as instruments of the state who use creative and cultural activities to provide a 'gloss for dispossession, displacement and, ultimately, social cleansing' (Pritchard 2017a).

Artwashing and monopolistic performance

In this binary model, public artworks that rely on their relationship with a particular place, space or site for their meaning are viewed as inherently political, and artists who conduct public works without obvious activist purposes, particularly on estates and other contested sites, are often treated with suspicion and hostility. For example, following a failed attempt to carry out a project in the car park of an east London estate the collective Performance Space released a newsletter online (2014), detailing how they had been forced to abandon their project when residents reacted angrily to their presence. The letter illustrates how the tensions that simmer underneath creative practices often lead to suspicion and mistrust of artists and cultural workers. Meanwhile, in an attack on 'hipsters' – the fashionable, culturally rich and economically mobile groups of usually young people who benefit from the gentrification that leads to social cleansing – Stephen Pritchard, an academic who writes about artwashing and gentrification, argued in the *Guardian* that artists have become the foot soldiers of the 'neoliberal state':

> Artists make the first move into post-industrial, post-welfare state wastelands like brownfield sites and council housing estates and sow the seeds of cultural capital. They attract hipsters before, eventually, being displaced by them and their new middle-class neighbours.
>
> (Pritchard 2016)

Although Pritchard's polemic here offers an extremely reductive view of the ways that artists operate in contested and rapidly developing sites, he does draw explicit attention to the conflicts, contradictions and tensions that artists making site-based estate works must navigate and that are often underplayed in scholarship about these works. Jen Harvie usefully explores the ways that artworks are compromised in the neoliberal landscape, pointing out that although artists often facilitate neoliberal agenda it is 'probably almost never artists' ambition to contribute to gentrification's negative social effects of exclusion and ghettoization' (2013: 11). Pritchard's work then, despite its problems, might be understood as a means to encourage artists to think more carefully about the politics of their practice.

Pritchard's argument also calls our attention to the politics of space, emphasizing the ways that site-based artworks themselves can enact what Michael McKinnie calls a 'monopolistic' politics. Here 'the relationship of performance to place is sometimes less interrogative, and more acquisitive, than is commonly acknowledged': privileging the performance or artwork over place rather than the other way around (2012: 22).

At the start of this chapter, I describe my experience of three located estate artworks I've encountered over the course of my research, which I return to below in more depth – *SLICK* (National Youth Theatre, 2011), *Seizure* at the Yorkshire Sculpture Park (YSP; Roger Hirons/Art Angel 2014) and 'The Wedding to the Bread' (Fourthland 2017). These works might all be considered 'monopolistic', and also all enact what might broadly be understood as 'artwashing' in one way or another. However, the first-hand accounts of my remembered experience offered above illustrate how, in practice, artworks rarely operate as straightforwardly as artwashing critiques might suggest. Rather, as my accounts narrate – and as discussed in relation to the mainstream theatre examples discussed in the previous chapter – the social, institutional and aesthetic elements of the works combine to offer audiences and participants dynamic and complex experiences that cannot be reduced to single political readings. These experiences are always ambivalent: their ultimate effect always depends on the political and social hinterland that individual audience members bring to the work and the material relationship between the performance, the audience, any other participants and the site. My accounts, above, deliberately move between my physical, embodied experience, my inner thoughts and emotions and my recollection of the artworks themselves to suggest how located estate artworks mediate between the inner and outer world of audience members experiencing them in particular ways. As scholar-practitioner Cecilie Sachs-Olsen argues, artworks that happen in the urban public realm, attempting to engage the 'public' in local issues or with local spaces, are useful precisely because they draw attention to the way that the city operates 'as an environment formed through various, often conflicting, social practices produced by diverse social groups' (Sachs Olsen 2017: 274).

In other words, any reading that might be made of these kinds of works relies on an interaction between their political context and the live, embodied, active engagement of an audience (who will receive the work very differently depending on their own relationship to the specific site). Although this is arguably true of any artwork, the nature of embodied spectatorship in located estate work takes on a particular importance because estate works are especially ambivalent. Charlotte Bell notes that estate artworks demand 'bodily presence in order to come into being' at the same time as 'they legitimately embody cultural monopolistic claims' (Bell 2014b: 312). This reliance on audience embodiment is what brings the works I discuss in this chapter into the frame of performance – even when, as in the case of the installation *Seizure*, they do not involve performers.

Site-specific performance on the estate

This chapter speaks broadly to the two categories that I describe as 'located' in the taxonomy offered in the introduction to this book ('located estate performance' and 'located arts practices "as" council estate performance'). However, the three examples I offer here can also all be understood as site-specific works (see the subcategories of located estate performance in the taxonomy), and, indeed, the language of site-specific scholarship is useful in thinking through the political structures of these works and how they might be understood to operate within the production of estate space.

McKinnie suggests that site-specific performance scholarship operates through three dominant tropes: heterotopia, in which the performance gestures beyond the performance site to other real and imagined spaces (see e.g. Tompkins 2012a); dialogue, in which the space operates to facilitate conversation between groups (see e.g. Kester 2004); and palimpsest, in which the ghostly layers of a site's lived history become visible through its performance (see e.g. Turner 2004). Although McKinnie is critical of the ways these models often elide the problematic politics of site-specific works by overlooking their monopolistic tendencies, I am interested in the ways that all of these models draw attention to the dialectical potential of site-specific practices.

Mike Pearson and Michael Shanks's definition of site-specificity also suggests the dialectical nature of the form:

Site-specific performances are conceived for, mounted within and conditioned by the particulars of found spaces, existing social situations or locations, both used and disused.... They rely, for their conception and their interpretation, upon the complex co-existence, superimposition and interpenetration of a number of narratives and architectures, historical and contemporary, of two basic orders: that which is of the site, its fixtures and fittings, and that which is brought to the site, the performance and its scenography: of that which pre-exists the work and that which is of the work: of the past and of the present.

(Pearson and Shanks 2001: 23)

This dialectical relationship between past and present (and, as I will discuss in relation to the examples below, future) is an important feature of located estate performance, wherein 'that which is brought to the site' relies on the contextual meaning afforded by the generic idea of the council estate, as well as whichever specific site(s) the work is located on. This is to make the fairly obvious point that the located estate performances I discuss rely on the fixed ideas about estates that circulate in the public imagination, which imbue often otherwise unintelligible works within a tangible political context and offer possibilities for meaning making.

So, too, we might understand located estate performance within Richardson and Skott-Myhre's articulation of the cultural politics of the hood – where the bounded location of the marginal inner city housing estate creates the conditions for oppression, but also for liberation and resistance, which are always most effectively staged *inside* that bounded location. This question of a located cultural politics, as Joanne Tompkins points out, is central both to site-specific practices themselves and also to the development of site-specific scholarship. She asks how the critique of located works might 'contribute not just to the development of a critical praxis, but also to the articulation of cultural activity as crucial to social well-being' (Tompkins 2012b: 4).

This chapter, then, works to consider site-specific performance as a located cultural politics, exploring how work made on estate sites creates, resists and responds to social, political and legal structures of power and their contextual realization on estates. Although I am uncomfortable with the idea that scholarship should work as advocacy for cultural activity, this chapter does begin to answer Tompkins's question around the role of scholarship – both by developing a critical praxis in relation to a specific type of site-specific practice and through taking seriously the possibility that works that are, on the one hand, instrumentalized and problematic in the way they enact a monopolistic acquisition of space also have possibilities to enhance well-being by harmonizing audiences with 'other' environments and to operate as a counter to the rapid and often violent takeover of our cities by corporations and investors.

Authenticity in located estate performance

In his 2016 work *Shattering Hamlet's Mirror: Theatre and Reality*, Carlson traces the emergence of 'environmental' and site-specific theatre practices within a wider history of theatre's complicated relationship with 'the real'. For Carlson, the appeal of performance taking place outside of the theatre building hinges on its material reality: the materially 'real' spaces into which audiences are invited. Carlson argues that located immersive works implicate audiences in a 'mimetic game' (118), where they themselves become responsible for deciding what blend of the fictional and real 'will determine the status of any theatrical element' (106). Importantly, he points out that moving outside of the theatre building and removing barriers between actor and audience have often operated to overcome the class segregation that existed in traditional modes of theatrical production and consumption (111).

The authentic appeal of located estate performance certainly resonates with Carlson's observations about the relationship between the real and the represented in site-based works more generally. The material reality of estates is often part of their 'authentic' appeal – an appeal perhaps, as I discuss below, rooted in the fascination with authentic objects of poverty that Karen Bettez Halnon (2002) has described as 'poor chic'. And, certainly, estate works are often ostensibly concerned with overcoming classed barriers to consumption.

However, as a distinct genre within the site-specific field, located estate works operate with a specific inflection of 'realness' and a specific relationship to reality. They are part of a wider genre of estate performance where conceptions of the real, as we have seen, are grounded in a socio-political context that means represented realness might always become an authenticating mechanism for stigmatizing ideas about estates that circulate in the wider culture, regardless of their 'actual' relationship to reality. The performances I discuss in this chapter turn away from the modes of social realism I explored in Chapter 2. Nonetheless the issues of authenticity that arise in relation to the works discussed here can still be understood within the model of the authentic real. These works have material consequence for the political, social and ideological structures that structure estate space and produce the wider landscape of social housing.

SLICK: Art and redevelopment, making sense of unresolved tensions

In 2010 the National Youth Theatre of Great Britain (NYT) announced a trilogy of large-scale, environmentally themed, site-specific performance events.

SLICK (2011) was the second of these projects. The first, *S'warm* (2010), was performed by 500 young people at Battersea Power Station and sites across London, exploring the potential impact of the threat to bee populations on the environment. *Flood*, the third planned production in the trilogy, appears to have been realized in reduced capacity at a performance in Manchester in 2012 (TakeTwoImages 2012). However, information about this performance is scant, and it is not listed in the archive of performances documented on the NYT's website.

SLICK was an immersive, participatory performance that took place on the Park Hill estate in Sheffield, a post-industrial city located in the north of England. Delivered by 220[2] young people under the direction of several established and emerging directors, including the NYT's associate director, Anna Niland, *SLICK* placed the audience at the centre of the action. On their arrival at the estate, audience members were cast as 'players' in the drama: gap-year students destined for voluntary work on a far-away island known as 'Utopia'. The estate's north block was, in the fictional world of the performance, the ship on which volunteers would travel, eventually discovering that Utopia was exploiting volunteers. As I describe in the opening to this chapter, the regeneration works, including scaffolding, tools and Urban Splash signs, were visible as spectators were led through the block. The story resolved as the audience disembarked from the ship, arriving at Utopia – a grassy square at the estate's centre – where the island's population rose up against the corporation exploiting them for profit. The performance culminated in a choreographed dance, featuring the 220-strong ensemble, which included aerial performers, who ascended the block's façade, lit by coloured floodlights that illuminated the building in neon colours.

The Park Hill estate has a fraught and complex history that can be mapped onto the wider history of estate decline and complexity that I outline in the introduction to, and the first chapter of, this book. Indeed, the narrative arc of *SLICK* might be understood as an allegorical critique of the estate's redevelopment: a utopian project that eventually falls prey to capitalistic exploitation. Completed in 1961, the estate once provided 995 homes for social rent, mostly for the largely working-class families employed by Sheffield's (now diminished) steel industry. Housing over 3,000 residents, the

Park Hill was designed to function as a community – with schools, shops, pubs, community centres, social clubs and a doctor's and dentist's surgery built into the concrete estate that overlooked the city. Housing allocation too prioritized community, as neighbours from the terraced houses that the estate replaced were given flats next door to one another, maintaining the existing networks that 'bind a community together' (ASH 2017a).

From its inception Park Hill was regarded as an architectural innovation – realizing the modernist 'streets in the sky' aesthetic that revolutionary architects such as Le Corbusier and Sant'Elia envisioned in their writings and drawings about the architecture that would define modernity (Heathcote 2017). The estate's four blocks were designed to recall terraced housing: elevated streets that ran along the flats from the first floor up were connected at each level and wide enough to accommodate the milk floats that completed their daily rounds.

Despite early recognition of its architectural value, however, the estate's local reputation suffered as the British steel industry began to flounder and unemployment soared. Park Hill fell into physical and reputational disrepair, partly as a result of housing policies that moved the most vulnerable onto the estate, partly as a result of wider disinvestment in council housing and partly as a result of the systematic devaluing of working-class culture that I reference in Chapter 1. By the late 1980s Park Hill was widely understood as a failure, and embodied all the negative connotations of estateness that I outline in the introduction, becoming associated with 'ugliness, social decay, drug use and family breakdown' (Dobraszczyk 2015). Nonetheless, in 1998, Park Hill was awarded English Heritage Grade II listed building status – meaning it is protected as a building of special interest – a move that both signalled the site's architectural importance and imbued the estate with a cultural cachet, potentially increasing its appeal to investors. Residents began to be moved out of the site in the 1990s, and by 2003, most of the estate's remaining residents had been evicted. In 2004, ownership of the Park Hill was transferred from Sheffield City Council to developers Urban Splash for the token sum of £1 (ASH 2017a).

Although the estate's north block has undergone redevelopment (phase one was completed in 2012), regeneration of the rest of the estate continues – albeit slowly and not without controversy. According to the campaign group Architects for Social Housing (ASH), just 26 of the 300-plus flats in the redeveloped north block are available for social rent. Meanwhile, in October 2016, a 'tent city' was set up on the estate, providing shelter for some twenty or more of Sheffield's homeless population and drawing attention to the wasted potential of the homes that sit empty on the derelict parts of the site.

Throughout the redevelopment, arts events have taken place on the estate, with arts and culture a key feature of the developer's vision for Park Hill's future (Urban Splash 2018). In April 2015 a temporary exhibition space was opened in the estate's former Scottish Queen pub, offering a programme of exhibitions, events and residencies. In November 2017, architect firm Carmody Groarke won a competition for an estimated £950,000 contract to design a £21 million permanent art space, including studios and a gallery, on the redeveloped site (Fulcher 2017).

The estate's history provides a spatio-political context from which to read the NYT's production. *SLICK* sits alongside a series of creative interventions on the Park Hill site that can easily be understood within an artwashing narrative – I return to this in more detail below. The realization of the project as part of the NYT's environmental trilogy, however, marks a shift in the company towards a more progressive and inclusive mode of work, complicating *SLICK*'s politics and inflecting its potential reception. An examination of the institutional context of this production reveals, once again, the importance of institutional frames in imbuing artworks with meanings that might disrupt, enhance, distort or complicate the meanings produced by the aesthetic, social and material aspects of the work.

Institutional ambiguity: NYT and social practice

The NYT is an organization with some prestige. Founded in 1956, it claims to be the world's first youth theatre and boasts an impressive range of high-profile alumni (NYT 2017).[3] The organization provides training and production experience, primarily in acting and stagecraft, for young people hoping to enter the professional theatre industry. Training is most frequently delivered through the membership programme, for which young people audition for a place on a summer course, on completion of which they may apply to take part in company performances. Members usually pay to take part in the summer school and for expenses when working in shows – including accommodation and travel.[4]

The NYT has a reputation for catering to middle-class young people and for perpetuating theatrical elitism. This reputation is to some extent justified. The company was founded by a former teacher from the fee-paying Alleyn's Boys' School, who directed young men from the school in Shakespeare plays during the holidays and quickly garnered support from prominent actors and industry figures, including the first company president, Sir Ralph Richardson. Until the mid-1990s the NYT's output was largely revivals of classical texts and newer texts by prominent contemporary writers (most of whom were men) – with a heavy emphasis on Shakespeare. These were mostly performed in London and occasionally at prestigious regional and international theatres (NYT 2017). Towards the beginning of the twenty-first century there was a shift, undoubtedly influenced by a shift in the theatre industry at large, towards new writing and devised productions. This shift in output also embraced the growing trend towards site-focused performance and outreach projects – part of the 'social' and 'spatial' turns – which were ostensibly socially engaged.

In an interview with the *Metro* newspaper in 2008 (Allfree 2008), the NYT's artistic director Paul Roseby acknowledged that the company had work to do in 'bridging the gap' between young people from different social and economic backgrounds. The establishment of a 'social inclusion' programme, through which young people from socially and economically disadvantaged backgrounds could take part in projects leading to performances and earn qualifications through accredited courses, was one way that the NYT attempted to overcome its elitist reputation. Although, as I have explored elsewhere (Beswick 2011a, 2015, 2018), these programmes often secured the exclusion they attempted to overcome by separating social inclusion and core NYT projects.

SLICK, then, can be understood within the NYT's larger institutional context as a work that indicated the organization's commitment to a more progressive, socially engaged practice. The 'inclusive' nature of the production was signalled in a number of ways. The Sheffield location positioned the work outside of London, both a symbolic move demonstrating the company's commitment to a 'national' theatre and a practical one, enabling members from outside of London and on lower incomes to take part without large expenses for travel and accommodation, bearing in mind that overnight accommodation in Sheffield is usually significantly cheaper than in London. Additionally, the large ensemble cast organized by several directors was a move away from the hierarchical mainstream industry model of performance – where a single director oversees a small cast of actors and stage technicians – for which the NYT is known.

The move towards large-scale ensemble work can be understood as ideologically symbolic, in that it positions the production within a lineage of politically progressive works by companies that have placed seemingly collaborative, non-hierarchical methods at the centre of their practice in one way or another – Joan Littlewood's Theatre Workshop (see Holdsworth 2006: 48), for example, or the feminist work of Red Ladder (see Reinelt 1986). The large cast also enabled the NYT to offer experience of taking part in a major production to lots of its members, creating a more egalitarian company environment than previously existed. Even within NYT membership, taking part in major productions is not guaranteed, given the number of members compared with the number of major shows staged annually,[5] leading to an internal 'elite' within the company, comprising those who are regularly cast in shows.

The site-specific form, along with its environmental theme, also framed *SLICK* as a 'social' work. As I discussed in the last chapter, taking a performance beyond the theatre or gallery space often operates to position that work in relation to wider social inequalities in one way or another. Using a council estate site immediately implicates *SLICK* in a class politics – here, it is one that is framed as progressive, socially engaged and celebratory. This positive, socially progressive nature of the work is not an inevitable reading offered by the estate location, so much as the combination of the estate location, the form and content of the production and the youth theatre context, which melded to produce an edgy, optimistic atmosphere that exerted an intoxicating energy over spectators. On the evening that I attended there was a real air of excitement and wonder as the performance ended. This was no doubt compounded by the spectacle of the finale, which evoked the complex embodied response Joslin McKinney has described as 'kinaesthetic empathy' – where 'sensorial, emotional and imaginative responses' (2013: 66) combine to produce an affective reaction to the scenographic spectacle that is 'almost beyond articulation' (63).

Authentic capitalism, artwashing and the sensuous manifold

McKinney's 'kinaesthetic empathy' resonates with Paul Crowther's (1993) articulation of the 'sensuous manifold', a 'phenomenological experience' (Palmer and Popat 2007: 301) whereby the conceptual and spectacular fuse to produce an embodied sensation that operates outside of language. Crowther's sensuous manifold is a useful model for thinking through a range of art practices, including performance (Scott Palmer and Sita Popat apply it to the analysis of digital dance works; I am suggesting that it is also a model for thinking about the politics of site-based and immersive performance). The concept articulates how the experience of art is 'a fundamentally presence-making experience, operating at the pre-reflective level of "body-hold" where the viewer or participant is arrested by the aesthetic effect' (Palmer and Popat 2007: 302).

For Crowther, the sensuous manifold is part of a complex ecology that exists between humans and their environments. The aesthetic experience of art operates as part of this ecology to enable a harmonizing between subject/

object divisions. Crowther's notion of the way that art functions as part of a human ecology values art aesthetically and rejects Marxist analyses of art as the institutionalization of the power-elite's interests and tastes, claiming that they are reductive – especially those that engage notions of 'discourse' (1993: 9).

But acknowledging the power relations at play within the creation, production and dissemination of artworks does not have to be reductive. And although it is undoubtedly the case that, at an aesthetic level, artworks operate sensuously to alert us, via an affective, harmonizing experience, to what it is to be human, this aesthetic experience is always mediated by an inevitable political context. That is to say that when it comes to art, power is always at play in one way or another. Indeed, the affective register through which art practices operate – giving birth to meaning through feeling – is the means by which artwashing so effectively elides the violence of regeneration and gentrification processes. In the context of estate gentrification, the sensuous manifold threatens to consume the site and its context, 'monopolizing' the estate with seemingly benign activities and interventions in order to realize profit without resistance for developers.

On the Park Hill this sensuous monopolization through art practices happens in various ways and often also involves appeals to authenticity. One example of this is the infamous 'I love you will you marry me' sign on the bridge between the north and west blocks. This sign, part of the Urban Splash regeneration of the estate, overwrites a line of an iconic graffitied proposal with neon lettering, recalling the neon works of contemporary British artist Tracey Emin. It is both a surprising, sensuous intervention and an appeal to working-class authenticity – garnering the development with the edgy, street credibility that graffiti, one of the 'four pillars' hip-hop, evokes. As ASH argue, 'I love you will you marry me'

> becomes an invitation to join the shiny new vision of Sheffield the transformation of Park Hill represents – no longer as the heartland of steel production in the North of England, but as a call centre for foreign-owned companies.
>
> (ASH 2017a)

In this way criticism of the work illustrates how companies like Urban Splash operate: profiting from the destruction of traditional working-class culture, while, at the same time, co-opting that culture to sell their product, seemingly with scant regard for the people left behind. For example, ASH (2017a) document how 'Jason', the man who authored the graffitied proposal, has received no funds or acknowledgement from Urban Splash. The mother of his since-deceased love interest told the *Observer* newspaper that the sign serves as an intrusion on her grief, an unwelcome reminder of her daughter. 'I'd like to go about life pretending that nothing's happened', she said. 'And you can't do that when her name's scrawled in such a public place' (Byrnes 2016).[6]

SLICK similarly co-opted working-class authenticity, engendering a politically neutralizing authentic affect. This affect is bound up in the site's 'realness' in at least two ways. Firstly, at a material level *SLICK* highlights how, as Carlson argues, drawing on Bert States, contemporary theatre practices continue theatre's history of a 'dynamic of "devouring the real in its realist forms"' (Carlson 2017: 15). In other words, the material reality of the site and its estate history are potent draws for audiences. The performance enabled a kind of 'poverty tourism' (Bell 2014b: 145) or 'poverty safari' (McGarvey 2017), offering access to 'real' council estate space and views over post-industrial Sheffield, without the threat of encounter with estate residents. Secondly, the performance engendered a spirit of authenticity similar to hip-hop 'realness' – where the real, youthful, energetic bodies of the performers interacted with the space to facilitate what Hanlon calls 'poor chic', a phenomenon that sees culture make 'recreational or stylish – and often expensive – "fun" of poverty, or of traditional symbols of working class and underclass statuses' (2002: 501). In *SLICK*, then, the urban realness of the site was underwritten by the energetic bodies of the young, multicultural cast of performers, whose physical presence brought the estate alive with a potent potential, melding with the scenographic interventions in the space to produce a sensuous, kinaesthetic affect.

As I recount in the opening to this chapter, after *SLICK*'s spectacular performance finale the audience were given canvas 'goody bags', which included leaflets and promotional materials detailing how to buy a flat on the redeveloped site. Indeed, the performance might be understood as a seductive showcase for the Urban Splash development, leading audiences through flats in the process of regeneration. Despite offering the illusion of audience freedom by allowing us to roam the space, our journey was carefully curated, enabling the performance to serve as a property viewing for potential buyers (art audiences, after all, are likely to include a majority of affluent middle-class professionals eligible for a mortgage). As we were guided around the north block, we were led past flats in the process of construction, with walls un-built so that the impressive scale of Park Hill's generous apartments were in clear view – as were the dazzling views of the city afforded from walkways and windows. In this way, *SLICK* reveals the ability of immersive and space-based performance to facilitate capitalist logic – or, as Harvie puts it, to 'cultivate an appetite for the claiming of private space' (2013: 109). Carlson describes how the successful works of immersive companies such as Punchdrunk offer an 'illusion of emancipation' that 'has important implications both for the theatre as an art form and as a social process' (2016: 116). He argues that

> [j]ust as modern theatre has at times almost obsessively consumed the surrounding real world, the operations of capitalism have sought to overtake this consumption by consuming this theatrical process, seeking to market and sell the 'real' experience as a product.
>
> (Carlson 2016: 116)

The 'body-hold' of the sensuous manifold is a powerful tool in capitalistic redevelopment processes, making critical distance from the artwork difficult and producing a viewer, who, overcome with the affective spectacle, becomes vulnerable to the 'product' on offer.

Paradoxes in utopia

In the introduction to her book exploring the relationship between dramaturgy and architecture, Cathy Turner argues that theatre offers utopian possibilities (2015: 1). Her work pays close attention to the ways that the material spatial elements of performance works interact with the narrative and dramaturgical elements, producing what psychoanalyst Donald Winnicott called 'potential space[s]', where the 'incongruity between dreamworld and reality is temporarily put to one side' (Turner 2015: 4). For Turner, this enables performances to create spaces of 'otherness' – and while she does not reductively celebrate theatre's function as a site of potential world-making, she does acknowledge the 'tempting and various' utopian possibilities of the form (Turner 2015: 15).

We can interrogate the paradoxes and tensions thrown up by the relationships between the material, aesthetic and institutional elements of *SLICK* by paying attention to its relationship with concepts of utopia. The utopian possibilities of theatre, as Jill Dolan argues, occupy an affective realm, where performance events might offer spaces in which 'an image of a better future can be articulated and even embodied, however fleetingly' (Dolan 2001: 457). Dolan's definition of utopia sees performance as a space where 'imaginative territories … map themselves over the real' (2001: 457). *SLICK* operated within this affective, territorial realm, the narrative and architectural aspects of the performance melding on site, as we have seen, to produce a sensuous aesthetic affect where the performative features of utopia, which include 'energy, abundance, intensity, transparency' (Dyer in Dolan 2001: 464) made visible fleeting, almost-tangible possibilities for a 'better future'. These utopian futures were 'imaginatively mapped' in a number of affective and literal ways: by temporarily altering the estate with vibrant performance energy and scenographic interventions – including vast walls built from plastic bottles, shimmering in the sunset; in the vision for the development offered by the tour of the block undergoing regeneration; and in the promotional leaflets given to audience members.

SLICK's seductive utopian affect was intensified by the 'whole performance event' (Dolan 2001: 457): by the experience of travelling to an unknown site, gathering in a vast, iconic space to watch young people perform in an impressively realized production – and no doubt further compounded by the fact that for many of the audience those young people were sons, daughters, siblings and friends.

However, this utopian affect was complicated by the unresolvable paradoxes of the estate site – in particular the 'ruin aesthetic' created by the 'ruin in reverse' of the Urban Splash development at Park Hill. As I argue elsewhere, a ruin aesthetic 'involves the stage space operating as a "dialectical landscape", which uses the "ruined resources of the past to imagine or re-imagine the future"' (Beswick 2015: 30). The ruin aesthetic that I describe draws on Robert Smithson's concept of the 'ruin in reverse' (1967: 72), where the topographical (or in this case, architectural) landscape facilitates a 'dialectical conversation between the past and the future' (Beswick 2015: 30). The physical, architectural reality of a building undergoing regeneration immediately instigates a dialectical interplay between past and future, as the palimpsest of the estate's history – that failed utopian project – sits visible in the ruins of the site itself, the vast empty buildings surrounding the development intruding on the utopian vision for the estate's future offered by the building works and glossy brochures. That is to say that the estate-as-performance-space is in conversation with Park Hill's history and, by extension, with the 'failure' of social housing in the public imagination, meaning the developer's vision for the estate manifests, at moments, as an impossible, utopian 'dream world' rather than a legitimate plan for the site's future.

Further complicating the utopian affect is the paradoxical narrative of the performance itself, a utopian critique of the capitalist tendency to use utopian ideals as a means to realize profit – the title suggesting the 'slick' means by which these tendencies are often realized. That the island of 'Utopia' around which the performance is set is revealed as an exploitative enterprise points to the ways that notions of utopia can function coercively, acting as ideal futures 'enforced at the expense of liberty' (Dolan 2001: 457). Narratively then, *SLICK* might be understood as a critique of the Urban

Splash development itself, albeit a critique that is obscured by the powerful affective register of the performance spectacle.

These paradoxical utopian affects illustrate the political complexity located estate artworks navigate. In a production of space the located estate performance, especially in the context of regeneration works, becomes a means through which theatre makers, and to an extent audiences, might engage in imaginative 'mappings' that produce the estate's future. While this utopian mapping has the possibility to resist dominant forces, it is also subject to co-option and exploitation by those dominant forces and the capitalist logic that drives them. This is especially the case where the cooperation of profit-driven corporations is necessary for the realization of art works – *SLICK* could not have been realized without the cooperation of Urban Splash, meaning it was inevitable that despite the socially progressive intentions of the NYT, tensions between the intentions of the performance and the politics of the site would arise.

Seizure: The generic estate, empty buildings and timeless beauty

Co-commissioned by the company Artangel and the Jerwood Foundation, *Seizure* was realized in 2008 at 151–189 Harper Road, a small council block awaiting demolition in the Elephant and Castle area of the London Borough of Southwark. Like *SLICK*, *Seizure* is a highly ambivalent work in which the material, institutional and aesthetic properties coalesce to produce paradoxical 'meanings' fraught with tension.

This was an installation that used a whole flat as its canvas. It is a piece that might more usually be considered within the realm of visual arts practices, although attention to the work in performance studies (e.g. Harvie 2011, Bell 2014b) suggests the way that it functions performatively within the wider estate discourse (as I will elaborate in more detail here). Working with a technique he had experimented with in other projects, Hiorns flooded a bedsit at the Harper Road site with copper sulphate solution, sealing the property for about three weeks (Trivelli 2011) to await the result. Once the flat was opened it was clear the experiment had worked: the space had become a crystal-encrusted cavern, completely transformed by the glimmering, jewel-like blue crystals that had formed over every surface. Like *SLICK*, *Seizure* created a spectacular world. Audience members could enter the space and move about the flat, experiencing its transformation. Despite the beauty of the work, Harvie points to the ambivalent ways that *Seizure* operated within an artwashing framework, contributing to 'the kind of localized artistic aura that frequently leverages processes of gentrification' while also appearing as a 'social work' that critiqued systems of social housing (Harvie 2011: 119).

Seizure was an immediately successful intervention in terms of its public reception. In her account of the work, scholar Elena Trivelli describes how, following its opening in 2008, queues formed outside the installation, with the positive response from both visitors and the press leading to the extension of the work to November 2008 (2011: 2). In 2009, Hiorns was nominated for the Turner Prize, and *Seizure* was reopened to the public from July 2009 until January 2010.

Staged in a building slated for demolition, *Seizure* was originally due to be destroyed along with the site that hosted it. Indeed, Trivelli positions *Seizure* as a work that is fundamentally about destruction. She describes how the chemical process that created the crystals caused the erosion of the flat's walls and argues that the act of opening the sealed apartment to see how the process had altered the space was also an act of destruction, 'shattering a work in progress' (2011: 5). The eventual, inevitable destruction of the work as part of Harper Road's demolition, Trivelli proposed, moved it outside of the logic of the capitalist art-market, as 'the material of the installation disappears with its experience and the production of the work consists in its destruction, thus finally creating the work of art as non portable and fundamentally non reproducible' (2011: 5).

Trivelli's reading of *Seizure's* resistance to the capitalist imperatives of the cultural industries was to prove naively optimistic. As the demolition of Harper Road approached, *Seizure* was acquired by the Arts Council, and a plan was made for its removal and relocation some 180 miles to the YSP – Europe's largest park of its kind, based near Wakefield in the north of England – where it would remain on loan as part of a ten-year agreement between ACE and the YSP. A large, concrete, mausoleum-like structure designed by architect Adam Khan was erected at the park to contain the flat, requiring audiences to cross 'a succession of thresholds' (Khan in Hiorns 2013: 31) to access *Seizure*. The installation opened in the summer of 2013 and remains on display at the time of writing.

As Bell argues, the 'nomadic spatial aesthetics' of *Seizure's* relocation 'imply an uneasy alliance between the social imperatives of site-specific activities and dominant modes of capitalist production which prioritize mobility' (Bell 2014b: 135). She proposes that its removal from Harper Road unfastens the installation from the narrative created by its council estate setting, complicating its site-specificity as 'the original "site" of the artwork no longer structures the wider experiences of engaging with the installation today' (Bell 2014b: 153).

A similar – though less critical – claim about the work's removal blurring its relationship with the estate site is made by Head of Arts Council Collections Caroline Douglas, in a slim volume published to celebrate *Seizure's* arrival at YSP. She writes,

> As an art object, *Seizure* is something between geology and pathology: a growth, a spasm in nature, an index of chemical time. It arrives here trailing shadows of its architectural origins, while at the same time disavowing their importance. It is pointless to ask what it is 'about' – the artist encourages us to understand it as 'unknowable'; perhaps the most accurate statement one could make is that *Seizure* exists in the response it creates within each individual who experiences it.
>
> (Douglas in Hiorns 2013: 6)

While it is self-evident that the installation is not 'about' any knowable thing (in the sense that it is an object, not a narrative) and that its relocation alters its relationship with the original site, I contend that it remains impossible to derive any meaning from the experience of *Seizure* without considering its relationship to the 'council estate' as a generic idea. As attention to the work itself, its articulation in YSP and ACE literature and scholarly analysis of the work reveal, *Seizure* frames, produces and positions the council estate in particular (and familiar) ways. It contributes to the so-called artwashing of social cleansing and operates firmly within the capitalist logic of the art market while, at the same time, offering moments where possibilities for seeing estate space differently manifest in the sparkling crystal ruin.

Ghosting estate discourse

Despite Douglas's assertion that Hiorns intends *Seizure* as an 'unknowable' work, it would be extremely difficult to experience the installation without the knowledge that it was once a council flat. *Seizure* does not only 'trail shadows' of its architectural origins, it is utterly shrouded in them. When I visited the YSP in 2014, details of the work's origins, including its original location at and removal from Harper Road, were on prominent display in the park's visitor centre. The *Seizure* exhibition page on the park's website, available at the time of writing, also details its origins at Harper Road, specifically referring to the fact that it was once a 'council flat' and to the 'social housing' context in which the work was made (YSP N.D.). Moreover, unlike many of the other works exhibited at YSP, which visitors might stumble across while ambling in the large, landscaped parkland, *Seizure* requires some effort and planning to visit. It is open only on weekends and during school holidays and is housed in an unprepossessing concrete structure – itself referencing archetypal brutalist council estate design – tucked away in a garden area of the park. At the entrance to the installation, park staff meet visitors and provide them with protective footwear. (I was told this was to stop shoes from bringing debris into the installation and to protect the crystals from damage, although in her account of seeing the work in Southwark, Bell writes that she signed a release form acknowledging the toxic nature of copper sulphate and was encouraged to wear gloves and boots in order to protect her body from the possible chemical effects (2014b: 134).) The requirement to cover feet, and the fact that only one small party of visitors at a time are able to enter the installation, means that audience members are likely to interact with the exhibition staff before entering the work and have time to ask questions about and discuss the installation with park staff, offering another opportunity to learn about its council estate origins.

I emphasize this council estate framing because it allows me to draw attention to the fact that the installation operates within a wider estate discourse, even away from its estate site. Clifford McLucas has articulated the relationship between a site and its performance in site-specific practice as 'host' and 'ghost' where, as Pearson and Turner paraphrase from McLucas's notes,

> [t]he 'host' is the extant building with its fixtures, fittings, ambiance; that which pre–exists the work; all that is *at* site, while the 'ghost' is that which is temporarily brought to and emplaced at site, that which remains spectral and transparent.
>
> (Pearson and Turner 2018: 99)

Although McLucas was not referring to installation work per se, the concept of 'host' and 'ghost' is useful for thinking about how the *idea* of the council estate as a generic place structures experiences of *Seizure* at YSP. The council estate flat is the 'ghost', temporarily emplaced at the 'extant' park, inside Khan's structure. The generic estate arrives as a 'spectral and transparent' entity that accompanies and envelops the work at its new host site. The ghostly nature of the relocated work was implied by an early title afforded to it by some publications (see e.g. Southbank Centre 2012), presumably changed once the exhibition opened, *Untitled (Seizure)*, which reflected the fact that the YSP display was a new work, ripped from its context, but appeared to acknowledge, by having the original title in parenthesis, that the context could not ever entirely separate itself from the original.

Indeed, although the Harper Road display of *Seizure* is often referred to as a site-specific work, in many ways the exhibit was never really about a *specific* site. It always relied on its relationship with a generic conception of the council estate and on the dominant public discourse about the generic estate for its impact. For Hiorns, who had initially intended to stage *Seizure* in the Robin Hood Gardens estate (the estate later acquired by the V&A that I mention in the introduction to this chapter), social housing is a failed idea. In an interview with the magazine *Artforum* he states:

> These kinds of buildings don't work; as a model they have not passed the test of time. Great symbols of collective will, which were treading on an individualistic attitude in the form of small, pokey flats. They give you very little architecture, the nominal amount of expression you're allowed to have, they were ungenerous in that respect.
>
> In the great social experiment these buildings inferred, they provided no room for movement, zero mobility to move further, they are completely static materially and emotionally.

> (Hiorns 2008)

The notion of social housing's 'failure' occurs again and again in accounts of *Seizure* – which often draw attention to the scale of the flat and its supposedly 'unlivable' proportions (see e.g. Williams 2008, Trivelli 2011, Harvie 2011). This interpretation of the installation as revealing the claustrophobic size of the property, and therefore of council housing in general, was surprising to me: I have lots of experience of visiting council flats in London – as I recount in the preface to this book I lived in one for a time as a child, friends and family lived in them while I was growing up and I worked for a number of years as a housing officer for a social housing provider, visiting properties in estates on at least a weekly, often a daily, basis. My experience is that, although they vary in size and are often overcrowded (because families grow and there is not the supply of larger properties to meet their needs) and run-down (due to lack of investment in maintaining properties), council flats in many London estates tend to be generously proportioned and often offer impressive views, giving a sense of space. Therefore, the cramped and claustrophobic nature of the installation was, for me, part of the flat's transformation: I didn't feel it was always uninhabitable, but that the crystals had diminished its size and made it so.

Although I have no idea about the experience of other visitors whose accounts of *Seizure* draw attention to the property as an example of housing failure, my own experience and interpretation of the work illustrate how one's lived experience necessarily shapes one's perception of an artwork.

This is to say that I presume many of those commenting on the installation's scale as if it were representative of the scale of council flats in general may have had limited experience of similar properties. In any event, none of those remarking on the flat's size acknowledged that its smallness was partly because this was once a bedsit: a property designed for single-person living, not family life.

The danger in understanding *Seizure* as representative in terms of scale is that it authenticates the social housing as 'failure' narrative, thereby justifying the demolition of Harper Road and sites like it. In this sense *Seizure*'s interpretation by visitors as revealing social housing's failure might be another way we can understand the work as artwashing – legitimizing the demolition of a building that was unable to serve a useful purpose. The fact that audiences can see for themselves the inhospitable nature of a 'real' council flat further authenticates the failure narrative.

Meanwhile, in interviews about the work Hiorns makes claims to an authentic knowledge of estate sites – he had once worked as a postman in Southwark and positions himself as familiar with not only the Harper Road estates but also other estates in the borough (see e.g. Hiorns 2013). These claims to belonging, in a now predictable way, operate again to 'authenticate' the failure narrative, making it difficult to conceive the work beyond a dominant paradigm in which the council estate is necessarily failed.

Institutions, the avant-garde and estates without people

Founded in 1985, Artangel is a company that centres site in its practice, moving beyond the gallery to commission works that happen in 'unexpected places' (Artangel 2017). These works are often staged as public artworks, free at the point of access and seemingly in dialogue with wider social and political concerns, although always ambiguously. They are also often positioned as what Grant Kester calls 'avant-garde', in that they are intricate and unknowable, revealing 'the inability of conventional language to grasp the infinite complexity of the world' (Kester 2004: 19). For example, Rachel Whiteread's now iconic *House* (1993) – a concrete cast of an entire family house in the working-class district of Bow in east London – garnered significant attention while refusing what Artangel co-director James Lingwood calls 'consensus'. 'It did not seek', he argues, 'to predetermine the ways in which people could respond to it' (Lingwood in Kester 2004: 20). However, as Kester argues, *House* did in fact elicit consensus from art critics and writers who saw the work as a comment on the fragmenting of the working-class community that had once defined Bow (2004: 20) – it was the wider public and the community of Bow itself who were unable to make coherent sense of the piece. In this way, Kester suggests, the work operated to divide the audience into 'philistine and cognoscenti' (Kester 2004: 22), reproducing modes of artistic production and consumption that privileged an already elite audience base.

Similar claims might be made about *Seizure*'s appeal. However, instead of dwelling on the reception of the work, I want to draw attention to the way that the language of the avant-garde used in its marketing, where it is presented as 'unknowable' and infinitely complex, conceal the actually quite straightforward ways that *Seizure* acted on site and beyond to facilitate a capitalist logic and to feed into dominant perceptions of estates as 'failed'.

At Harper Road the installation utterly consumed the site, serving it up for further consumption by viewers and finally destroying the site in order that the work might be saved for circulation in an art market that ultimately operates through a capitalistic logic. Bell positions *Seizure* as an example of 'creative destruction', drawing on economist Joseph A. Schumpeter's term which describes 'how markets under capitalism revolutionize the economic structure from within' (Bell 2014b: 154).

She draws attention to Artangel's ideological privileging of individual private donations on its website, despite their receipt of public funding from ACE as a National Portfolio Organization, and further monies from the Jerwood Foundation (Bell 2014b: 297). Bell highlights how Artangel offer rewards and benefits to private donors, dubbed 'angels', including 'an annual signed limited edition artwork'.

> Given the fact that many of Artangel's commissions are site-specific and what co-director Lingwood claims 'events' ... the concept of property ownership and the tangibility of a signed 'artwork' encircles projects that seem to prioritize social engagement and support into capitalist rhetoric and circulation.
>
> (Bell 2014b: 297)

As Bell argues, Artangel's enterprise is largely framed around a neoliberal logic that privileges artworks over the spaces where they are staged. In this model estates co-opted as 'art' 'are afforded a protection and longevity they do not receive as homes' (Bell 2014b: 148). The violence of the estate's demolition is therefore effectively 'artwashed' – and is further concealed by the removal of people, as residents of the estate, from any conceptual frame.

Indeed, the most striking thing about *Seizure* – particularly in terms of my framing of it as estate performance – is the extent to which any consideration of people is absent from the work, its marketing and its public and scholarly reception. *Seizure* both literally and figuratively depicts an empty estate, void of the sustaining energy of life. The absence of people (and particularly the invisibility of residents as audience members in narratives of the work) operates to produce the generic estate as an ideology rather than a lived place, which makes it easier to dismiss the whole project of social housing as 'failed', closing down the possibility of readings where the complex and meaningful ways that estate place is lived become visible.

Beauty/resistance: Moving beyond time

Notwithstanding its overarching narrative of estate failure, *Seizure* is undoubtedly a beautiful work. When audience members give accounts of their experience, in scholarship and journalism, they invariably break into poetic language in an attempt to describe the jarring affect of the installation. In *Wallpaper* magazine, for example, *Seizure* is called 'a sprawling carpet of sparkling blue copper sulphate crystals … spread virulently over the walls' (*Wallpaper* 2009). Trivelli refers to the work as a 'dark blue dream' (2011: 3), while Harvie describes the flat as a 'decidedly unhomely giant blue-toothed maw' (2011: 115). These descriptions have a searching quality, with the use of metaphor suggesting a kinaesthetic affect that is almost 'beyond words' and which embodies some of the qualities of the sensuous manifold I described in my account of *SLICK*. Just as in that work, here too the sensuous manifold threatens to elide the violence of estate demolition and provide a gloss on social cleansing. Nonetheless, the particular quality of beauty adds a distinct affective dimension, which also offers possibilities for reframing the estate outside of dominant discourses – providing moments where the utopian promise of a 'better future' might manifest. James Thompson suggests that a 'beauty affect' can act as a powerful critical tool, central to a radical politics (2009: 152). Mojisola Adebayo argues that beauty 'can get us thinking rationally and critically about those who have been considered ugly by society', harmonizing us with that which is considered other (Adebayo 2015: 154).

It is the beauty affect of the work where I propose there are possibilities for disrupting its place in the dominant narrative of estate 'failure'. This is not to say that everyone or even necessarily anyone who sees the work will be able to conceive it entirely without the dominant frame. Instead, an emergent idea of what the estate is, might be or might have been can come into view, at moments, as the affective experience of being in a space utterly and mesmerizingly transformed takes affective hold. This happens as what Steve Dixon calls a kind of 'stepping to one side or outside of [time]' (Dixon 2011: 96), a phenomenon that is perhaps especially pertinent in sites that are 'other' and which therefore offer the potential to be understood through a range of lived practices and theoretical positions.

Fiona Anderson, for example, discusses the time-shifting quality through which we might understand marginal spaces in her essay on the gay cruising spaces of 1970s New York. According to Anderson, photographs of the waterfront ruins that served as cruising spaces for homosexual men towards the end of the late twentieth century are often framed as contemporary 'Pompeii': a failure narrative where the ruined landscape morally intrudes on the sexual excesses the photographs document, evoking the AIDS crisis and suggesting a 'homophobic causal relation between cruising and the development of HIV/AIDS'. Anderson rejects the 'Pompeii' readings of these documents, arguing that we might, instead, see them operating 'outside of normative temporal and social markers'. In these ruin spaces, she proposes, and in the documents that recall them, there was a 'sense of … peculiar timefulness … where images of the past and present raced "back and forth" incoherently' (Anderson 2015: 136).

The queering of time that Anderson describes in the waterfront ruins is also made possible by *Seizure*, which reconfigures a ruined space to create an affective layering that destabilizes the past, so that it becomes 'unmoored from a normative linear connection' (Anderson 2015: 143). While the estate ghosting that I argued inflects the work ensures that the past is always in a dialectical interplay with the present, the beauty affect pulls us into a contemplation of site where past, present and – especially at YSP, where it is unmoored from its content and has an uncertain destiny – possible futures 'race back and forth incoherently', allowing viewers to see and experience the space differently. This magical, shimmering cavern is beyond any estate realism that dominates popular representation, affording the possibility to know and think about estates in potentially emancipating ways, where the estate might be something dazzling rather than only a failed idea.

Elaine Scarry points to beauty's potential to take one out of time and inspire deliberation, stating that

> What is beautiful prompts the mind to move chronologically back in the search for precedents and parallels, to move forward into new acts of creation, to move conceptually over, to bring things in relation, and does all this with a kind of urgency as though one's life depended on it.
>
> (Scarry 2006: 30)

This sense of moving unsteadily through time in contemplation goes some way to describing the affective register through which *Seizure* operates aesthetically, layering the flat with possibilities, fuelling the imaginative potential of the space and ensuring a unit of social housing life beyond the estate. There is future for a space that, otherwise resigned to its fate as a site of demolition, was once only conceivable as a ruined relic of the past.

'The Wedding to the Bread': Tricky politics, resident engagement and inauthentic ritual

In the summer of 2017, the art collective Fourthland, in collaboration with the filmmaker Rosalind Fowler, conducted a series of visits to the homes of residents on the Wenlock Barn estate in east London. Carrying a collection of artist-made objects wrapped in a length of cloth, they performed a ceremony in each home: ringing a bell, laying the objects on the cloth and reading a short statement from a small scroll. Once the ceremony was finished the artists asked their hosts to bring objects of their own to the table. From these interactions with residents, all kinds of material encounters emerged: some of the residents dressed in their wedding outfits; some offered the artists meals; one woman brought the umbilical cord of her most recently born child to the table, explaining that in Bangladesh, the country where she was born, the tradition is to bury the cord in the soil on family land and to cut off and weigh the hair and fingernails from the baby, donating the value of their weight in silver to the poor.

From these exchanges the artists worked with residents to develop short ceremonial scenes, filmed against a sculptural backdrop in the community 'back garden'. The scenes were edited into a seventeen-minute film called *I Feel Like Doing This*, in which gestures became abstracted ideas that referenced the stories, rituals and practices residents had shared during the visits, unhinged from specific contexts. So, for example, the umbilical cord tradition was embellished and, in the film, a giant umbilical cord is buried in a huge mound of earth by the Bengali mother, costumed in her wedding dress, while, in another scene, a white English woman acts as the scales weighing the hair and fingernails.

I Feel Like Doing This was screened in the communal 'back garden' on the Wenlock Barn estate in October 2017, after a ceremony, 'The Wedding to the Bread', which I performed at Fourthland's invitation to an audience of gathered residents and locals. Acting as a ceremonial 'officiator', I narrated a brief history of British social housing, emphasizing its ideological roots in community and collectivity, and invited residents to take vows committing to the future of social housing. After the ceremony we all stood in a circle as residents offered small gestures that represented how they felt about life on the estate, which were repeated as we recited our vows. The event culminated in a feast, where we shared the bread that was set out on a makeshift altar along with food and drink provided by Fourthland and the estate's residents. The film and the 'Wedding to the Bread' ceremony both emerge from Fourthland's decade-long engagement with Wenlock Barn, revolving around a series of community gardens that the collective has helped to establish across the estate.

Wenlock Barn is the largest estate in Shoreditch, a neighbourhood that straddles the London boroughs of Hackney, Islington and Tower Hamlets. It comprises a series of blocks, the first opened in 1949 – although all homes in the blocks were originally social housing tenure, Right to Buy and the ongoing regeneration of the estate mean that many of the homes are now privately owned and rented, with several of the newer blocks almost entirely private tenure. Like many large estates of broadly modernist design, Wenlock Barn has garnered a reputation for crime and so-called anti-social behaviour, becoming an archetypal 'dreadful enclosure' – a reputation that is used to justify the site's regeneration and move to mixed tenure housing (see e.g. Space Syntax 2009). Despite – or perhaps as a result of – the threat of regeneration, in 2006 residents of Wenlock Barn enforced their legal right to manage their homes, and the estate is now run as a TMO, which means a resident-led board oversee the day-to-day management and organization of the estate.[7]

Fourthland, a partnership between artists Louise isik Sayarer and Eva Knutsdotter Vikstrom, first began working on the Wenlock Barn estate after responding to a 2008 call for a regeneration commission funded by the Shoreditch Trust. The call asked for proposals from artists who might make temporary use of green spaces on the estate site for a festival happening in the area, a commission that might easily be framed as artwashing because of its place within the wider regeneration process. Seeing an opportunity for more than a one-off engagement, Fourthland responded to the call, suggesting that instead of making a temporary intervention on the estate they might instead start a longer-term project, working with residents to create a sustainable garden space. This idea appealed to the residents who were invited to participate in deciding on the winning commission, and work on the Growing Kitchen garden began. In collaboration with residents, a garden space with thirty-five allotments, a herb border, a pond and a bread-oven barbecue was developed and eventually handed over to residents who now manage and run the space. This first project also included performance elements and the sharing of recipes, which were gathered in a community cookbook.

In the years since the Growing Kitchen project, Fourthland have continued to work with residents on the estate, running projects funded by a range of organizations including ACE, the London community foundation and the Big Lottery Fund, often with match funding from the TMO. Projects have involved the creation of food-share gardens, an orchard and the 'back garden' – a second resident-led garden space with allotment plots for food growing – as well as performance interventions such as the film and 'wedding' ceremony I describe above. Fourthland are now so embedded in the day-to-day life of the estate that they are listed as a permanent community project on the TMO's website (wenlockbarntmo 2018).

Unlike the other projects I have explored in this chapter, which took over already empty estates as 'one-off' works, attracting 'outsiders' onto estate sites, Fourthland's 'Wedding to the Bread' is part as an ongoing portfolio of work that is embedded on-site and which, despite operating, at least initially, as part of the wider ongoing regeneration of Shoreditch, has residents at the heart of the practice. Sally Mackey has referred to site-specific work that requires sustained engagement with participants and involves an element of place-making as 'place-specific'. She proposes that in place-specific practice site is 'deeply emplaced, both as a material location and as part of people's everyday lives' (Mackey 2007: 186); the work produced demonstrates the 'materiality and psychological construction of that place' (Mackey 2007: 185).

'The Wedding to the Bread' ceremony meets Mackey's definition of the place-specific. This is estate located work that, rather than drawing on existing generic estate tropes to present a narrative to outsiders, becomes about working with residents to discover and create what *this* estate is or might be – enhancing residents' sense of belonging and emplacement. It demonstrates how located work can usefully critique estate regeneration processes and provide a 'holding space' through which residents' voices can be heard. Nonetheless, this kind of work is also bound up in existing systems and structures of power that enact and reinforce injustices that exist beyond the estate, demonstrating how instrumental located artworks, no matter how well-conceived and embedded, can rarely overcome overarching power structures, and often even rely on those unequal structures for their existence.

Tricky politics and monopolistic care

Fourthland's work operates in a realm we might understand as 'applied' arts – in that it is art practice made for and with the community, led by professional artists who are 'outsiders', enacting a progressive, broadly leftist politics. Playwright and theatre-maker Mojisola Adebayo has criticized the term 'applied' for fostering what she calls 'politricks', noting that the term 'omits its politics and this admission is politically tricky' (Adebayo 2015: 123).

Although Fourthland do not use the term applied to describe their work, the 'tricky' power dynamics that Adebayo identifies in applied practices might, at least on first examination, be applied to Fourthland's work, and particularly to 'The Wedding to the Bread' ceremony.

Adebayo refers to the problematic ways that 'mostly young, able bodied middle-class white women ... will often be "applying" their drama to black boys, people who are working-class, people who are minorities and people with disabilities' (Adebayo 2015: 126). Certainly, Louise isik Sayarer, Eva Knutsdotter Vikstrom and Rosalind Fowler present as 'able bodied, middle-class white women', university-educated and with growing reputations as professional artists, having exhibited at galleries in London and undertaken residencies nationally and internationally. In reality, of course, identities are rarely straightforward, and class, ethnicity and disability are difficult to gauge from presentation alone. Fourthland's website suggests the complexity of identity and indicates the intersections the artists work from – isik Sayarer's heritage is described as 'Turkish-English' and Knutsdotter Vikstrom as 'Norwegian/Swedish.' My point in drawing attention to their 'white middle-class' presentation, then, is not to suggest that this is an accurate label for these individuals, it is instead to highlight the fact that artists working in community settings are often bound up in a tricky politics which operate within wider systems and structures where inequalities related to class, race and disability do not disappear. Fourthland are afforded a position of relative power on the estate – setting up, running and organizing community spaces and performance events. The fact that they are paid for their work, while residents' (who are overwhelmingly working class, black, Asian and other ethnic minorities) involvement is not usually financially remunerated is one way that the unequal power dynamic plays out in practice. As Pritchard points out, such unequal power dynamics can lead to what he calls 'community artwashing', where artists monopolize community bonds, harvesting and monetizing 'intangible elements of people's lives' and using community work to promote their own art practice and further their careers. Pritchard points out the ways that community engagement projects taking place as part of regeneration processes are often used as case studies by developers, 'validating the displacement of the very people ... who gave their social capital away for free' (Pritchard 2017b).

The invitation given to me to conduct a ceremony at 'The Wedding to the Bread' performance might also be understood as politically 'tricky' within an artwashing context. I too present as white, middle class and able bodied and was invited to the estate in my capacity as an academic (I did not know any of the artists involved in Fourthland prior to the event): a university lecturer working on estate art asked to share some of my knowledge about estate history. This immediately positions me as an 'expert', potentially recreating the hierarchies that exist beyond the estate where academic and 'outsider' knowledge is frequently privileged over the lived, embodied knowledge of residents themselves. The fact most of the residents in attendance were from black, Asian and other ethnic minority groups further reinforces my privileged position in this environment. Indeed I grappled with these tricky politics when deciding whether to accept the invitation: to what extent is my engagement in this event exploitative and patronizing to those very people who form the audience for my performance?

To suggest that 'The Wedding to the Bread' and Fourthland's wider body of work is politically tricky is not to accept Pritchard's simplistic critique where all artworks taking place in the context of regeneration necessarily operate only to facilitate gentrification processes. As Sachs Olsen (2017) suggests these totalizing 'instrumentalization' narratives do not pay sufficient attention to the nuances of socially engaged practices operating within a neoliberal era, which must negotiate a fraught political landscape – both resisting and becoming complicit within problematic power structures. Pritchard's narrative also comes dangerously close to suggesting that any change, disruption or exchange in an attempt to materially invest in a neighbourhood is necessarily exploitative.

Thompson proposes that applied practices might acknowledge their tricky politics by 'linking the care and resilience hoped for in those private projects with the subtly subversive politics of public performance' (2009: 40). The move between private care and politically subversive public work is one way that Fourthland negotiate the tricky politics of located estate practice – working with diligence, thoughtfulness and respect for the voices, differences and autonomy of residents themselves.

Care ethics, intuition and embedded critique

My concerns about accepting the invitation to officiate at 'The Wedding to the Bread' ceremony dissipated as soon as I arrived at the event, an hour or so before it was scheduled to begin. Children from the estate were milling around the garden, helping to set up – parents arrived later, along with other residents and locals, laying out food that we would later share on a long table. One woman set out a small stall where she sold herb infusions and pamphlets about the medicinal uses of plants. Observing the interactions between the artists and residents it seemed that Fourthland were deeply embedded within the day-to-day practice of the estate, that they were liked and respected by those who lived there. It was clear that the artists liked and respected the residents too – there was a sense of ease, comfort and playfulness: of private, meaningful relationships between participants and a tangible care taken over the organization of the day and the well-being of everyone in the space.[8]

It is difficult to describe this affective 'care' register without resort to anecdote, 'sense' and intuition, leading to the kind of writing that feels unscholarly. Perhaps this is because of the ways that knowledge is produced, reified and gendered: in an article positing an aesthetics of care Thompson points to its feminization, noting that 'both the institutional and private practices of care tend to be marginalized, gendered and devalued' (2015: 432). He draws on the feminist field of care ethics to delineate the ways that care can foster 'an affective solidarity and sense of justice' (432). An ethics of care, Thompson argues, 'should also be understood as a critique of a society where the habit of caring for others is devalued, placed at the whim of the market and radically under resourced' (435).

On their website Fourthland point to the roots of their work in the 'feminine', emphasizing that a feminine methodology allows an 'honouring' of the other. In an interview with me about their practice Knutsdotter Vikstrom described the ways the company try to work intuitively: suggesting that the gardens become 'holding space' where residents might be honoured with time and attention. In the making of *I Feel Like Doing This*, for example, each of the short scenes was filmed over the course of a day, and residents who elected to be part of the film were honoured at the filmings: food and drink was provided for each participant and their friends and family, who were invited along so that the filmings became celebratory ceremonies in their own right. So too, the organization of the gardens is an intuitive process, where Fourthland work alongside residents, with sensitivities to cultural differences, to ensure the fairness and sustainability of the project – a process that the TMO refers to as 'cultivating care' (wenlockbarntmo 2018). Fourthland explain:

> We wanted people from all cultures to feel that they had a role within a place. Meaning that we didn't want to limit the format to anyone, meaning that if you would have had flyers or forms or any of those things you would have excluded a lot of people, because there are many people who don't speak English for example. So they might have felt intimidated to come, or felt that they didn't have a role in that place. So because of the organic input from the onset, people just came because they felt they could offer something. And because many people came it just ended up being that people from all cultures came, and particularly a lot of Turkish and Kurdish community, Bangladeshi, there was a lot of West African, Jamaican … It kind of relies on people being sort of

holders of the understanding that it's a mixed community space, a mixed diversity space. Because an actual waiting list wouldn't really work in a formal sense.... So we have had to adopt this more different, almost like a tree approach to the waiting list, relying on the fact there was this trust, and whoever was doing that, they were selecting from that place of actually having a mixed space for everyone.

(My interview with Fourthland 2018)

Politically tricky issues of payment for the film were confronted head on and dealt with intuitively too, with Fourthland adding a community percentage to the sale of prints from the film, to be shared with the residents involved in the project as an acknowledgment of their participation and work.

My concerns about arriving as an expert 'outsider' had also occurred to Fourthland, who explained that the decision to invite a non-resident to participate in the 'wedding' had been taken carefully, and that in fact I was the first 'outsider' invited to participate in a performance. They explained that framing my talk as part of a ceremony where vows were taken meant that I was able to attend in a way that felt legitimate, rather than patronizing.

We have always been cautious about inviting people in suddenly who might come in without [sharing our] intentions – and the idea about the vows that is by nature a little bit more formal ... allows permission of formality. It wouldn't have worked for you to do a talk, so the performativity of knowledge exchange was crucial.

(My interview with Fourthland 2018)

Understanding Fourthland's practice as operating within an aesthetics of care draws attention to the ways that the collective negotiate the tricky politics that inevitably run through their work and resist the neoliberal systems that necessitate their practice. Thompson's assertion that care aesthetics should be understood as a critique is relevant here, Fourthland state that their intuitive approach is an 'indirect critique' of gentrification processes (my interview 2018), which so often work against intuition and care, imposing top-down visions for the future of sites that ultimately destroy what is already there.

Mythmaking and the subversion of authenticity

At the centre of 'The Wedding to the Bread' ceremony was a mythmaking process, where the authenticity of cultural rituals offered by the residents was playfully subverted in order to facilitate the 'place-making' that Mackey defines as a key component of place-specific work. Unlike registers of authenticity I have explored in other parts of this book, where practices call on registers of 'the real' to authenticate their work in one way or another, the wedding ceremony deliberately disavowed notions of the authentic and the sacred. Roland Barthes asserts that myths emerge as representations which silence alternative narratives (Barthes 1973) – as we have explored in this book, the cultural myth of the failed council estate powerfully silences alternative ways of understanding estate spaces. Fourthland push back against failure narratives by creating new myths that enable other ways of being in and coming to know estates.

Instead of using 'realness' as a means of imbuing the work with a cultural cachet that might appeal to estate outsiders, playful subversions of the authentic work here to open up possibilities for the estate space and reify the importance of the garden as site where residents are able to work with artists to resist the regeneration processes that threaten their homes. Fourthland explained to me, for example, how they strategically choose new garden sites for projects in an attempt to save community space that might otherwise be built on.

Using a wedding ceremony, a practice that is familiar in all cultures, and merging this with a celebration of bread – a food that Fourthland note is both universal and culturally specific – allowed the quotidian garden space to become a site of magic and possibility. The introduction of me as an officiator and academic 'expert' added another layer to the ceremony, as my reflections on the history of social housing, focusing on the positive instead of the problematic elements of this history, blurred the real and the mythical, opening up a space where those in attendance could imagine what this site might be, reflect on their relationship to it and contemplate possible futures. The playful register of the performance was reflected in the audience response to the material: several were uncertain about the origins of the bread wedding ceremony, asking whether this was a traditional English ritual. 'No', the artists replied, 'but it could be.'

The creating of the gardens as quasi-mythical spaces is part of the process of 'place-making', where, Mackey tells us, the work fosters and reflects the material and psychological construction of place. So too the subversion of the authentic works to resist the unfolding regeneration processes, as the 'public good' of the spaces is acknowledged, upending the 'dreadful enclosure' narrative and preventing the common spaces from being sold as development sites (my interview with Fourthland 2018). In this way the work operates as what I have elsewhere termed 'spatial critique', a *spatialised* form of critical resistance to dominant discourses' (Beswick 2011b: 434, emphasis in original) where those implicated by those discourses are given the opportunity to participate in the production of their own reality. As Chantelle Mouffe argues, despite the tendency to frame art practices as facilitating dominant narratives, critical artistic practices *can* question the dominant hegemony (2007). This kind of critical resistance might also be understood as part of a wider struggle – a 'cultural politics of the hood' (see Beswick 2016b), where on-site practice, as I will explore in the next chapter, can paradoxically unhinge the work from its specific context, connecting the struggle for space, voice and legitimacy in *this place* to national and global struggles happening elsewhere.

Critical ambivalence

The analyses I have offered in this chapter (and to an extent in the previous chapter) are deliberately ambivalent. On the one hand this is because ambivalence and attention to nuance are essential in identifying the paradoxical politics that characterize the estate performance field. However, the ambivalence that I offer here also serves as a deliberate, critical response to the increasingly reductive debates about public artworks, on estates and elsewhere, that permeate public, scholarly and online conversations about these practices. Too often discussions of located artworks exist in a binary, irreconcilable model (as I suggest in the introduction to this chapter) where the artist is either a useful agitator in estate activism or else an artwasher complicit in neoliberal regeneration processes – leading to further reductive discussions and interpretations of politically contentious works. This both diverts attention from those in power who are responsible for social cleansing and puts artists in the position of having to angrily defend their practice, rather than inviting them to critically assess the impact of their work in the spaces and communities where they take place.

An example of the way this reductive binary plays out can be seen in Roman Vasseur's response to criticism of his work on 'Let Us Pray for Those Now Residing in the Designated Area' – a three-year project, which took place between 2007 and 2010 and involved a series of temporary commissions erected in the public space of Harlow New Town. The project was an attempt by the local council, according to their press release, to 'promote a spirit of place' (Essex County Council N.D.), in the run-up to a redevelopment of the dilapidated town. Vasseur responded to accusations of political complicity by making the patently ridiculous argument that, as an artist, he was able to opt out of the political context in which the work operated. As Josephine Berry-Slater and Anthony Iles (2011) have pointed out, despite Vasseur's assertions that the artist's impulse to 'express their sensuous beings' leads them to be 'disloyal to communities of politics', his work in Harlow 'is not without specific aims, or the desire to have some lasting impact' (118). Berry-Slater and Iles highlight that as part of the project Vasseur took on a curatorial role with politically influential responsibilities, such as selecting a developer-planner and offering an architectural review of the proposed redevelopment. They use Vasseur's work in Harlow to argue that, when creating works for public spaces, the artist is always engaged in a kind of 'social war' – where she is neither able to overtly collude with the political aims of the institutional gatekeepers, due to art's requirement for autonomy, nor to effectively 'opt out' of the political context of the work as the boundaries between gallery art and street art (and indeed institutions and located performance practices) are blurred (Berry-Slater and Anthony Iles 2011: 118). I argue that although located estate works are often clearly complicit in destructive regeneration processes, and at their worst can be understood as facilitating social cleansing, there are, nonetheless, also often possibilities for reading these works in resistant ways. Calling on artists to be mindful of the impacts of their practice should not mean calling for them to stop making work. Even within highly compromised circumstances, there is possibility for performances and other artworks to open up new ways of seeing, where they might intervene in the dominant discourse – an idea I return to in more detail in the conclusion to this book. Neither should we forget that many working-class people, some of whom have lived or still live on estates, are also artists and audiences.

Resident artists

I came to realize how easy it is to be seduced by this dominating story; to conflate, without any available evidence to the contrary, these perceived experiences with lived ones and assume tenants have been clamouring to escape.[1]

(Roberts 2018: 129)

*

I mark a theatrical intervention on my own performativity rather than allow the fetishization of my home by someone else. Understanding the currency of representation, this becomes a political point for me ... On this occasion I become a participant in the staging of my own politics.[2]

(McCarthy 2010)

*

We are here.

(Fugitive Images 2015)

*

The music video for Skepta's MOBO award-winning grime single 'Shutdown' (2015) is set in the concrete courtyard of the iconic Barbican estate, a brutalist development in the City of London. In the context of the video, the Barbican's buildings evoke the aesthetic of an inner-city council estate. Flanked by an army of his baseball-cap-wearing peers, smoking and tapping at mobile phones, on 'Shutdown' Skepta celebrates the spirit of community and resistance that exists in Britain's urban working-class communities. Unlike many of the brutalist estates in London, the Barbican was not built as social housing and, as house prices in inner London have soared, it has become known for housing 'stockbrokers and intellectuals ... [in] an atmosphere of ease and comfort' (Hatherley 2008: 34). It is part of the Barbican complex that includes the Barbican Centre for performing arts and is adjacent to the Museum of London and the Guildhall School of Music and Drama: elite art institutions that are often (as discussed earlier in this book) understood as inaccessible to the working classes. In this way 'Shutdown' offers a quite complex spatial critique, where the Barbican stands in for the council estate, but, at the same time, is not a council estate, troubling understandings of brutalist estates as hot-houses for crime and violence.

In the run-up to the 2017 general election, Skepta's video was sampled by performance artist Mark McGowan, the 'Artist Taxi Driver'. In his video 'Theresa May's Tory Magic Money Tree', McGowan attacks the austerity measures that have eroded access to public services and cultural institutions ('Your community centre, shut down / Your library, shut down'). By using sections of the 'Shutdown' video, McGowan further emphasizes the critique the original video offers, drawing attention to the sharp divide between life for those living on the Barbican and life for those on council estates whose communities are being literally 'shut down'.[3]

In another example of grime music offering a critique of dominant estate narratives, at the 2018 Brit Awards, the artist Stomzy called on the Grenfell tower tragedy to deliver a searing message to Prime Minister Theresa May:

> Yo, Theresa May where's the money for Grenfell?
> What you thought we just forgot about Grenfell?
> You criminals, and you got the cheek to call us savages
> You should do some jail time, you should pay some damages
> We should burn your house down and see if you can manage this
> MPs sniff coke we just smoke a bit of cannabis
>
> (Guardian News 2018)

Standing in front of a looming three-tiered structure, in which people dressed in balaclavas sat at regular intervals along each tier, Stormzy opposed the negative stigma associated with council estate residency. He celebrated black British culture and blamed the government, politicians and the media for portraying estate residents as 'savages' while leaving survivors of the Grenfell fire to fend for themselves, despite the millions of pounds of public donations made to assist survivors in the wake of the disaster. As Stephen Crossley (2017) details, words such as 'savage' have a long history in describing the poor working classes and are intimately bound up with the colonial project the British Empire conducted across the globe. Crossley traces the way that racially loaded language used to describe and exoticize those residing in 'the far flung corners of the British Empire' came to be used in the project of 'domestic colonisation' (2017: 17) to describe the conditions of the working poor living in Britain, who were also subject to exploitative practices carried out by the state. Stormzy's summoning of this word connects the racial and class injustices that resulted in the Grenfell disaster (see Hanley 2017b).

Meanwhile, in the recording of the live performance, as the camera pulls back, the structure behind Stormzy resembles the silhouette of an archetypal brutalist estate (presumably this perspective was obvious to the live audience throughout the performance). This effect brings the estate space to the stage in a defiant show of strength, where the threatening estate building, with its balaclava-clad inhabitants, seems to reinforce Stormzy's power: turning the 'threat' of the estate back on the government.

I draw attention to these examples of grime music because this chapter is focussed on the voices of estate residents, and grime (a UK development of hip-hop that also has influences in garage, ragga and jungle music) is a very visible form through which British council estate residents have been able to speak back to dominant estate narratives in the contemporary culture, bringing the voices of those who live on estates to bear on a mainstream discourse that so often overlooks them. I also draw attention to grime because its origins in grass-roots hip-hop culture position it as a very obvious example of what I described in Chapter 1 as an articulation of the global hood, where modes of resistance and survival developed in the marginalized inner cities of North America are appropriated and articulated globally.

As hooks argues, to inhabit the margins is to be located at both a place of oppression and opposition; clinging to the margin can 'nourish one's capacity for resistance' (1990: 150). It is easy to understand the hood, with its association with crime and violence – and its co-option by corporations and media industry – as yet another damaging, stigmatizing conception of the council estate. But, as I mentioned in Chapter 1, I am interested in thinking about how positioning the council estate as part of a global hood allows us to understand ostensibly local, grass-roots work as part of a global network of resistance. Positioning the estate as hood is a means of 'clinging to the margin' and a way of understanding how seemingly local acts can resonate nationally and around the world, drawing attention to the transnational nature of injustices caused by neoliberalism and the way resistance to injustice also resonates transnationally. The global resonances of these local practices are enhanced by the accessible, easy and relatively inexpensive dissemination enabled by social media platforms such as YouTube, Instagram and Twitter (which also undoubtedly have their own exploitative politics, an articulation of which is beyond the scope of this book). Stormzy's use of the word 'savages' and the wide dissemination of his performance online is one example of how we might read British hood politics as articulating the 'transnational' nature of injustice in a form that has potential global reach.

Voices from the margin

Amplifying and analysing voices from the margins is both a matter of enriching scholarly and public knowledge about contested places and a matter of survival for those who live in marginalized conditions (Beswick 2016a). David Roberts points out how narratives of council estates that elide resident experience are 'incomplete', enabling 'persistent accusations of [estate's] unsuitability' as homes 'to go unchallenged' (Roberts 2018: 130). This contributes (as we saw in the previous chapter of this book) to the legitimization of regeneration programmes that displace residents, decimate social housing stock and contribute to social cleansing. Nick Couldry (2010), meanwhile, argues that 'there is no short-cut to understanding neoliberalism's consequences for people's daily conditions of voice without listening to the stories people tell us about their lives' (114). Couldry proposes that space is important in the struggle for voice, suggesting that the 'articulation of space' can 'affect the articulation of narrative' (125).

Couldry's emphasis on space resonates with Richardson and Skott-Myhre's assertion that it is works that take place within 'the bounded space of the hood itself' (2012: 19) that have the most potential to resist those dominant, stigmatizing conceptions of marginalized hood spaces. In order to understand how estate residents resist dominant narratives and speak back to power, it is important to think about how work made by artists on the estates where they live feeds into what Richardson and Skott-Myhre call the cultural politics of the hood (see Chapter 1), where resistance might happen because networks of self-production move beyond the dominant discipline of 'the media, the state or the market' (2012: 19).

Residents speak back

The council estate has proven a potent 'bounded' site for performing resistance to the dominant discourse surrounding social housing and the resulting social cleansing of rapidly gentrifying neighbourhoods. The grime examples I mention at the start of this chapter, where the estate is brought to the stage or screen to facilitate a political critique, illustrate one way that the estate site can be used to 'speak back'. Another means of mobilizing estate space is illustrated by on-site campaigns where residents stage resistance to ongoing regeneration, gentrification and redevelopment projects. For example, the Carpenters estate occupation, part of the Focus E15 campaign launched by a group of young mothers who were served eviction notices from a hostel in Newham, east London, where they were living with their children. The Focus E15 campaigners occupied the disused estate (also in Newham) for a period of just over two weeks during September and October 2014. The occupation, which received significant press attention, highlighted the violence of redevelopment projects that sever people from their homes and local networks. It drew attention to the fact that council housing capable of providing entirely adequate living conditions was left empty so that developers might profit from the site.

When I visited the occupation, I was struck by the way that the campaigners used the space to 'perform' their messages. The estate was altered scenographically, with large handmade banners, adorned with slogans that drew attention to injustices the occupiers were resisting and the violence regeneration projects have visited on those who live in Newham: 'These people need homes', 'it was a lovely community', 'social housing not social cleansing'. The building that was under occupation acted as a kind of carefully performed stage too, visitors to the site were shown around the flat where campaigners were living – a well-proportioned family home that retained the cosy interior decoration presumably left over from former residents who had been evicted. We were encouraged to take photographs and share them on social media to draw attention to the habitable conditions of the property. However, when I tried to photograph other flats in the block, which were in poorer condition, I was asked to delete the photographs, which complicated the simple (but nonetheless true) 'these homes are habitable' message the campaigners wished to disseminate. On site, the Focus E15 group were able to maintain a control over the campaign and its messages that might have been difficult elsewhere.

Artists who live on estates also often use estate sites to voice resistance to processes of neoliberal takeover facilitated by regeneration. For example, the academic and artist Lynne McCarthy offered her own artistic response to the 'Market Estate Project' (2010), an initiative in which seventy-five artists were invited to make work on the soon-to-be-demolished Market estate in Islington, north London, where McCarthy was living at the time. In a conference paper documenting her experience of the project, McCarthy described the video-projection installation she had created, shown in her flat. This work documented her domestic life as she prepared to move out from her home. She juxtaposed images of her daily life with a recording of a party scene held by former residents of the property that she had managed to obtain. As McCarthy explains in the quotation at the start of this chapter, the staging of her work was a performative intervention that deliberately disrupted the politics of space played out by the Market Estate Project, where outsiders were invited to make work about a place where they did not live: this was McCarthy's means of resisting the fetishization of her home.

As these examples illustrate, the use of site can powerfully assist estate residents in asserting their agency and voicing opposition to top-down processes in which they are often powerless to intervene. Although the redevelopment of the Carpenter's estate was not stopped by the Focus E15 campaign, and while McCarthy had to leave her home to make way for the redevelopment of the Market estate, the ability to voice resistance in both these cases importantly draws wider attention to the human costs of regeneration processes – and enables residents to assert some control over the narrative of those processes.

Resistance in the hood: Art and control

Art and creative practices might appear trivial and ultimately futile in the wider context of the housing struggle (and hence are often overlooked in scholarly accounts of council estates), but as Daniel Miller documented in an ethnographic study of a London estate, 'we have to regard apparently trivial activities as deriving from profound concerns' (Miller 1988: 370). As I proposed in the introduction to this book, residents have a profound need to tell their own stories about the spaces where they live. More generally, control over one's life is an important factor in maintaining good physical and mental health – for example, a review of studies into the relationship between work and health concluded that it is those individuals with less control over their jobs, rather than those with more pressurized jobs, who are at increased risk of stress-related heart conditions (see Virtanen et al. 2013). This suggests that it is the level of agency individuals have to exercise control in key areas of their lives which relieves or exacerbates stress – indicating the ways that creative practices staged by residents on estates, who assert displays of control even in spite of their ultimate futility, might be vital for those residents' survival, regardless of any ultimate 'success' in intervening in redevelopment and demolition processes.

In the remainder of this chapter, I offer readings of three estate artworks, made by artists about estates where they have lived: performance and visual artist Jordan McKenzie's *Monsieur Poo-Pourri* series, Fugitive Images' film *Estate: A Reverie* and Jane English's autobiographical solo performance *20b*. These artworks all emerge from the artists' experiences of living on estates in east London, an area that has undergone rapid gentrification since the turn of the twenty-first century, with formerly working-class districts quickly becoming fashionable and expensive cultural 'destinations' targeted by property developers. Focussing on three works created in this area during and in response to ongoing regeneration offers an insight into the cultural politics that circulate in a particular locale, at a particular historical moment – but resonate beyond. There is an interplay in all these works between the specific circumstances of the places they emerge from and the wider landscape of local, national and global housing crises. I explore the strategies the artists use to disrupt dominant narratives, drawing attention to the ways they opt out of top-down institutional relations and trouble conceptions of the authentic real that run through much estate representation.

Artworks that are brought to estates by outsiders, or brought to outsiders by institutions, as we have seen, can often articulate an ambivalent politics and become complicit in reinforcing dominant ways of knowing estates. Work produced on estates about estates by estate residents is usually directly oppositional in one way or another and although this does not mean the works are not also ambivalent, it is perhaps easier to understand them as resistance and to clearly locate them in a global 'hood' cultural politics.

Below, I have outlined three broad strategies used by resident artists, strategies that articulate a cultural politics of the hood, enabling a 'speaking back' from the bounded estate site. I use these strategies as ways to discuss the works I explore in this chapter. Although I use each strategy to think through a single work, I do not suggest that these strategies do, or can, work in isolation from one another. They are, instead, ways of identifying the resistant qualities of resident-led estate performance and linking them to movements and tactics employed beyond council estate activism. In other words, these strategies are a means of framing and understanding the politics of grass-roots estate artworks in a way that might more clearly link them to a global context. These strategies also resonate with the resistant qualities of works explored elsewhere in this book, such as *DenMarked* and 'The Wedding to the Bread' ceremony.

1. Subversion (Jordan McKenzie)

Subversive practices work deliberately against reductive council estate narratives that circulate in the dominant discourse. They undermine spectator expectations of estates and playfully upend reductive stereotypes of these spaces.

2. Yearning (Fugitive Images)

Resident-led oppositional practices often operate in a register that might be understood as 'yearning': what hooks describes as a 'longing for critical voice', an affective response to oppressive conditions 'that wells in the hearts and minds of those whom ... narratives have silenced' (1990: 27). Yearning strategies offer deep and deeply thoughtful insights into the everyday life of estates that affords residents a 'critical voice'.

3. Revenge Nostalgia (Jane English)

'Revenge nostalgia' is a term I have adopted from the artist Laura Oldfield Ford. The word 'revenge' emphasizes the emotionally affective political quality of estate artworks, suggesting that nostalgia is not necessarily reductive and can, in fact, offer complex, oppositional depictions of working-class communities that counter dominant and dangerous political narratives that devalue and displace them (see also Beswick 2015).

Jordan McKenzie's *Monsieur Poo-Pourri* films: Subversive humour, art theory and the politics of the everyday

'Monsieur Poo-Pourri' is an aristocrat who has fallen on hard times and finds himself marooned in east London, living in a tower block on a council estate in Bethnal Green. Created by artist Jordan McKenzie, the Poo-Pourri character is a subversive, satirical persona, whom McKenzie performs, both on his estate and elsewhere – including in the streets and at arts festivals – to draw attention to issues of class, space and power. McKenzie himself is an established visual and performance artist, who has been working professionally since the early 1990s, with exhibitions, shows and residences nationally and internationally, and teaching positions at prestigious art institutions including as a drawing instructor at the University of the Arts, London. He is also a council estate resident who lives in a social rented flat on the Approach estate in Bethnal Green. The Poo-Pourri series offers a mediation of life on the estate that overturns the regularly repeated negative narrative tropes we have explored throughout this book, using comedy to imbue the estate with a sense of play and possibility.

The short film *Monsieur Poo-Pourri Takes a Tour of His Estate* (2010), for example, begins as the aristocrat prepares for a day of horse riding. In the film, McKenzie's flat doubles as Poo-Pourri's home and we watch him, dressed in britches and a riding helmet, take a journey through the estate building, navigating corridors and descending the block in a lift. He exits through the communal doors, traversing the grounds of the estate on a homemade hobby-horse. The film – with its footage of the moving lift and bird's-eye view of the estate grounds – makes spirited use of the vertical possibilities provided by the height of the tower block where the flat is located, as well as affording viewers a sense of the vertiginous unease that comes from living up high. This playful paradox creates an affective representation that conveys a sense of everyday life on a council estate, reflecting geographer Richard Baxter's (2017) findings in his work on the Aylesbury estate, where 'vertical practices' were revealed as both a significant way that residents living in high-rise flats come to know their homes – forging a sense of belonging through playful and sensuous engagement with verticality – and a means by which the experience of living at height becomes, at times, uneasy.

Monsieur Poo-Pourri Takes a Tour of His Estate is also a satirical comment on housing and wealth inequality. Poo-Pourri practices his council estate as if it were the estate of the landed gentry: as if the communal space belonged to him alone. As Marquard Smith argues, in Poo-Pourri, 'McKenzie looks to mock the tactless unpleasantness of the aristocracy who, redundant but far from passing away, carry on governing England driven ... by an unremitting contempt for the poor' (Smith 2014: 8). The film also overturns stereotypical images of modernist, high-rise estates as concrete wastelands, highlighting the ample green spaces the Approach estate provides for those who live there, and the possibilities of those spaces for facilitating leisure, exploration and fun.

In *Monsieur Poo-Pourri Travels the World* (2010), another film in the series, Poo-Pourri plans to explore the world by boat, but, finding himself overwhelmed by the prospect of travel, 'its dirt and noise', he decides simply to 'imagine it'. The bathtub in McKenzie's flat becomes Poo-Pourri's boat. Dressed in a long striped nightshirt he sits in the tub, reading a map of the world, which he covers in salt and submerges in the water. The surreal work, as Kemp-Welch notes, is a 'double-edged' critique of poverty and the emancipatory potential of the imagination.

> Though he plays the part of a 19th century neurotic, McKenzie is also clearly commenting on the problems of our times. Lying in a dingy bathroom, he dreams of escape – from disempowerment, confinement, and the experiential poverty these bring. But as always with McKenzie the critique is double-edged. For the power of the imagination – it's potential for enchantment – is not only being ridiculed but also celebrated – which is not to say that reality is not disappointing: it is.
>
> (Kemp-Welch 2014: 27)

If the dominant narratives we have seen so far in this book tend towards using sensational aspects of estate life (drug dealing, violence, sexual impropriety, demolition) to fetishize and sustain the status quo, here McKenzie subverts that dynamic, offering a hyper-mundane register that, while seemingly banal, gives way to complex and nuanced representations of space that illuminate the possibilities for finding the sensational in the everyday by practicing space differently. By making works that are obviously 'not real' McKenzie rejects the 'authentic real' register that dominates representations of estate sites. His playful, humorous engagement with mundane spaces is not only a means to ridicule and subvert discourses of power, his estate work also actively facilitates conversations with 'high' art theory that is often understood as belonging to the elite cultural domains that exclude social housing residents.

Estate antics: Minimal traces

Poo-Pourri is part of a wider body of work that McKenzie has made on and about his estate. These works are variously designed to intervene in or comment upon wider power structures and they retain traces of the dialogue with art theory that McKenzie has staged elsewhere. For example, many of his estate works can be understood as emerging from ideas articulated in the minimalist discourse that he has explored in works not connected to his estate, such as 'Andre Dance' (2008) and 'Serra Frottage' (2010).

Minimalism is an art movement that emerged in New York during the 1950s and 1960s and is characterized by the idea that 'art should be its own reality and not be an imitation of some other thing' (Tate N.D.). In other words, minimalist artists did not attempt to present an 'alternative' reality, but instead wanted the viewer to respond to the materials in front of them. Kemp-Welch uses Anna Chave's essay 'Minimalism and the rhetoric of power' to argue that minimalism is an unlikely form in which to deliver any resistant political critique – it was an anti-utopian aesthetic that did not 'challenge the institutional or financial foundations of the art world' (Kemp-Welch 2014: 4). According to Chave, the minimalist movement failed effectively to leverage resistance to the violence of the state during the 1960s and instead came to act as a 'valorization of power' that neglected to offer 'something different' to the status quo in which 'the patriarchal overvaluation of power and control … can be held to account for all that is politically reprehensible and morally lamentable in the world' (1992: 272).

In his estate works, McKenzie both uses and rejects minimalism's refusal to propose an 'alternative' world – co-opting the basic materials at his disposal to fashion a relentless engagement with everyday materiality that distorts the status quo so that it becomes something more than real, but never loses its relationship with material reality. The minimalist artist Carl Andre's statement that his art would 'reflect not necessarily politics but the unanalysed politics of my life' can be seen in McKenzie's approach to estate-based art practice. Andre's assertion that 'Matter as matter rather than matter as a symbol is a conscious political position, I think ...' (Chave 1992: 265) appears to inflect McKenzie's artistic engagement with his home, where the basic matter and materials of the estate and the surrounding area are co-opted, in their raw state, and thus happen to *become* political. As Smith notes,

> Because of his familiarity with the local and locale, and his estrangement and alienation from it, [McKenzie] is capable of turning our attention to the consequences of our economic system's banalization, downgrading, and in fact assault on the everyday; and on England's citizens.
>
> (Smith 2014: 37)

For example, for 'Border Patrol' (2014–2015) McKenzie positioned himself as a 'guardian of the border' (McKenzie N.D.), collecting objects that had been used as doorstops to wedge open the communal doors to his block of flats. The collection of objects includes folded lengths of cardboard, brightly coloured children's toys and a pen, melted out of shape – they are exhibited either in their raw form or as life-size photographs displayed on white backgrounds (the objects are also available to view on McKenzie's website). 'Border Patrol' uses the 'unanalysed' material politics of the physical estate threshold, troubling dominant discourses of estate residents as a threat to outsiders by positioning outsiders as a threat to the estate. As McKenzie explains,

> The back door space in my block of flats is seen as a tense crossing space by my neighbours where the inside meets the outside. Gangs, individuals, addicts and dealers use the corridors and stairwell and in order to gain access use a multitude of found objects as 'door stoppers'.
>
> (McKenzie N.D.)

'Border Patrol' might also be understood as a reference to the politics of immigration that inflect estate space – the title suggests national border protections, referencing the way that the council estate is called upon in right-wing media discourse around welfare benefits, positioned as a contested site on which immigrants are depicted as sinister undesirables whose presence amplifies the intrinsic danger of these places. While 'Border Patrol' does not create a utopian alternative vision of the estate, the incongruous objects, particularly the brightly coloured toys and plastic containers, do suggest the vibrancy of estate life and certain sense of mystery, intrigue and possibility – although this is again double-edged: the vibrant objects sit alongside the mundane, dirty and industrial (newspaper cuttings, cigarette butts, lumps of cement). As Kemp-Welch argues, McKenzie's work (like the minimalists') critiques the idea of utopia by '[reinforcing] its artificiality' (Kemp-Welch 2014: 12), continually undermining any utopian register that hovers into view.

Other interventions McKenzie has made on his estate include Lock Up Performance Art (LUPA 2011–2013), a series of events for which McKenzie (working in collaboration with artists Kate Mahony and Aaron Williamson) commissioned well-known and emerging live artists to stage performance works in a garage he rented in the car park. As he explained in an interview recorded on a DVD of his practice released by the Live Art Development Agency (LADA), LUPA made use of the materials available on site – it was a small, local event that eventually attracted large audiences from both the 'art world' and the estate itself:

> I have a lock-up garage on the estate where I live and we thought it would be interesting to site low-fi performance-based works in the estate. The way that it works is that the buildings surround it, so it sort of becomes like a natural theatre. We used to get the electricity from the local shop opposite. We ran an illegal bar from the car boot. Just charged for hot gin. Which that would then pay for the rent of the space … I think the first one we did had about six people, and now we can have audiences up to about 200.
>
> (transcribed from LADA 2014)

Despite the work appealing both to art audiences and his neighbours, McKenzie resists framing LADA as an 'outreach' project patronizingly attempting to 'bring' art to the estate. Rather, his neighbours' interest in the work was an unexpected consequence of making use of available materials – a politics emerging from his engagement with matter:

> One of the most delightful and amazing things about that was when one of the residents walked up to me and said, 'Can I have a word with you?' And I thought, 'Oh here we go. He's gonna be, he's gonna slam it and say it's terrible', and what he said was that 'We love it. And the council want to build on the green spaces around the estate and we need to use them more in order to be able to defend them. So would LUPA please come and use the allotment, the play area etc. etc.' So in a way we were being used – they were incorporating us into their strategy to be able to

maintain the green spaces that they have. So I thought what an amazing consequence. Which I couldn't foresee.

(transcribed from LADA 2014)

Poo-Pourri too makes use of the physical space and its matter – although it rejects minimalism's anti-imitation emphasis. Poo-Pourri both creates imaginative possibilities for the estate and disrupts them. Here McKenzie fashions a decidedly alternative world – but one that maintains its engagement with material reality. As McKenzie describes, for Poo-Pourri, 'Everything becomes this kind of fantasy terrain, he's looking at a window but he's not looking at a window, or in my case a tower block, he's seeing a castle. A kind of an enchantment of space. So on one level its really banal but I think on another level it really enchants space' (transcribed from LADA 2014). Thus, as I expand below, the Poo-Pourri character engenders the kinds of 'art theory' critiques leveraged by McKenzie's other estate works, with the character giving way to ideas that are far more complex than the simple delivery and stripped-back presentation might first imply.

Subverting the *flâneur*

In *Monsieur Poo-Pourri Points at Things* (2010), the third film in the series, the aristocrat ventures beyond his estate home, idly roaming the neighbourhood where he lives, pointing at things he comes across (a manual worker cleaning the stairs outside the tube station, a paper cup of Pepsi left on top of a rubbish bin, a poster of the council estate pop star Cheryl Cole, a lamp post, discarded cigarette butts, a pigeon, a copy of the now defunct tabloid newspaper the *News of the World*) with a silver-tipped wooden cane. In this video McKenzie plays with the idea of the *flâneur*, the idle wanderer, a figure that first emerged in nineteenth-century Paris, where the rapidly developing city made way for a new bourgeois class of (white) man, who could stroll the streets as an uninterrupted observer and write about what he saw. As Elizabeth Wilson notes, the *flâneur* was a response to '[t]he development of a consumer and spectacular society on a scale not previously known', which 'represented opportunities for progress, plenty and a more civilized populace' (1992: 91). McKenzie's playful invocation of the *flâneur* figure in contemporary Bethnal Green serves to highlight some of the criticisms of the *flâneur* that have emerged from feminist and black scholars and raises questions about what it means to walk in city spaces today – as well as questions about the classed and gendered nature of privacy that Lisa McKenzie draws attention to in her discussions around the routine invasion of working-class women's privacy by the state (discussed in Chapter 1).

The classed and raced nature of Poo-Pourri's privilege is evident in his deep contrast to his surroundings. An aristocrat in a working-class district, where many of the inhabitants are black and brown skinned, and where the things he 'points' at (the street-cleaner, Cheryl Cole, the *News of the World*) are often symbolic of working-class life. On one level the pointing works as a humorous intervention that, in the live moment of its action, bemuses and amuses those who witness Poo-Pourri's antics – as with McKenzie's other estate works it exists in a hyper-mundane register that subverts the 'sensational mundane' that pervades representations of working-class spaces and people. Occasional comments from passersby ('What's up there?' someone enquires off-camera, before a young woman looks directly at the lens and asks, 'What are you pointing at?') not only indicate the impossibility of invisibility for this anachronistic aristocratic *flâneur* but also highlight the privilege McKenzie is afforded, as a white man in his 'upper class' costume, to dominate the space and dictate its rules, to raise curiosity but never fear apprehension.

Thus *Monsieur Poo-Pourri Points at Things* raises questions about who gets to walk idly and freely in public space – questions that are particularly pertinent given the council estate resonances of the Poo-Pourri project and the rapidly gentrifying, working-class, multicultural milieu that McKenzie navigates in his film. As the case of Mark Duggan, which I outlined in Chapter 1, has highlighted, tension between (working-class) black people, particularly young men, and the police are often heightened due to issues of street policing and the targeting of black men for 'stop and search'. The 'stop and search' laws, which enable police to apprehend those they have 'reasonable grounds' to suspect of crime, are at least three times more likely to be used on black people (Home Office 2017), meaning that the ability to walk freely is a raced as well as a classed privilege. The raced implications of walking have become pertinent in contemporary debate, as the figure of the *flâneur* has re-emerged alongside a renewed interest in walking practices, such as psycho-geography. In 2018, for example, Eclipse Theatre staged a UK tour of a show titled *Black Men Walking* that illuminates hidden histories by inserting black walkers into the English landscape, foregrounding stories located in spaces and practices from which black narratives have often been obscured. The privilege (middle-class) white people are given to both walk freely and dominate stories of public space is not only national, but resonates with international concerns and politics too – once again revealing the power bounded estate practices have to speak beyond the local. As the writer Teju Cole pointed out in a Facebook post responding to the targeting of black people by law enforcement in the United States, 'Flanerie is for whites' (Cole 2018) – a point movingly evidenced in Garnette Cadogan's essay 'Walking while black' (2016). McKenzie's Poo-Pourri evokes these tensions while strolling obliviously, commanding the local terrain.

Subversion: Incongruous strategies

In an essay exploring the subversive strategies used by the feminist art collective The Guerrilla Girls, Anna Teresa Demo proposes incongruity as a means through which the collective 'engender a comic politics of subversion' (2000: 134). For Demo, incongruity is a key feature of subversive politics. 'The use of terms, images or ideologies that are incongruous', she explains, 'reorders – even remoralizes – a situation or orientation in a process akin to consciousness-raising' (2000: 134). She illustrates how The Guerrilla Girls scrutinize the 'everyday', making use of the comic frame in order to provide 'a unique vantage point from which to see the inaccuracies of a situation' (134). Demo's articulation of an incongruous subversive strategy is useful for thinking about the way McKenzie's Poo-Pourri series intervenes in estate discourse to facilitate a complex 'reordering' or 'remoralizing' of estate space.

Like the Guerrilla Girls, Poo-Pourri uses incongruous comic tactics – placing the aristocrat in a council block and challenging the audience to make sense of his unlikely behaviour. Poo-Pourri subverts conventional understandings of estate space by drawing attention to its playful potential, undermines the 'authentic real' by 'enchanting' estate space with obviously fictional, contrived scenarios and challenges notions of ownership over 'elite' art by removing art theory debates from the gallery and university and staging them on the estate where he lives.

McKenzie does not work entirely outside of the art market, however. He has staged the Poo-Pourri works at festivals and exhibitions[4] and relies on commissions and a patchwork of funding, including from LADA and ACE, to realize his practice. The Poo-Pourri film series, however, was made and produced without commission or external funding and circulates beyond the conventional 'art world' as well as within it. The online dissemination of Poo-Pourri on videos on McKenzie's website (where documentation of two of the films from the project sits along with much of his other practice) might be understood as subversion of power, placing ownership of the work outside of the control of dominant art markets. McKenzie's tendency to share his work through videos also troubles notions of spectatorship, often keeping the primary audience (witnesses to the live acts documented in the videos) unclear about his motivations, serving 'to undermine the idealism of performance as a genre committed to the direct power of live action' (Kemp-Welch 2014: 12) by placing the online viewer in a privileged position. These disruptions of power and destabilizations of dominant discourse – along with McKenzie's refusal to fit any stereotype of social housing resident – evidence the ways estate artists working subversively in their own homes can offer opposition to the versions of the estate dictated by the media, the state and the market: taking control of their own representation while still having fun.

Fugitive Images' *Estate: A Reverie*: Home *un*making, gentrification and yearning on an east London council estate

Estate: A Reverie (2015) is a 'creative documentary' (Mortimer 2014) feature film made by the art collective Fugitive Images, a company founded by residents to produce work in response to changes happening on the Haggerston West and Kingsland estates as they underwent regeneration. The film was funded through a patchwork of organizations, including ACE, who now hold the film as part of their collection. Nonetheless this was a project made from within the community, rather than in response to any commission. It was filmed by artist and director Andrea Luka Zimmerman over a seven-year period as she and her neighbours – who lived on the Haggerston estate in Hackney – prepared to move out to make way for a redevelopment of the site. Zimmerman has said that the film seeks

> to capture the genuinely utopian quality of the last few years of the buildings' existence, a period when, because demolition was inevitable, a sense of the possible, of the emergence of new, but of course time-specific, social and organizational relationships developed, a fresh understanding of how the residents might occupy the spaces of the estate.
>
> (Lux N.D.)

Estate is a complexly woven film that layers observational documentary footage with dramatic performance, role play and what Zimmerman describes as 'interventions in public space and with a wider public' (Fugitive Images N.D.). These interventions include the portrait series 'I Am Here', in which huge photographs of residents replaced the orange boards that had been erected externally to cover windows of empty properties. The photos served to remind those passing by that the estate was still inhabited. In the documentary, we see the portraits being mounted in the windows of an externally facing block as Zimmerman explains the rationale behind the project: 'So you know what they said? "Time to go." And then they left flats of us here. Out of sight, out of mind. Well, we weren't, and we aren't.... So you know what we said? "We are here."'

About halfway through the film, there is a scene shot in the home of an ageing disabled resident named Jeff. We watch through an open doorway as Jeff explains to a visiting representative who has come to assess his home – presumably sent by the housing association or local authority – the difficulty he has navigating the flat. He can't get out, he tells her, because he is now using a chair and is unable to make his way down the steps that lead up to his front door. He has lived in the flat for thirty years. 'When I first come here', Jeff says, 'they said, "you won't be in here long because we'll pull them [the estate's blocks] down"'. The sense of precarious uncertainty that emanates from this scene with Jeff, the feeling of living, suspended, in a kind of extended limbo, waiting for your home to be torn down, to be moved somewhere else, clinging to what you have in the meantime, drives the emotional affect of the film. This a precarious, fraught utopia.

The Haggerston estate was part of the Haggerston West and Kingsland 'prestige' estates, made up of blocks built by London County Council (which was replaced by the Greater London Council) on either side of the Regent's Canal between 1928 and 1953 (this canal-side location made the properties prime development opportunities later on). The estates were intended to house families as part of slum clearance programmes; as Zimmerman and Lasse Johansson explain in a book project documenting Fugitive Images' work on Haggerston West and Kingsland, these sites were initially intended to 'improve not only the living conditions of the residents but also their moral character' (2010: 5). In *Estate: A Reverie*, we see how even from their inception the estates and their inhabitants were viewed with suspicion by outsiders. In historical footage interspersed into the film, two local women discuss the residents on the new development, making it clear that they understand their incoming neighbours as dirty and morally inferior.

In a now familiar trajectory Haggerston West and Kingsland fell into decline and disrepair, especially after management of the sites was handed from the Greater London Council to Hackney Council in the 1980s, when some of the estates' residents were permanently moved elsewhere to make way for refurbishments, fracturing the established sense of community. By the 1990s Haggerston had become known as a 'sink estate', with a reputation as the 'heroin capital of Europe' (Zimmerman and Johansson 2010: 7). In 2007, residents voted for a regeneration package that would demolish the original development and build a new one in its place.[5] Ownership of the buildings was transferred from Hackney Council to London and Quadrant Housing Association (L&Q) in preparation for the site's redevelopment, and in the seven-year period leading up to the demotion residents were afforded unusual freedom to make use of estate space without interference from L&Q. Zimmerman describes this as both an idyllic and sad time. *Estate: A Reverie* captures this period, where residents lived with an enduring sense of loss, but came together to support one another, produce artworks and host community events in spaces across the estate. The film demonstrates how, during this transitional period, the conditions for creating a utopian, albeit temporary, community-led space became possible. Zimmerman describes it as

> the thickening of the moment when you know you are going to lose something. Suddenly you see what's there and you know it's not going to be there anymore. It's that kind of time-warp – like you know you're going to lose something, then suddenly your eyes open. It's about exploring that.
>
> (Mortimer 2014)

The last block on the Haggerston estate was demolished in 2014. Although the residents were given properties on the newly developed site and, unlike in many other London developments, were not forced to move away from the neighbourhood they had called home, the fraught politics of gentrification nonetheless run through the regeneration. In order to finance the new estate buildings, the development doubled in density to include private and shared ownership properties – a phenomenon that Fugitive Images argue embodies a Thatcherite economics of 'a trickle down effect, which claimed that the creation of wealth in an area would trickle down and benefit its poorer parts' (Zimmerman and Johansson 2010: 11).

> The problem with this is two-fold. First, it embodies a logic of 'aspiration', where one should continually desire to have 'more'. Second, it could also be argued that when luxury developments, designer shops, artisan bakeries, high-end food markets etc., begin to crop up in a poor area there is an additional side-effect, which is that these opposites – rich and poor – tend to amplify each-other and, rather than any trickle-down, they even further articulate the vast socio-economic difference that exists between them.
>
> (Zimmerman and Johansson 2010: 11)

The film deals with these tensions and anxieties, shedding light on the ways that estate residents come to terms with their changing neighbourhood and make sense of the gaze that incoming, wealthier occupants place on these social housing 'natives'. A young resident says that, although she enjoys some of the new shops and cafes, her friends often feel unwelcome in the higher-end stores that have sprung up at the local Broadway Market. At one point the residents gather to discuss how their estate has become something of a cultural 'destination', filmed by art students and tourists. They disagree about how offensive they find this intrusion; one resident remarks that she doesn't mind, while another says that she feels it frames them as 'unfortunate'. In another scene, several of the Haggerston residents gather on the balcony of a block overlooking the estate's courtyard, staring down at a guided tour that is being held there as part of Hackney's 'Open House' initiative – offering access to notable architecture in the borough. 'I wonder what the tour guide's telling them?' a resident jokes, 'That we've just finished cleaning chimneys?!'

Distorted realism

The overarching story told by *Estate: A Reverie* is 'true' in the sense that it documents real events. However, the film itself engages a number of forms and registers, distorting the 'fly-on-the-wall' realism that dictates the estate documentary genre and is the dominant form used in the poverty porn television programmes discussed in Chapter 1 of this book. Zimmerman works poetically, juxtaposing conventional documentary footage with unexpected compositions. The film opens, for example, with a child, sitting in the snow, holding a chicken as sheep wander, bleating loudly behind him. This image references a story told later in the film, in which an early resident of Haggerston, unable to bring the farmyard animals he had lived with in his 'slum' property, took his own life once he moved onto the estate, gassing himself inside his flat with his dog – a story that points to the ambivalent origins of Haggerston: not only a place of community, but a place where people were homed after losing their communities. The opening image also calls on questions of the divide between the rural and the urban and invites the viewer to look at the estate and its possibilities anew by offering us an unusual framing of the space.

This layering of forms, Zimmerman explains, was an intentional method, designed to communicate the complexity of estate life:

> This hybrid aspect of the film developed not out of a desire to be aesthetically 'avant-garde' but rather because the various devices were simply the most productive in terms of conveying both the layered aspects of the site, historically, architecturally and socially, and also the similarly textured identities the residents found themselves living

within, in terms of how they were viewed by peers, social agencies, and the neighbouring public.

(Fugitive Images N.D.)

Estate's 'textured' employment of forms usefully reveals how dominant narratives and stories we receive about estates and perceptions of residents that circulate in the public imagination are deeply embedded in history and culture. For example, in *Estate* we see a group of residents rehearsing and performing scenes from a stage adaptation of Samuel Richardson's classic novel *Clarissa* (1748). This reference to the novel nods to the fact that buildings on the Haggerston were named after Samuel Richardson ('Clarissa Road', 'Samuel House', etc.), using an elite literary figure as part of the attempt to 'improve' the original tenants. As they rehearse the play, the residents discuss the themes and ideas it expresses; one points out that a key concept that runs through the novel is about the divine and retributive nature of justice – if an injustice happens and is deserved, we are wrong to pity the victim. In the context of the injustices delivered on the estate's residents displayed elsewhere in the film, this statement illuminates the ways that the dominant discourse disavows pity for estate residents, whose 'morally inferior' behaviour positions them as deserving figures of injustice: a discourse that was literally manifested in the naming of the Haggerston estate's buildings.

Similarly, the erection of the 'I Am Here' photographs references the ways that developers often use images to erase working-class lives, conjuring a vision of a gentrified middle class who will live on newly redeveloped estate sites. It is common for hoardings to be erected around regeneration sites that depict affluent couples and families – often white skinned – surrounded by expensive furniture and consuming luxury goods, such as expensive coffee. These images communicate the message that incoming residents who will live on the new development are not the working classes who previously inhabited the site (regardless of whether that is actually the case).

The poetic juxtaposition of the everyday with stories, performances and interventions from across the estate's history works to give an affective sense of the ways that reality is constructed and conveys the complex lived texture of that constructed reality for Haggerston's residents.

Home *un*making

We might consider *Estate: A Reverie* as a documentation of the nuanced process of home *un*making. Richard Baxter and Katherine Brickell's (2014) introduction of the term 'home *un*making' to the vocabulary of home studies offers a means by which we can think through the complexity of the process documented in the film. As Baxter and Brickell posit, studies of home have tended to focus on issues of homemaking and attachment, ignoring the various processes by which we become detached or removed from our places of home. This oversight in home studies means there is a lacuna in our understanding about the ways in which homes are unmade, a lacuna that extends from wider discrimination of certain types of people, spaces and experiences 'that do not fit an ideal model' (Baxter and Brickell 2014: 139). Like homemaking, home *un*making is a process that is both consciously enacted and unfolds in response to the environment. A 'precarious' series of activities 'by which material and/or imaginary components of home are unintentionally, deliberately, temporarily or permanently divested, damaged or even destroyed' (Baxter and Brickell 2014: 134).

Importantly, home homemaking and *un*making are not binary concepts that articulate the positive and negative aspects of attachment to one's home, but are in dialectical interplay as home is made and unmade in multiple physical and imaginative ways as we find our place(s) in the world. The ambivalent *un*making/making process is encapsulated in a scene towards the end of the documentary where residents throw belongings and items of furniture they no longer need from the balconies into a skip in the courtyard. As they do so an elderly resident walks slowly to the skip and places his old television gently on top of the rubbish. 'You see', he says, confronting his conflicting feelings as he unmakes and remakes his idea of home in anticipation of moving on, coming to terms with the prospect of change, 'I didn't want it [to] smash up.'

Yearning

In her seminal essay collection *Yearning: race, gender and cultural politics,* hooks argues that the term 'yearning' offers a useful means of articulating the intersectional 'depths of longing' that emerge from conditions of oppression across 'race, class, gender, and sexual practice' (1990: 12). She articulates the complicated ways that 'yearning' brings together different registers of longing that embrace the hopes and dreams of the oppressed and those from privileged groups who long for change:

> All too often our political desire for change is seen as separate from longings and passions that consume lots of time and energy in daily life. Particularly the realm of fantasy is often seen as completely separate from politics. Yet I think all of the time black folks (especially the underclass) spend just fantasizing about what our lives would be like if there were no racism, no white supremacy. Surely our desire for radical social change is

intimately linked with the desire to experience pleasure, erotic fulfilment and a whole host of other passions.

(hooks 1990: 13)

hooks's 'yearning' is a means through which we can understand the cultural politics of *Estate: A Reverie*. It is also a way we can think about the raced as well as the class politics it depicts, with many of the residents in the film from black and other ethnic minority communities. The film evokes the 'fantasy' register both by offering ways of *seeing* the estate differently (as a bucolic farmyard covered in snow in the opening shot, for example) and showing us ways that residents *practiced* the estate differently in its final years: creating folk art, staging performances, making artistic interventions on the site and living apparently in harmony and solidarity side by side (perhaps class solidarity here is a means of erasing the 'white supremacy' that hooks refers to). The 'longing' that hooks describes runs through the film affectively, summoned through the layering of forms described above as well as through the use of diegetic and non-diegetic music. A folk musician playing the accordion appears several times through the film, her wistful, melancholic songs ('now's the time to hitch up and be strong/ though our heart is breaking') drawing the sense of yearning from the screen into the viewer.

Zimmerman explains that the film's affective quality, what I am calling the 'yearning' affect (although she doesn't use that term), is a deliberate strategy 'offering a certain tone of memory, subjective of course, but one grounded in a common experience of living with difference' (Fugitive Images N.D.). Though the yearning here speaks from a specific site, it also, as hooks suggests this kind of political yearning might, opens up possibilities for understanding 'common ground' where 'differences might meet and engage one another' (hooks 1990: 13). The temporary utopian community depicted in the film, Zimmerman suggests, could act as a kind of template for 'ways of being in the city; a more inclusive and supportive form of social and personal interaction, taking place within a more porous and collectively focussed urban environment' (Fugitive images N.D.). This suggests one way that the documentary might resonate beyond Haggerston, offering an indication of how a located cultural politics of the hood can speak beyond a specific site, calling for recognition and action from those elsewhere who are also yearning for change.

Jane English's *20b*: Demolished estates, domicide and revenge nostalgia

How do you speak back from a site that doesn't exist anymore? Jane English's nostalgic project *20b* (2015–2017) explores this question. *20b* is a devised performance in which English attempts to recreate her childhood home, a flat on the Brooks estate in Plaistow, in order to come to terms with her feelings about its demolition and resist the 'failure' narrative that enabled its demise. In the show, which has toured regional, fringe and subsidized theatres and arts centres across England in various iterations, English offers a nostalgic account of her life on the estate and narrates her struggle to accept its destruction.

The version of the performance I saw at Camden People's Theatre in 2017 was performed by English herself as a one-woman show. It begins as she recounts a recurring dream where she returns to flat 20b. English tells us that she didn't say goodbye to the estate before she left and that memories of her unresolved relationship with the place she once called home haunt her despite the years that have passed since its demolition.

As the performance progresses, English attempts to reconstruct her lost home from photographs, memory fragments and maps. At one point she reveals a replica of the block she has fashioned from cardboard boxes. She wants to remember exactly what it was like and wants us to know the place too. Guiding the audience through each cardboard replica flat in the block where she lived, English brings the space and her neighbours to life with nostalgic stories that elicit the sensory experience of living on the estate and celebrate the vibrant multicultural community – evoking the smells, sights and textures that made the place real.

> If not sunbathing, I think of her peeling potatoes because she was always making homemade chips. Her flat often smelt of hot cooking oil, and dog, and bleach and dettol cos she was always cleaning up after the dogs. And hash, because if Angela didn't have a cup of tea in her hand, it was a spliff.
>
> (English N.D.)

These recollections are delivered in a sentimental tone that risks replicating the kinds of reductive working-class nostalgia discussed in Chapter 1, but unlike those forms of politically neutral nostalgia, here English engages a political register. She takes us through documents that connect the destruction of the Brooks estate with the wider gentrification of London's East End – tracing the council's decision-making process and justification for the demolition.

Moving the performance further beyond a reductive nostalgia rooted in her personal memories of childhood, English recounts her attempts to find her neighbours during the research process for making the show. Her conversations with them demonstrate the lasting impact living on the estate has had on the lives of its residents, as well as the ambivalent feelings former residents have about the estate now. Recalling some of the more difficult aspects of estate life such as poverty, crime and violence, English is careful not to fall entirely into sentimentality. Nonetheless, the show highlights that the estate holds both treasured and terrible memories and that it is the demolition of her home, not its existence, which is the source of English's pain and the pain of her neighbours, who also describe dreaming about the estate years after its demolition and longing to return there. In one moving scene, English plays a recording of a conversation with her neighbour, Trevor, who tells her about his experience of returning to the area after gentrification, realizing that he is no longer welcome or able to live there:

> *Three hundred grand for a flat. In Stratford, up the top. Literally there* [sic] *plan is to wipe out anyone who is not making enough money. Cos even people who is working, working class people, cant afford for their places.*
>
> (English N.D., original emphasis)

At the end of the show, English plays a recording where her mother describes returning to the estate on the afternoon after they had moved out. Detailing how she made her way through the abandoned property, looking at objects they had left behind, her mother explains how she came to terms with the fact that this was no longer their home. Sitting on the balcony of the flat, contemplating the familiar view, she disassociated completely from the space:

> *[W]e'd only just moved that morning and it felt completely alien to me, and that it just wasn't home anymore, everything, the essence of us didn't exist there anymore ... I just left with a sort of shrug of the shoulders that it was just, it was just over. It was just gone.*
>
> (English N.D., original emphasis)

Institutions and creative control

20b is English's first solo work. It was developed as a passion project – by which I mean it was driven by the artists' desire to speak, and not through a commission or call made by institutional gatekeepers. Although English worked with a number of institutions to create the performance – attending artist development programmes run by Friction Arts, Birmingham Repertory Theatre and Bryony Kimmings Ltd – and eventually secured funding from ACE, moving between institutions enabled her to maintain control and assert a creative voice that operates outside of the dominant discourse. This is not a performance aimed at a middle-class audience, and it makes no attempt to appeal to those who are 'outsiders' by presenting life on the estate as 'other'. In fact, English relishes the mundane details of estate life. Her stories seem designed to resonate with other people who have lived on council estates. She recalls answering the public telephone in the street outside her block, where she would field calls for neighbours who didn't own a phone; describes how, on a visit to an abandoned block of flats in Aston, Birmingham, 'the wire mesh safety glass above the doors, the exact same lino tiles that were in our building' create an uneasy familiarity (English N.D.). The tone of delivery asks the audience to identify with rather than to 'learn' from the representation – highlighting, again, how working outside of conventional institutional frameworks can enable a platform for estate residents' voices that does not cater to the middle-class mainstream for whom the estate is other.

The venues where English has shown the work, notably the Theatre Royal Stratford East, Camden People's Theatre in London and Slung Low in Leeds, are predominately fringe institutions that are committed to fostering relationships with local communities and reflecting their concerns. None of the venues had creative input into *20b*, but, as with *DenMarked*, staging a working-class story on a stage where working-class people are likely to visit and allowing the artist creative control enabled the performance to feel deeply connected to an urgent wider context. There is no sense that English is attempting to assert her authenticity in order to offer an 'authentic real' version of the estate – although, undoubtedly the fact that this is a 'real' story is part of its appeal. Nonetheless, this realness does not remain untroubled. The nostalgic register of *20b*, and English's own admission that her memories tend to paper over the cracks of the less desirable aspects of estate life – along with the obviously 'not real' estate space, fashioned from cardboard boxes – emphasize, in fact, that this version of the council estate is decidedly not the real thing; English's estate can only ever exist as a memory.

Domicide

20b is a personal account of the emotional consequences of what the geographer John Douglas Porteous has termed domicide. 'Domicide' describes 'the planned deliberate destruction of someone's home, causing suffering to the dweller' (Porteous and Smith 2001: 19). The invention of the term, as Frances Heywood notes, 'makes it possible to give a voice to all the feelings and understanding that the victims of the process have been unable to articulate' (Heywood 2003: 269). Despite the introduction of the concept of domicide to the field of home studies, however, the ways that the loss of home impacts on those forcibly removed from the places they live in remain relatively underexplored in both scholarship and culture. In this context, English's work develops our sense of the ways that homes impact on the psyche and the process of grieving that is necessary to move on from the loss of home – as well as illuminating the specific human impacts of gentrification in east London.

English's performance of her experience of domicide enacts a tale which, like all love stories, is at once not only highly specific but also profoundly human. She tells the audience about the behaviour induced by her loss: returning to the estate on covert visits, during which she would feel more and more anger about the decision to destroy her home and the lack of care taken to preserve any aspect of the space:

> Well, I knew the building was going to be demolished, so I'd kind of prepared myself for that, but I never expected they would get rid of the trees. That really upset me. Because they were so big, they were massive and beautiful. And they just fucking uprooted them.
>
> (English N.D.)

English's devising process – her attempts to recreate a physical space that no longer exists in order to let it go – exemplifies how expressions of domicide might be conceived as part of the homemaking and *un*making process I described in the previous section.

Speaking to the importance of re-making the 'bounded' physical estate site, English explained to me how – unable to invite the audience into the estate to experience what was lost – she wanted to affectively place them in her former home. Much of the devising and developing process involved working out the most effective way to do this. First, she made an installation for one person at a time in an empty unit space with a patio door, which she turned into a version of her living room as it looked after she'd moved out.

> My mum helped me to make it actually, put speakers inside this arm chair – so audience members would sit in the arm chair, and there were bits of the story that I told, about the moving and that experience. And then I left the space and then [a recording of] my mum telling the story came out of the chair.... When my mum had helped me make the chair she also made a backdrop, which was a view from the balcony drawn on a big bit of canvas that was hung up

behind the patio doors backwards, so it just looked blank. And then, as my mum was telling the story about looking at the view, there were lights behind it so it lit up and you could see the view behind it for a moment, and then it disappeared.

(My interview with Jane English May 2017)

The evolution to a cardboard recreation of the estate came as the performance developed and English realized she would need a means of staging the space for larger audiences, in a way that she could tour to different venues.

20b, although a highly specific and personal story, nonetheless resonates with a broader local national and global political picture. The gentrification of east London is part of a global neoliberal project, predicated on a rapid urbanization that displaces and unhomes citizens, mostly against their will. David Harvey calls this '[a] process of displacement and … accumulation by dispossession' (2008: 24). He points to the invasion of hillside neighbourhoods in 1990s Seoul, slum clearance projects in Mumbai, gentrification projects in the Bronx and mooted plans to develop Brazil's favelas to highlight how the violent, local displacements of people form a global injustice, delivered by an ideology where the accumulation of capital is the core driver of the political economy. *20b* gives voice to the human cost of the political status quo: a 'speaking back' that might resonate beyond the local, but which, nonetheless, enables a victim of a global injustice to take control of her specific experience.

Revenge nostalgia

In 2015, the visual artist Laura Oldfield Ford gave a talk about her drawings of abandoned council estates (and other former working-class sites) at Queen Mary University of London. During the Q&A discussion afterwards, she described the aesthetic of her drawings, which document the ways state policies have systematically devalued and destroyed working-class communities and spaces, as 'revenge nostalgia'. Like the 'rage' in the 'council estate rage' aesthetic I described earlier in this book, revenge in this phrase should not be misunderstood as an uncritical reactionary position: it is a term that encompasses the affective quality of politically and critically engaged nostalgia, able to connect specific stories to the wider injustices delivered on working-class communities. The term revenge acknowledges the difficult emotional terrain that results from those injustices and gives us a means by which to understand emotionally inflected, angry and reflectively nostalgic works as critically important in the landscape of the housing crisis and its connection to the devaluing of working-class culture. As I have argued elsewhere,

> The 'revenge' in this useful phrase highlights the political quality of estate artworks; it suggests that nostalgia is not necessarily reductive and can, in fact, be operationalized to offer complex, oppositional depictions of working-class communities that counter dominant and dangerous political ideologies. 'Revenge nostalgia' may usefully describe the critical potential of Boym's ambivalent model – the term 'revenge' being expedient in this context for describing the affective qualities of the interplay between the specific and the general, in which restorative nostalgia is co-opted to facilitate a reflective social critique that impacts other spaces and places, in one way or another.
>
> (Beswick 2015: 37)

The demolition of Brooks Road is both a specific event and a symptom of wider local, national and global crises. Social housing users across the globe are disempowered, 'powerless up to the point where they can't even argue against the destruction of their self-made living arrangements within the strict planning system that was superimposed on them in the first place' (Engel 2011: 73). The nostalgic tone of *20b* is shot through with a piercing critical awareness of this wider context – and at moments, such as the visit to the Birmingham estate, offers a glimpse into the wider political landscape that is both angry and necessary.

Institutions, the Arts Council and the impossibility of 'grass-roots'

In this chapter I have framed resident-led works as examples of grass-roots practice that operate to one degree or another outside of dominant media, state and market forces. Although all the works I discuss are 'grass-roots' in the sense that they emerge 'from the ground up' as part of an embodied, emplaced context, none of them circulate entirely outside of the wider capitalist context in which we are all embroiled. These are professional artists, whose work relies to some degree on the support of institutions and the state for funding, audience creation and sustainability. In earlier chapters of this book I have been highly critical of ACE and the ways in which its language erases class and reinforces an elitist system.

However, it is also important to acknowledge that, despite the limits of its discourse, ACE provides opportunities for working-class artists and enables a landscape of art and performance practice that would be difficult to sustain in a model where artists had to rely on commercial commissions and philanthropy. This is to say that, as with all the arguments I have set out in this book, the creation of a 'cultural politics of the hood' is nuanced and does not and cannot be realized entirely without the systems and structures that organize the art market and the creative economy more widely. This doesn't mean that the power of these works is negated – but it does underline that, however far we try to remove ourselves from the structures that structure inequality, we find ourselves also structured by the prevailing system, navigating as best as we can within it.

Conclusion: Three thoughts

Capitalist realism

This book has sought to explore the role of performance and performative practices in producing estate space. Throughout the book I have returned again and again to issues of authenticity, with discussions of what I have called the 'authentic real' emerging as a central concern. As I have outlined, concepts of authenticity in relation to estates operate ambivalently, always threatening to subsume a single depiction under a burden of representation, where it comes to stand as a total version of 'real' council estate space. While the cultural preoccupation with authenticity can and does offer platforms for estate residents to tell stories through their own lens, so too claims to authenticity are co-opted by institutions and individuals to ward off criticism and to suggest that what is presented on stage (or screen, or in the estate itself) is unproblematically 'true'.

My attempt to address the role of the authentic real in estate representation is influenced by Mark Fisher's argument in *Capitalist Realism*. As Fisher proposes, late capitalism operates through discourses of reality, which resonate globally and result in a 'sense of exhaustion, of cultural and political sterility' (2009: 7); capitalism's realist logic, he argues, occupies 'the horizons of the thinkable' (8), where it becomes impossible to imagine any alternative to the status quo. It is useful to think about the role of artistic form in this context; it is perhaps no coincidence that realism has emerged as the dominant representational form in late capitalism. As Michael Vanden Heuvel has noted, 'realism simply replicates existing – and therefore arguably bourgeois, patriarchal, racist, oppressive and oedipal – discourses, and functions as a mode of conciliation, assimilation, adaptation, and resignation to those discourses' (1992: 48). As we have seen throughout this book, social realism particularly has mostly failed to usefully intervene in discourses surrounding class and council estates, and concepts of authenticity and reality frequently emerge across forms as a means by which claims to progressive politics can be laid with little threat to the structures that create injustice. In Chapters 2 and 3, I drew attention to how centring material reality in representations of estates can risk the engendering of poverty safari, where outsiders can consume authentic estateness from a safe distance. In this way, realism (and its residue in the form of the authentic real in avant-garde forms) serves to confirm the impression that the state of affairs depicted by the artwork is a 'reality' from which there is no escape – other than to literally escape via social mobility.

Realist forms that shore up the status quo, rooted in a wider culture of the authentic real, are not limited to representations of the English estate. We see similar depictions in popular global representations of marginal urban spaces. The films *La Haine* (1995) and *Girlhood* (2014), for example, are realist depictions of French housing projects (or *banlieue*) on the outskirts of Paris, which resonate, in their depiction of a 'dreadful enclosure', with representations of the council estate we have seen throughout this book – albeit in a different national context. Similarly, US hood movies (e.g. *Boyz in the Hood, Menace II Society*, see Chapter 1) use realist forms and claims to authenticity to position marginal spaces of the American inner city as containers for social issues that have local, national and global resonances. We might think about how discourses of 'lack', of violence, poverty, racial inequality and lawlessness in representations of various marginal home-spaces (the favelas of Rio de Janeiro in the film *City of God* (2002), or the slums of Mumbai in the movie *Slumdog Millionaire* (2002), for example) often rely on realist conventions that serve to reify and often fetishize the marginality they reveal. In this way, council estate performance, as a nationally bounded practice, can be understood as a specific iteration of a global politics of realist representation that creates 'the horizons of the thinkable'. Future analysis might more fully trace the implications of this transnational picture.

This criticism doesn't mean that performance and other art practices are utterly unable to bring about change or to offer possibilities for seeing and being differently – there are always gaps in the created reality. Chapter 3 particularly demonstrates how even highly compromised works have the potential to be read in ways that disrupt the dominant order. 'The Wedding to the Bread' ceremony, discussed in that chapter, illustrates how deep commitment to anti-realism, to myth-making based in care, can change the practice of space in constructive ways and even intervene in forced gentrification processes. So too the examples of resident-led performance in Chapter 4 indicate how pushing against reality might productively challenge the ways we understand and practice estates: those resident-led works give us a sense of how performances of resistance can foster feelings of control as we attempt to survive in the often hostile prevailing culture.

*

The spatial ecology

I approached this study with the belief that theatre and performance forms have a tangible effect on the production of spaces, and I have demonstrated how such an effect might be powerfully co-determined by the spatial conditions of performance. This has revealed the limits that exist in creating resistant practices in particular contexts. As Bharucha has argued, to suggest that performance has the ability both to open up understanding of social problems and address those problems runs the risk of 'seriously reducing or conflating the socio-political registers of different realities and contexts' (Bharucha 2011: 374). Thus, I propose that we might better understand the spatial operation of estate performance practices via what I call the 'spatial ecology'.

As a term, 'spatial ecology' draws upon two distinct theories. The first is Lefebvre's theory of spatial production, where space is created as dynamic and inherently political interaction between perceived, conceived and lived experiences. The second is Paul Crowther's notion of 'ecology' as a complex term that addresses the interaction between human beings and their environments. For Crowther, human ecology 'focuses on such things as the relations between subject and object of experience, the personal and the collective, and the particular and the general' (Crowther 1993: 5). He argues, as I outlined in Chapter 3, that such relations are often unstable and that aesthetic experience of art enables a harmonizing to occur between subject/object divisions. The artwork, he says, operates as part of the human ecology via the 'sensuous manifold', where the sensual and conceptual are fused.

The 'spatial ecology' that I propose acknowledges that while artistic and other cultural practices can, as Crowther argues, facilitate radical and complex modes of perception and enjoyment, so too the political, *spatial* dimensions of artistic practices often promote or sustain the interests and ideals of particular power-elite groups. Cultural practices usually emerge from, or are reliant upon, systems that are structured in a way that shores up existing power relations. Berry-Slater and Iles warn that we must be careful not to buy into 'fictitious fantasies of production' (2011: 119), whereby social commentary is conflated with direct political action.

I have suggested throughout *Social Housing in Performance* that the institutional contexts from which performance practices operate profoundly influence the way those practices filter into the culture and create possibilities for resisting dominant discourse. I have also suggested that the existing habitus of audience members will shape their readings of and interactions with artworks. As Agbaje argued in an interview I conducted about the critical reception of her estate play *Off the Endz*, 'there is no such thing as a balanced view'. Individuals are always burdened with their perspective, which is a result of their particular lived experience. This has implications for considering the role of theatre institutions in the production of space, because performance work creates meaning not only through its aesthetic effects and rhetorical design but also via the interplay between that design and the contexts from which the work emerges, and the lenses through which theatre makers and audiences view it. It also has implications for qualitative performance analysis, which is also shaped and organized, in part – and despite the theoretical and empirical work that enables researchers to claim objectivity – by the habitus of researchers and the institutional and social contexts in which research is produced and received.

This book does not escape the implications of the spatial ecology: it too uses dominant estate tropes at times, slipping into a register of authentic real (particularly in the preface). So too, the academic language that I have used and, perhaps more importantly, the price of this volume (and academic books more broadly) means its contents will be out of reach to many of those for whom it might be of interest. Both performance practices and research practices require a diverse range of approaches and perspectives to reflect the multiplicity of estate experience, to provide access to a variety of audiences and to challenge dominant estate discourse effectively.

The concept of spatial ecology acknowledges the sensuous processes that feed into the creation, reception and perception of artworks, but stresses that artistic practices are both organic and organized forms of intervention – which operate to produce, reinforce, sustain and question received notions of space and place. It supposes that the experience of art is highly ambivalent. The ostensible integrity of the artist producing an artwork with which to harmonize her subject/object relationship with the world – or conversely of the artist/activist using their funded practice as a call to arms for the staging of a political resistance – is called into question when specific practices function deliberately to harmonize uncomfortable or unstable subject/object relations, thereby operating to silence legitimate concerns regarding the power imbalances that exist in particular spaces. Whether the makers of the work are complicit in the process or not, their commission or selection and the cooperation of gatekeepers – such as theatre institutions or private or public funders – in the staging of estate performance means that performance is always, at least partly, in service of the political structures through which the production of social spaces is controlled.

Once again I emphasize that the role of performance in the production of space cannot be understood without a consideration of the relationship between the aesthetic affects and the institutional, material and social contexts from which individual examples emerge. Because of the centrality of the council estate in public discourse, special attention to the nature of its representation is necessary in order to appreciate how council estate performance operates as part of this spatial ecology – producing sites that play a central role in the identity and governance of the United Kingdom. This book has offered estate performance such attention and as such serves in its totality as an approximation of the spatial ecology of council estate performance.

*

Estate performance: Hope

As I draw this book to a close, making final edits in the summer of 2018, council estates show no sign of losing their prominent place in the public imagination. Indeed, the inquiry into the Grenfell Tower fire, an inflated property market, particularly in the south east of England – making home ownership an impossible luxury for all but the very wealthy – and the uncertain political and economic landscape in the wake of the vote to leave the European Union have intensified national attention around issues of housing security and the role of the state. These conditions have emerged at a time of some change in the political rhetoric – if previous government policy from both sides of the political spectrum over the past three decades has more or less explicitly sought to reduce the role of social housing, now leaders of both the Conservative and Labour parties have suggested social housing must feature in 'fixing' the broken market (see e.g. Chakrabortty 2017, Gibb 2017). In August 2018 the government published the social housing green paper, which sought, among other things, to 'tackle stigma and ensure that social housing can be both a stable base that supports people when they need it and support social mobility' (Ministry of Housing, Communities and Local Government 2018).

The dominant discourse shows signs of shifting, then, and the role of artistic and activist performance practices in contributing to this shift should not be overlooked. If we were to map a recent history of a political change in how we speak and think about housing, we might look, for example, to the documentary film *Dispossession: The Great Social Housing Swindle* (2017) as a cultural flashpoint. Directed by the independent filmmaker Paul Sng under his Velvet Joy Productions company, it was screened in dozens of independent showings across the country, which included live Q&As with the director, housing activists and academics.

Sng was also commissioned to use footage from the film to make a shorter television documentary, *Social Housing, Social Cleansing*, shown on Channel 5 in 2018. The film gives a thorough if didactic account of the social housing crisis and its human impact. *Dispossession* garnered attention from mainstream newspapers (see e.g. Moore et al. 2017, Muir 2017) and significant celebrity support. Jeremy Corbyn, leader of the Labour Party, attended one of the later screenings after it was shown at The World Transformed, an event held adjacent to the Labour Party Conference, in 2017. Indeed, Corbyn's speech at the Conference that year appeared to allude to *Dispossession* or at least to the activism from groups who feature in it, with the language of his speech – 'no social cleansing', 'forced gentrification' and so on – seemingly referencing slogans used by housing campaigners. The film, along with sustained activism from groups like ASH and grassroots campaigns such as the Focus E15 occupation discussed in Chapter 4, amplified by the public outrage over Grenfell, appears to have inflected the tenor of political discussion and public debate. I write this not to suggest that *Dispossession* operates outside of a spatial ecology or the limits of the authentic real: indeed, as ASH (2017b) point out one of the film's limits is that it reveals the reality of the housing crisis but lacks 'any solutions'. Nor do I argue that we are necessarily on the cusp of a radical shift in the dominant council estate discourse. But I want to point out that emergent, resistant works can and do filter into the mainstream. As Mouffe argues,

> Today artists cannot pretend any more to constitute an avant-garde offering a radical critique, but this is not a reason to proclaim that their political role has ended. They still can play an important role in the hegemonic struggle by subverting the dominant hegemony and by contributing to the construction of new subjectivities.
>
> (Mouffe 2007)

Total pessimism about the ability of art to enact a political dimension belies its potential, and artists' commitment to the politics of their estate practices reveals the possibility (however limited) that we might come to understand the value of secure, safe, subsidized, social housing outside of a 'failure' narrative. Despite its limits, art still offers us the opportunity to make our reality different.

Notes

Introduction: The council estate, definitions and parameters

1 The term 'discourse' is used here after Foucault (1971); it refers to the relationship between knowledge and power, presuming that power is controlled by what is known and by those who are able to create that knowledge.

2 The origins of the term 'chav' are contested, however; alternative understandings posit the term to have derived from the Romany *chavi* meaning 'child' (see Quinon N.D. for an example of the popular debate over the word's etymology).

3 The terminology is not consistent between countries. In some parts of Scotland the more common, often derogatory, colloquial phrase is 'scheme', for 'housing scheme'.

4 As I explain in more detail below, 'social housing' is an inexact term for council estates, as many estates are now mixed tenure with owner-occupiers and private renters living alongside social renters.

5 Of course, social housing exists in other parts of the United Kingdom, and much of the debate here can be extrapolated and applied beyond England. However, there are some differences in the policy and governance of estate spaces in the United Kingdom's different countries, a detailed discussion of which is beyond the scope of this book. So too, there are differences in the ways spaces of social housing are culturally understood and practiced. In Irvine Welsh's novel *Porno*, the character Sick Boy reminds us that the word 'estate' is routinely used to describe the sprawling homes of the landed gentry. He remarks that using the word 'estate' to describe state housing is laughably English. 'That's the English', he says, 'ridiculously pompous to the last. Who else would be grandiosely deluded enough to call a scheme an estate? I'm huntin', fishin' shootin' Simon David Williamson from Leith's Banana Flats Estate' (2002: 33). Although this statement is a humorous device in the novel, pointing both to the character's cynicism and his Scottish nationalist politics, the quotation also suggests the potential problems of presenting English examples and cultural understandings as if they reflect the United Kingdom in its entirety.

6 Although English/UK estate representation has been explored by scholars in journal articles and as a smaller element of wider comparative studies (see Burke 2007, Watt 2008, Taunton 2009, Cuming 2013 and 2016) and in PhD theses (see Goodwin 2013, Bell 2014b, McCarthy 2018).

7 There is also a geographical bias towards London. This is, in part, a personal decision: my experience of council estates has been a driving

motivation for this research, and because I came to the project with
experiential knowledge of London estates it made sense to focus the
work in the city that had been my home and my place of work, and on
performance practices about the types of estates I was most familiar
with, staged in buildings I was easily able to access. Additionally, the
representation of the council estate in the popular media – and on the
nationally significant London stage – also tends to focus on London
estates as part of a general bias towards London that the British media
and artistic elite are often accused of.

8 The term 'social housing' is fairly imprecise and wide-ranging in both its use
and its scope. 'Social housing' is generally used to refer to subsidized rented
housing provision. Paul Reeves defines the term as 'housing provided by
local authorities and housing associations … and extended to cover housing
managed by these properties, regardless of ownership'. Reeves argues that
the key feature of social housing is that it is 'non market' and 'allocated
principally on the basis of housing need rather than effective demand'
(2005: 2). Although, generally speaking, we can consider council estates
under the umbrella term of 'social housing' many council estates are either
partly or entirely owner occupied or private rented. Usually this is because
individuals have purchased their homes or because private companies have
developed properties and sold or rented them privately for profit. In such
cases the properties in question would not usually be considered 'social
housing', because they operate within the principles of effective demand.
However, to further complicate the picture, increased provisions for low-cost
(or 'affordable') mortgages and shared ownership schemes mean that the
line between owner occupation and 'social housing' is sometimes blurred
(Reeves 2005: 2). Additionally, properties that are not part of a council estate,
including street properties and sheltered accommodation, might also be
considered social housing if they operate outside of effective demand.

9 The precise definition of 'spare bedroom' has been a central feature of the
national debate over this policy. A discussion of the intricacies of the policy
is beyond the scope of this investigation, but an overview of this welfare
reform is available at the National Housing Federation website (2013).

10 This is because pre-existing policy already placed restrictions, in relation to
accommodation size, on housing benefit for private renters (see Wilson 2017).

11 This strategic framework indicated that the Arts Council were prioritizing
funding for socially engaged work, particularly work that targeted young
people (2010: 19) and diverse communities in areas where 'engagement
in the arts is low' (2010: 30). It was updated in 2013, and that iteration
of the report is titled *Great Art and Culture for Everyone* (Arts Council
England 2013).

12 However, these dates oversimplify a more complex picture. The introduction
of estates to the United Kingdom was a gradual process, which Alison
Ravetz (2001) traces from the nineteenth century (see also Boughton
2018). Indeed, state-subsidized housing projects continue to the present

day – although these contemporary examples tend to differ from the
twentieth-century projects in that the latter are often implemented and
managed by private companies, who are offered subsidies to include social
rented properties in mixed tenure buildings.

13 The Garden City movement, developed by Ebenezer Howard, influenced
the design of many of Britain's estates and New Towns in the first half of
the twentieth century. The utopian ideal of the Garden City principle was
to create living environments with idyllic green spaces, well-proportioned
houses and accessible public buildings (Ravetz 2001, Reeves 2005). The
Progress estate in Eltham, South East London, is an example of an estate
whose design is based on Garden City principles.

14 A TRA is a group of tenants and leaseholders that represents the interests
of those living on a particular estate. They will often hold regular open
meetings, to which all residents are invited. These meetings are usually
attended by representatives from the housing association or local authority
responsible for overseeing the management of the estate. The TRA offers
residents the opportunity for consultation, dispute resolution and advice on
issues relating to the running of the estate.

15 This section develops and repeats work first published in *Performance
Research* (Beswick 2016b).

1 Quotidian performance of the council estate

1 © Grant Kester, 2004, *Conversation Pieces: Community and Communication
in Modern Art*, University of California Press.

2 Harpurhey is not, in fact, an estate as such; it is a neighbourhood in
Manchester, although there are estates in the area. That it is presented as an
estate by the BBC, however, is very revealing in terms of drawing attention
to the way that estates are made to 'stand in' for class, antisocial behaviour
and poverty in popular media representations.

3 My use of the term 'the real', as I expand below, explores how notions of
absolute authenticity and truth operate in representations that purport to
depict 'real life'. Although this conception of 'the real' has some resonances
with the Lacanian use of that term, I am not mobilizing Lacan's model.

4 Some of the material in this section is developed from and repeats material
published in an article I co-wrote with Charlotte Bell (see Bell and Beswick
2014), which emerged from our parallel doctoral research on theatre and
social housing.

5 The *Sun* newspaper offered an initial reward of £20,000 for information
leading to Shannon's return. This later increased to £50,000 (BBC 2017).

6 There is not space to offer an in-depth account of the vast media coverage
of the Matthews case here, but Cotterill's article gives a very detailed and
thorough reading. See also Jones (2011).

7 See Chapter 2 for a more detailed discussion of social realism.

8 The title was changed in the online version to 'Superstar Cheryl Cole overcomes council estate adversity'.

9 The acronym 'Wag' is a colloquial abbreviation of the phrase 'wives and girlfriends', it was used widely in the newspaper press (particularly tabloid newspapers such as the *Sun*, the *Daily Mail* and the *Mirror*) in Britain throughout the 2000s to refer to the female romantic partners of Premiership footballers.

10 She has also performed under her maiden name 'Cheryl Tweedy' and, after divorcing her footballer husband Ashley Cole and remarrying, as 'Cheryl Fernandez-Versini', as well as simply 'Cheryl'.

11 This section is developed and repeats material from an article that first appeared in *Performance Research* (Beswick 2015).

12 Interestingly, discourses of exceptionalism also allow middle-class people to position their success as 'exceptional', as a result of hard work and talent. This means middle-class culture can avoid examining the structural conditions that create 'social closure' where the working class are marginalized from certain elite positions and institutions dominated by the middle class.

13 Some of this material is rehearsed in a chapter that first appeared in *Theatre, Dance and Performance Training* (Beswick 2018).

14 Of course, there are clear distinctions to be made between the kind of sensational tabloid journalism I have mentioned elsewhere and policy initiatives that intend to address inequality. However, in mentioning these different orders of the 'quotidian' in the same chapter I am intending to demonstrate how the dominant discourse establishes and then reinserts itself in insidious ways at different levels of the 'every day'. We will consider ways in which it is possible to push against this dominant discourse in later chapters.

15 'Scruffs' is a colloquial term for casual clothing, such as tracksuit bottoms, while 'uggs' is a term for boots made by 'Ugg' – an expensive brand of comfortable footwear, which became very fashionable in the late 2000s.

16 Cole did not appear on *Pop Idol*; she was a contestant on *Popstars: The Rivals*.

17 The 'why aye pet' refers to a Newcastle colloquialism, understood to be spoken by working-class people with strong Geordie (Newcastle) accents.

18 This section is developed from and repeats material that was first published in *Performing (for) Survival: Theatre, Crisis, Extremity* (Beswick 2016a).

2 Class and the council estate in mainstream theatre

1 Indeed, quite how we measure or categorize class is an ongoing debate across sociology and related disciplines (see Savage 2015). Hence I deliberately avoid offering a concrete definition or series of

measurements here, rather I see the category 'working class' as an imprecise and dynamic term, with economic, social, educational and cultural dimensions.

2 A collective established by the journalist Bridget Minamore, playwright Sabrina Mahfouz and producer Georgia Dodsworth, Critics of Colour aims to broaden access to the theatre industry by expanding diversity in criticism.

3 I rehearsed this idea in the *Journal of Contemporary Drama in English*, some sentences from this chapter appear in that article (Beswick 2014).

4 The West End production of *The Curious Incident of the Dog in the Night Time* moved to the Gielgud Theatre in 2014, after the ceiling of the Apollo collapsed during a performance. It ran until June 2017.

5 'Coching' is slang term, deriving from Jamaican patois that means, more or less, 'relaxing or staying idly in one place, often at home'.

3 Located on the estate

1 See Watt 2009, Lees and Ferreri 2016, ASH 2017a and Minton 2017 for a more in-depth discussion of the social cleansing debate and how it plays out in relation to specific estate regenerations.

2 In media coverage of the event different outlets offer different estimates for performer numbers in the show. The figure of 220 is given by one of the directors in an amateur news video about the production available online (SteelTVonline 2012).

3 Including Helen Mirren, Daniel Craig, Daniel Day-Lewis, Chiwetel Ejiofor, Colin Firth, Rosamund Pike, Orlando Bloom, Catherine Tate, Ben Kingsley, Derek Jacobi, Timothy Dalton, Matt Lucas and Hugh Bonneville.

4 Courses for 2017 ranged from £450 to £989. Accommodation is charged at between £465 and £950 (NYT 2017). There are competitive bursaries to enable low-income young people to participate in the core programme.

5 The NYT accepts an average of 500 members each year. In the archive of NYT productions the latest numbers available at the time of writing are for the years 2015, when ten shows were staged, and 2016, when fourteen shows were staged. This includes shows by the core and social inclusion arms of the company.

6 Although Claire's name does not feature as part of the neon sign it is still visible as part of the original graffiti.

7 TMOs are not necessarily benevolent organizations and, as the Grenfell Tower fire indicates, are also as vulnerable to corruption and oversight as other types of social housing management.

8 Of course, everyone in the space does not mean 'all estate residents' and it is more than likely that there are residents on the estate who feel less warm towards Fourthland and their work – and indeed many who don't engage with it at all. This is part of the tricky politics of site-based applied work.

4 Resident artists

1 © David Roberts, 2018, *Performing Architectures: Projects, Practices, Pedagogies*, Methuen Drama, an imprint of Bloomsbury Publishing Plc.
2 © Lynne McCarthy, 2010, 'The agency of the applied body', Theatre Applications conference, Central School of Speech and Drama.
3 The use of the original video in this new performance is an example of 'sampling', a hip-hop technique usually used with aural material, where sections of an original work are taken and reused in a different song. I point this out to highlight how hood conventions growing out of grassroots hip-hop techniques are appropriated, both within and beyond hip-hop forms to stage resistance globally.
4 *Monsieur Poo-Pourri Takes a Dip* was a commission for the b-side arts festival, and McKenzie has received support from the Live Art Development Agency to realize projects such as the DIY training initiative 'Look at the e(s)tate we're in' – a workshop he ran on his estate for other artists making socially engaged practice.
5 While this means the regeneration was ostensibly the residents' choice, Minton has evidenced how community consultation processes are often corrupt and fail to reflect the will of the residents, with frequent allegations of 'ballot rigging' (2017: 72).

References

Adebayo. M. (2015), 'Revolutionary beauty out of homophobic hate: A reflection on the performance *I stand corrected*', in G. White (ed.), *Applied Theatre: Aesthetics*, 123–55, London: Bloomsbury.

Adiseshiah, S. (2016), ' "Chavs", "gyppos" and "scum"? Class in twenty-first century drama', in S. Adiseshiah and L. Lepage (eds), *Twenty-First Century Drama: What Happens Now?*, 149–71, Basingstoke: Palgrave Macmillan.

Allen, K., Tyler, I., and De Benedictis, S. (2014), 'Thinking with White Dee: The gender politics of austerity porn', *Sociological Research Online*, 19(3). Available online: https://doi.org/10.5153/sro.3439.

Allfree, C. (2008), 'Bridging different worlds for the National Youth Theatre', *Metro*, 11 August. Available online: http://www.metro.co.uk/metrolife/259154-bridging-differ- ent-worlds-for-nationalyouth-theatre (accessed 16 January 2013).

Anderson, F. (2015), 'Cruising the queer ruins of New York's abandoned waterfront', *Performance Research*, 20(3): 135–44.

Antoniou, K. (2013), 'Interview: Simon Stephens on the new production of his play Port', *Riot*, 21 January. Available online: https://run-riot.com/articles/blogs/interview-simon-stephens-new-production-his-play-port (accessed 7 February 2018).

Appiah, K. A. (2006), 'Whose culture is it?', *New York Review of Books*, 9 February. Available online: http://www.nybooks.com/articles/2006/02/09/whose-culture-is-it/ (accessed 15 March 2018).

Artangel (2017), 'About us'. Available online: https://www.artangel.org.uk/about_us/ (accessed 16 May 2018).

Arts Council England (2010), *Achieving Great Art for Everyone: A Strategic Framework for the Arts*. Available online: http://www.artscouncil.org.uk/media/uploads/achieving_great_art_for_everyone.pdf (accessed 21 November 2013).

Arts Council England (2011), *Arts and Audiences: Insight*. Available online: http://www.artscouncil.org.uk/sites/default/files/download-file/arts_audience_insight_2011.pdf (accessed 15 May 2018).

Arts Council England (2013), *Great Art and Culture for Everyone: 10-Year Strategic Framework 2010–2020*. Available online: http://www.artscouncil.org.uk/media/uploads/Great_art_and_culture_for_everyone.pdf (accessed 27 January 2014).

Arts Council England (2015), *Developing Participatory Metrics*. Available online: http://www.artscouncil.org.uk/sites/default/files/download-file/CC_participatory_metrics_report_July_2015_FINAL.pdf (accessed 30 March 2017).

ASH (2017a), 'Sheffield tent city and the social cleansing of Park Hill estate', *Architects for Social Housing*, 30 January. Available online: https://

architectsforsocialhousing.wordpress.com/2017/01/30/sheffield-tent-city-and-the-social-cleansing-of-park-hill-estate/ (accessed 18 April 2018).

ASH (2017b), 'Dispossession the great Labour party swindle', *Architects for Social Housing*, 14 December. Available online: https://architectsforsocialhousing.wordpress.com/2017/12/14/dispossession-the-great-labour-party-swindle-2/ (accessed 22 June 2018).

Aston, E., and Reinelt, J. (2001), 'Building bridges: Life on Dunbar's Arbor, past and present', *Theatre Research International*, 1(3): 285–93.

The Audience Agency (2017), *Up Our Street*. Available online: https://www.theaudienceagency.org/audience-spectrum/up-our-street (accessed 1 February 2018).

Back, L. (2005), '"Home from home": Youth, belonging and place', in C. Alexander and C. Knowles (eds), *Making Race Matter: Bodies, Space & Identity*, 19–41, Basingstoke: Palgrave Macmillan.

Barnett, D. (2016), 'Simon Stephens: British Playwright in dialogue with Europe', *Contemporary Theatre Review*, 26(3): 305–10.

Barrett, M. (2016), ' "Our Place": Class, the theatre audience and the Royal Court Liverpool', PhD thesis, University of Warwick.

Barthes, R. (1973), *Mythologies*, trans. A. Lavers, New York: Hill & Wang.

Battersea Arts Centre (2017a), 'Our history'. Available online: https://www.bac.org.uk/content/38622/about/our_history/our_history (accessed 7 February 2018).

Battersea Arts Centre (2017b), 'How we programme'. Available online: https://www.bac.org.uk/content/37398/create_with_us/how_we_programme/how_we_programme (accessed 7 February 2018).

Bauman, Z. (2001), *Community: Seeking Safety in an Insecure World*, Cambridge: Polity Press.

Baxter, R. (2017), 'The high-rise home: Practices of verticality in London', *International Journal of Urban and Regional Research*, 41(2): 334–52.

Baxter, R., and Brickell, K. (2014), 'For home *unmaking*', *Home Cultures*, 11(2): 133–43.

BBC (2008), 'Parties clash over Shannon case', *BBC News*, 7 December. Available online: http://news.bbc.co.uk/1/hi/uk_politics/7769889.stm (accessed 30 March 2017).

BBC (2017), 'Shannon Matthews: The kidnap hoax that shocked the UK', *BBC News*, 6 February 2017. Available online: http://www.bbc.co.uk/news/uk-38881419 (accessed 15 May 2018).

Bell, C. (2013), 'The inner city and the "hoodie"', *Wasafiri*, 28(4): 38–44.

Bell, C. (2014a), 'Cultural practices, market disorganization, and urban regeneration: Royal Court Theatre Local Peckham and Peckham Space', *Contemporary Theatre Review*, 24(2): 192–208.

Bell, C. (2014b), 'On Site: Art, Performance and the Urban Social Housing Estate in Contemporary Governance and the Cultural Economy', PhD thesis, Queen Mary University of London.

Bell, C., and Beswick, K. (2014), 'Authenticity and representation: Council estate plays at the Royal Court', *New Theatre Quarterly*, 30(2): 120–35.

Bennett, T., Savage, M., Silva, E. B., Warde, A., Gayo-Cal, M., and Wright, D. (2009), *Culture, Class, Distinction*, London: Routledge.

Berry-Slater, J., and Iles, A. (2011), 'No room to move: Radical art and the regenerate city', in *Social Housing: Housing the Social ... ment*. Amsterdam: SKOR.

Beswick, K. (2011a), 'A place for opportunity: *The Block*, representing the council estate in a youth theatre setting', *Journal of Applied Arts and Health*, 2(3): 289–302.

Beswick, K. (2011b), 'The council estate: Representation, space and the potential for performance', *Research in Drama Education: The Journal of Applied Theatre and Performance*, 16(3): 421–35.

Beswick, K. (2014), 'Bola Agbaje's *Off the Endz*: Authentic voices, representing the council estate: authorship and the ethics of representation', *Journal of Contemporary Drama in English*, 2(1): 97–122.

Beswick, K. (2015), 'Ruin lust and the council estate: Nostalgia and ruin in Arinze Kene's *God's Property*', *Performance Research*, 20(3): 29–38.

Beswick, K. (2016a), 'A trialectical cusp: Between the real and the represented: At the bus stop in SPID Theatre Company's 23176', *Performance Research 'On Dialectics'*, 21(3): 27–36.

Beswick, K. (2016b), 'The council estate as hood: SPID Theatre Company and grass-roots arts practice as cultural politics', in L. Peschel and P. Duggan (eds), *Performing (for) Survival: Theatre, Crisis and Extremity*, 163–84, Basingstoke: Palgrave Macmillan.

Beswick, K. (2018), 'Playing to type: Industry and invisible training in the National Youth Theatre's *Playing Up 2*', *Theatre, Dance and Performance Training*, 9(1): 4–18.

Bharucha, R. (1993), *Theatre and the World*, London: Routledge.

Bharucha, R. (2011), 'Problematising applied theatre: A search for alternative paradigms', *Research in Education: The Journal of Applied Theatre and Performance*, 16(3): 365–84.

Bolton, J. (2012), 'Capitalizing (on) new writing: New play development in the 1990s', *Studies in Theatre and Performance*, 32(2): 209–25.

Booth, R. (2018), 'Botched refurbishment fuelled Grenfell Tower fire, says leaked report', *The Guardian*, 16 April. Available online: https://www. theguardian.com/uk-news/2018/apr/16/botched-refurbishment-fuelled-grenfell-tower-fire-says-leaked-report (accessed 18 April 2018).

Boughton, J. (2018), *Municipal Dreams: The Rise and Fall of Council Housing*, London: Verso.

Bourdieu, P. (1977), *Outline of a Theory and Practice*, Cambridge: Cambridge University Press.

Boym, S. (2001), *The Future of Nostalgia*, New York: Basic Books.

Brabin, T., De Piero, G., and Coombes, S. (2017), *Acting up report: Labour's enquiry into access and diversity in the performing arts*. Available

online: https://d3n8a8pro7vhmx.cloudfront.net/campaigncountdown/
pages/1157/attachments/original/1502725031/Acting-Up-Report.
pdf?1502725031 (accessed 1 February 2018).

Brigden, C., and Milner, L. (2015), 'Radical theatre mobility: Unity Theatre, UK,
and The New Theatre, Australia', *New Theatre Quarterly*, 31(4): 328–42.

Burke, A. (2007), 'Concrete universality: Tower blocks, architectural modernism
and realism in contemporary British cinema', *New Cinematic Journal of
Contemporary Film*, 5(3): 177–88.

Butler, J. (1999), *Gender Trouble: Feminism and the Subversion of Identity*,
London and New York: Routledge.

Byrnes, F. (2016), 'The tragic story of Sheffield's Park Hill bridge', *Observer*. 21
August. Available online: https://www.theguardian.com/global/2016/aug/21/
tragic-story-of-sheffield-park-hill-bridge (accessed 21 August 2017).

Cadogan, G. (2016), 'Walking while black', Lithub, 8 July. Available
online: https://lithub.com/walking-while-black/ (accessed 15 May 2018).

Cameron, D. (2016), 'I put the bulldozing of sink estates at the heart of
turnaround Britain', *Sunday Times*, 10 January. Available online: http://www.
thetimes.co.uk/article/ive-put-the-bulldozing-of-sink-estates-at-the-heart-
of-turnaround-britain-rtcgg2gnb6h (accessed 10 January 2016).

Carlson, M. (2008), 'National theatres: Then and now', in S. Wilmer (ed.), *National
Theatres in a Changing Europe*, 21–33, Basingstoke: Palgrave Macmillan.

Carlson, M. (2016), *Shattering Hamlet's Mirror: Theatre and Reality*, Ann
Arbor: University of Michigan Press.

Case, S. (2008), *Feminism and Theatre*, Basingstoke: Palgrave Macmillan.

Castella, T., and McClatchey, C. (2011), 'Gangs in the UK: How big a problem
are they?', *BBC News*, 12 October. Available online: http://www.bbc.co.uk/
news/magazine-15238377 (accessed 21 November 2013).

Cavendish, D. (2013), 'Port, National Theatre, review', *Telegraph*, 29 January.
Available online: http://www.telegraph.co.uk/culture/theatre/theatre-
reviews/9835229/Port-National-Theatre-review.html?mobile=basic (accessed
7 February 2018).

Chakrabortty, A. (2017), 'Jeremy Corbyn has declared war on Labour councils
over housing', *Guardian*, 27 September. Available online: https://www.
theguardian.com/commentisfree/2017/sep/27/jeremy-corbyn-labour-
councils-housing (accessed 4 June 2018).

Chambers-Letson, J. T. (2013), *A Race So Different: Performance and Law in
Asian America*, New York: New York University Press.

Chan, T. W., Goldthorpe, J., Keaney, E., and Oskala, A. (2008), *Taking Part
Survey Briefing No. 8 Attendance and Participation in Theatre, Street Arts
and Circus in England: Findings from the Taking Part Survey*, London: Arts
Council England.

Chave, A. (1992), 'Minimalism and the rhetoric of power', in F. Frascina and J.
Harris (eds), *Art in Modern Culture: An Anthology of Critical Texts*, 264–81,
London: Phaidon.

Clapp, S. (2013), 'Port – review', *Observer*. 3 February. Available online: https://www.theguardian.com/stage/2013/feb/03/port-lyttelton-simon-stephens-review (accessed 7 February 2018).

Coatman, A. (2017), ' "Rita, Sue and Bob Too" at the Royal Court', *London Review of Books*, 19 December. Available online: https://www.lrb.co.uk/blog/2017/12/19/anna-coatman/rita-sue-and-bob-too-at-the-royal-court/ (accessed 1 February 2018).

Cocker, H. L., Banister. E. N., and Piacentini. M. G. (2015), 'Producing and consuming celebrity identity myths: Unpacking the classed identities of Cheryl Cole and Katie Price', *Journal of Marketing Management*, 31(5–6): 502–24.

Cole, C. (2012), *Cheryl: My Story*, London: HarperCollins.

Cole, T. (2018), Teju Cole Facebook. Available online: https://www.facebook.com/Teju-Cole-200401352198/ (accessed 15 May 2018).

Costa, M. (2013), 'Arinze Kene: At Home, I'm Nigerian. I go out and I'm a British Kid', *Guardian*. 25 February. Available online: http://www.theguardian.com/stage/2013/feb/25/arinze-kene-gods-property (accessed 21 November 2013).

Cotterill, J. (2010), 'Mugshots and motherhood: The media semiotics of vilification in child abduction cases', *International Journal for the Semiotics of Law*, 24(4): 447–70.

Couldry, N. (2010), *Why Voice Matters: Culture and Politics After Neoliberalism*, London: Sage.

Cresswell, T. (2004), *Place: A Short Introduction*, Malden: Blackwell.

Cox, D. (2010), 'Clio Barnard's The Arbour is out of lip-synch with reality', *Guardian*, 25 October. Available online: https://www.theguardian.com/film/filmblog/2010/oct/25/clio-barnard-the-arbor-dunbar (accessed 1 February 2018).

Crossley, S. (2017), *In Their Place: The Imagined Geographies of Poverty*, Bristol: Policy Press.

Crowther, P. (1993), *Art and Embodiment: From Aesthetics to Self-Consciousness*, Oxford: Clarendon Press.

Cuming, E. (2013), 'Private lives, social housing: Female coming-of-age stories on the British council estate', *Contemporary Women's Writing*, 7(33): 28–45.

Cuming, E. (2016), *Housing, Class and Gender in Modern British Writing*, Cambridge: Cambridge University Press.

Cunningham, J., and Cunningham, S. (2012), *Social Policy and Social Work*, London: Sage.

Damer, S. (1974), 'Wine Alley: The sociology of a dreadful enclosure', *Sociological Review*, 22(2): 221–48.

Daus, P. (2000), 'Rita, Sue and Bob too/A state affair', *Guardian*, 9 December. Available online: https://www.theguardian.com/stage/2000/dec/09/theatre.artsfeatures1 (accessed 1 February 2018).

De Certeau, M. (1984), *The Practice of Everyday Life*, Los Angeles: University of California Press.

De Jongh, N. (2009), 'Cruel cartoon not very nice', *Evening Standard*, 12 February. Available online: http://www.standard.co.uk/goingout/theatre/cruel-cartoon-not-very-nice-7412614.html (accessed 13 August 2013).

Demo, A. T. (2000), 'The Guerrilla Girls comic politics of subversion', *Women's Studies in Communication*, 23(2): 133–56.

Department for Digital, Culture, Media and Sport (2016), *Taking Part Survey*. Available online: https://www.gov.uk/guidance/taking-part-survey (accessed 1 February 2018).

Dixon, S. (2011), 'Theatre, technology and time', in J. Pitches and S. Popat (eds), *Performance Perspectives: A Critical Introduction*, 89–97, London: Routledge.

Dobraszczyk, P. (2015), 'Sheffield's Park Hill: The tangled reality of an extraordinary brutalist dream', *Guardian*. 14 August. Available online: https://www.theguardian.com/cities/2015/aug/14/park-hill-brutalist-sheffield-estate-controversial-renovation (accessed 18 April 2018).

Dolan, J. (2001). 'Performance, Utopia and the "Utopian Performative"', *Theatre Journal*, 53(3): 455–79.

Dolan, J. (2016), 'Code switching and constellations: On feminist theatre criticism', in D. Radosavljević (ed.), *Theatre Criticism: Changing Landscapes*, 187–200, London: Bloomsbury Methuen.

Duarte, F. (2011), 'Interview – Zygmunt Bauman on the riots', *Journal of Social Europe*, 15 August. Available online: http://www.social-europe.eu/2011/08/interview-zygmunt-bauman-on-the-uk-riots/ (accessed 21 November 2013).

Duckworth, V. (2015), 'Getting by: Estates, class and culture in austerity Britain by Lisa McKenzie', *Times Higher Education*, 29 January. Available online: https://www.timeshighereducation.com/books/getting-by-estates-class-and-culture-in-austerity-britain-by-lisa-mckenzie/2018137.article (accessed 30 March 2017).

Dunbar. A. (2000), 'Rita, Sue and Bob Too', in A. Dunbar and R. Soans (eds), *Rita Sue and Bob Too/A State Affair*, 11-82, London: Methuen.

Edwards, J. (1998), 'The need for a "bit of history": Place and past in English identity', in N. Lovell (ed.), *Locality and Belonging*, 147–67, London: Routledge.

Ellen, B. (2012), 'Cheryl Cole: "I've dined with Prince Charles but I've also sat in a crack den" ', *Observer*. 27 May. Available online: https://www.theguardian.com/theobserver/2012/may/27/cheryl-cole-interview-barbara-ellen (accessed 31 March 2017).

Ellis, C., Adams, T. E., and Bochner, A. P. (2011), 'Authoethnography: An overview', *FORUM,* 10 January 2011: *Qualitative Social Research* 12(10). Available online www.qualitative-research.net/index.php/fqs/article/view/1589/3095 (accessed 15 April 2014).

Engel, L. (2011), 'After social housing: towards a flexible Utopia', in *Social Housing: Housing the Social … ment*. Amsterdam: SKOR.

English, J. (N.D.), *20b*. Unpublished.

Essex County Council (N.D.), *Spirit of Place*. Available online: http://www.essex.gov.uk/Activities/Arts%20Services/Public-Art/Documents/Genius_Loci.pdf (accessed 7 February 2014).

Etherton, M., and Prentki, T. (2006), 'Drama for change? Prove it! Impact assessment in applied theatre', *Research in Drama Education: The Journal of Applied Theatre and Performance*, 11(2): 139–55.

Everyman (N.D.), 'Everyman history'. Available online: https://www.everymanplayhouse.com/about-us/everyman-history (accessed 1 February 2018).

Fandom (N.D.), 'Vicky Pollard', *littlebritan.wika*. Available online: http://littlebritain.wikia.com/wiki/Vicky_Pollard (accessed 19 June 2018).

Farmer, C. (2016), 'Tattoo lover Cheryl adds yet another inking to her collection as she unveils shocking new cleavage etching', *Daily Mail*, 18 May. Available online: http://www.dailymail.co.uk/tvshowbiz/article-3595911/Tattoo-lover-Cheryl-adds-inking-collection-unveils-shocking-new-cleavage-etching.html (accessed 31 March 2017).

Fisher, M. (2009), *Capitalist Realism: Is There No Alternative?* Ropely: 0 Books.

Fitzmaurice, S. (2012), 'She's keeping her head down: Cheryl Cole tweets picture of herself in backless silver dress stood in a prayer-like pose as she gets focused ahead of tour', *Daily Mail*, 21 September. Available online: http://www.dailymail.co.uk/tvshowbiz/article-2206184/Cheryl-Cole-tweets-picture-backless-silver-dress-stood-prayer-like-pose-gets-focused-ahead-tour.html (accessed 31 March 2017).

Forman, M. (2002), *The 'Hood Comes First: Race, Space and Place in Rap and Hip Hop*, Middletown: Wesleyan University Press.

Forrest, R., and Murie, A. (1985), 'Restructuring the welfare state: Privatization of public housing in Britain', in W. van Vliet, E. Huttman and S. Fava, *Housing Needs and Policy Approaches: Trends in 13 Countries*, 97–109, Durham: Duke University Press.

Forsyth, A., and Megson, C., eds (2009), *Get Real: Documentary Theatre Past and Present*, Basingstoke: Palgrave Macmillan.

Foucault, M. (1971), 'Orders of a discourse: Inaugural lecture delivered at the Collége de France', *Social Science information*, 10(2): 7–30.

Fourthland (2018), website. Available online: http://fourthland.co.uk (accessed 18 April 2018).

Friedman, S., and O'Brien, D. (2017), 'Resistance and resignation: Responses to typecasting in British acting', *Cultural Sociology*. Available online: http://journals.sagepub.com/eprint/VxWyY6g7vdrKKzbwqkRx/full (accessed 23 July 2017).

Fugitive Images (N.D.), 'Estate a reverie'. Available online: http://www.fugitiveimages.org.uk/projects/estatefilm/ (accessed 15 May 2018).

Fulcher, M. (2017), 'Exclusive: Carmody Groarke wins £21 million Park Hill gallery contest', *Architects Journal*, 7 November. Available online: https://www.architectsjournal.co.uk/news/exclusive-carmody-groarke-wins-21m-park-hill-gallery-contest/10025046.article (accessed 22 August 2018).

Gallagher, K., and Neelands, J. (2011), 'Drama and theatre in urban contexts', *Research in Drama Education: The Journal of Applied Theatre and Performance*, 16(2): 151–56.

Gardner, L. (2018), 'Is British theatre guilty of failing the working class?', *The Stage*, 14 March. Available from https://www.thestage.co.uk/features/2018/gardner-is-british-theatre-guilty-of-failing-the-working-class/ (accessed 16 May 2018).

Gibb, K. (2017), 'Theresa May's speech and the challenge to expand English social housing', *The Conversation*, 5 October. Available online: https://theconversation.com/theresa-mays-speech-and-the-challenge-to-expand-english-social-housing-85218 (accessed 4 June 2018).

Gidley, B., and Rooke, A. (2010), 'Asdatown: The intersections of classed places and identities', in Y. Taylor (ed.), *Classed Intersections: Spaces, Selves, Knowledges*, 95–116, Aldershot: Ashgate.

GirlsAloudFan79 (2014), 'Cheryl Cole – Piers Morgan Life Stories (Uncut)'. Available online: https://www.youtube.com/watch?v=MrlkeP2TpYE&t=1410s (accessed 31 March 2017).

Goodwin, G. J. (2013), 'Poetry of the Council Estate: A Lefebvrian Approach', PhD thesis, University of Surrey.

The Graham Norton Show (2014), 'Cole shows off new bum tattoo – The Graham Norton Show'. Available online: https://www.youtube.com/watch?v=icLK1J0n9I0 (accessed 7 February 2012).

Graña, C. (1989), *Meaning and Authenticity, Further Essays on the Sociology of Art*, New Brunswick and Oxford: Transaction Publishers.

Grenfell Action Group (2016), 'KCTMO – Playing with fire!', 20 November. Available online: https://grenfellactiongroup.wordpress.com/2016/11/20/kctmo-playing-with-fire/ (accessed 18 April 2018).

Guardian News (2018), 'Stormzy at the Brit Awards: Yo, Theresa May, where's the money for Grenfell?'. Available online: https://www.youtube.com/watch?v=iZ3PTJ7gWoM (accessed 16 May 2018).

Hall, S. (1997a), 'The work of representation', in S. Hall (ed.), *Representations: Cultural Representations and Signifying Practices*, 13–74, London: Sage.

Hall, S. (1997b), 'The spectacle of the other', in S. Hall (ed.), *Representations: Cultural Representations and Signifying Practices*, 223–90, London: Sage.

Halnon, K. B. (2002), 'Poor chic: The rational consumption of poverty', *Current Sociology*, 50(4): 501–16.

Hancock, L., and Monney, G. (2013), 'Welfare ghettos' and the "broken society": Territorial stigmatization in the contemporary UK', *Housing Theory and Society*, 30(1): 46–64.

Hanley, L. (2007), *Estates: An Intimate History*, London: Granta Books.

Hanley, L. (2016), 'Cameron cannot "blitz" poverty by bulldozing housing estates', *Guardian*, 19 January. Available online: https://www.theguardian.com/society/2016/jan/19/cameron-poverty-bulldozing-housing-estates (accessed 30 March 2017).

Hanley, L. (2017a), 'What do we mean when we say "white working class"?', *Guardian*, 23 March. Available online: https://www.theguardian.com/world/2017/mar/23/what-do-we-mean-when-we-say-white-working-class (accessed 16 May 2018).

Hanley, L. (2017b), 'Look at Grenfell Tower and see the terrible price of Britain's inequality', *Guardian*, 16 June. Available online: https://www.theguardian.com/commentisfree/2017/jun/16/grenfell-tower-price-britain-inequality-high-rise (accessed 27 June 2018).

Harling, R. (2017), 'Balfron Tower the artwashing of an icon', *Urban Transcripts Journal*, 1(3). Available online: http://journal.urbantranscripts.org/article/balfron-tower-artwash-icon-rab-harling/ (accessed 1 February 2018).

Harpin, A. (2011), 'Land of hope and glory: Jez Butterworth's tragic landscapes', *Studies in Theatre and Performance*, 31(1): 61–73.

Harris, A. (2012), 'Art and gentrification: Pursuing the urban pastoral in Hoxton, London', *Transactions of the Institute of British Geographers*, 37(2): 226–41.

Harvey, D. (2008), 'The right to the city', *New Left Review*, 53, 23–40.

Harvie, J. (2011), 'Democracy and neoliberalism in art's social turn and Roger Hiorns' seizure', *Performance Research*, 16(2): 113–23.

Harvie, J. (2013), *Fair Play: Art, Performance and Neoliberalism*, Basingstoke: Palgrave Macmillan.

Hatherley, O. (2008), *Militant Modernism*, Ropley: 0 Books.

Hattersley, G. (2008), 'Sink estate superstar', *Times*, 7 December. Available online: https://www.thetimes.co.uk/article/superstar-cheryl-cole-overcomes-council-estate-adversity-n553qs7d7js (accessed 15 May 2018).

Haydon, A. (2016), 'A brief history of online theatre criticism in England', in D. Radosavljević (ed.), *Theatre Criticism: Changing Landscapes*, 135–54, London: Bloomsbury Methuen.

Heathcote, E. (2017), 'From sink to swank – in defence of Britain's brutal estates', *Financial Times*, 15 January. Available online: https://www.ft.com/content/7ae5d134-bacf-11e5-bf7e-8a339b6f2164 (accessed 18 April 2018).

Henley, D. (2015), *More Reasons to Love Libraries*. Available online: http://www.artscouncil.org.uk/blog/more-reasons-love-libraries (accessed 30 March 2017).

Heywood, F. (2003), 'Domicide: The global destruction of home', *Housing Studies*, 18(2): 269–72.

Higson, A. (1984), 'Space, place, spectacle', *Screen*, 25(4–5): 2–21.

Hiorns, R. (2008), *Seizure*, edited by James Lingwood, London: Artangel.

Hiorns, R. (2013), *Seizure 2008/2013*. Arts Council Collection/Pureprint.

Holdsworth, N. (2006), *Joan Littlewood*, Abingdon: Routledge.

Holdsworth, N. (2007), 'Spaces to play/playing with spaces: Young people, citizenship and Joan Littlewood', *Research in Drama Education: The Journal of Applied Theatre and Performance*, 12(3): 293–304.

Home Office (2017), 'Stop and Search'. Available online: https://www.ethnicity-facts-figures.service.gov.uk/crime-justice-and-the-law/policing/stop-and-search/latest (accessed 15 May 2018).

hooks, b. (1990), *Yearning: Race, Gender, and Cultural Politics*, Boston: South End Press.

Hunt, T. (2018), 'Displaying the ruins of demolished social housing at the Venice Architecture Biennale is not "art-washing"', *Art Newspaper*. 28 May. Available online: https://www.theartnewspaper.com/comment/displaying-the-ruins-of-demolished-social-housing-is-not-art-washing-the-v-and-a-is-a-place-for-unsafe-ideas (accessed 22 August 2018).

Huq, R. (2006), *Beyond Subculture: Pop, Youth and Identity in a Postcolonial World*, London: Routledge.

Hyder, E., and Tissot, C. (2013), 'That's definite discrimination': Practice under the Umbrella of Inclusion', *Disability and Society*, 28(1): 1–13.

Innes, C. (2000), *A Sourcebook on Naturalist Theatre*, London: Routledge.

Iyer, S., Kumar, A., Elliot-Cooper, A., and Gebrial, D. (2018), 'Marxism and identity politics', *Historical Materialism*, 29 May. Available online: https://www.versobooks.com/blogs/3853-marxism-and-identity-politics (accessed 22 August 2018).

Jeffries, M. (2010), 'Cheryl Cole defiant over on-screen spat with Wagner', *Daily Record*, 22 November. Available online: http://www.dailyrecord.co.uk/entertainment/celebrity/cheryl-cole-defiant-over-on-screen-1076508 (accessed 4 April 2017).

Jensen, T. (2014), 'Welfare commonsense, poverty porn and doxosophy', *Sociological Research Online*, 19(3). Available online: http://dx.doi.org/10.5153/sro.3441 (accessed 27 June 2018).

Jephcott, A. P. (1971), *Homes in High Flats*, London: Oliver and Boyd.

Jestrovic, S. (2005), 'The theatrical memory of space: From Piscator and Brecht to Belgrade', *New Theatre Quarterly*, 21(4): 358–66.

Johnson, C. (2010), 'X Factor: Drama as furious Cheryl Cole lays into Wagner for branding her "just a girl from a council estate who got lucky"', *Daily Mail*, 21 November. Available online: http://www.dailymail.co.uk/tvshowbiz/article-1331595/X-Factor-2010-Cheryl-Cole-lays-Wagner-branding-lucky-council-estate-girl.html (accessed 4 April 2017).

Johnson, K. (2014), 'Theatres are not catering for the working class majority', *Guardian*, 15 September. Available online: https://www.theguardian.com/culture-professionals-network/culture-professionals-blog/2014/sep/15/working-class-people-subsidised-theatre (accessed 1 February 2018).

Jones, B. (2010), 'The uses of Nostalgia: Autobiography, community publishing and working class neighbourhoods in post-war England', *Cultural and Social History*, 7(3): 355–74.

Jones, O. (2011), *Chavs: The Demonization of the Working Class*, London: Verso.

Jones, S., Hall, C., Thomson, P., Barrett, A., and Hanby, J. (2013), 'Re-presenting the 'forgotten estate': Participatory theatre, place and community identity', *Discourse: Studies in the Cultural Politics of Education*, 34(1): 118–31.

Jowitt, J. (2013), 'Strivers v shirkers: The language of the welfare debate', *The Guardian*, 8 January. Available online: http://www.guardian.co.uk/politics/2013/jan/08/strivers-shirkers-language-welfare (accessed 3 June 2013).

Kearns, A. Kearns, O., and Lawson, L. (2013), 'Notorious places: Image, reputation, stigma. The role of newspapers in area reputations for social housing estates', *Housing Studies*, 28(4): 579–98.

Kelleher, J. (2009), *Theatre & Politics*, Basingstoke: Palgrave Macmillan.

Kemp-Welch, K. (2014), 'Jordan McKenzie and the Rhetoric of Power', *Jordan McKenzie*, exh. cat., London: Arts Council of England; York: Yorkshire Sculpture Park.

Kester, G. H. (2004), *Conversation Pieces: Community and Communication in Modern Art*, Berkeley and Los Angeles: University of California Press.

King, P. (2006), *Choice and the End of Social Housing: The Future of Social Housing*, London: Institute of Economic Affairs.

Kitossa. T. (2012), 'Habitus and rethinking the discourse of youth gangs, crime, violence and ghetto communities', in C. Richardson and H. A. Skott-Myhre (eds), *Habitus of the Hood*, 123–42, Bristol: Intellect.

Kitwana, B. (2005), *Why White Kids Love Hip Hop: Wankstas, Wiggers, Wannabes, and the New Reality of Race in America*, New York: Basic Civitas.

LADA (2014), *Jordan McKenzie Occupations 1996–2013* [DVD], London: Unbound.

Laing, S. (1986), *Representations of Working-Class Life 1957–1964*, London: Macmillan.

Lavender, A. (2016), *Performance in the Twenty-First Century: Theatres of Engagement*, Oxon: Routledge.

Lawler, S. (2005), 'Disgusted subjects: The making of middle-class identities', *Sociological Review*, 53(3): 429–46.

Lawler, S. (2012), 'White like them: Whiteness and anachronistic space in representations of English white working class', *Ethnicities*, 12(4): 409–26.

Lay, S. (2002), *British Social Realism: From Documentary to Brit Grit*, London: Wallflower.

Lees, L., and Ferreri, M. (2016), 'Resisting gentrification on its final frontiers: Learning from the Heygate estate in London 1974–2013', *Cities*, 57: 14–24.

Lefebvre, H. (1991), *The Production of Space*. Trans. D. Nicholson-Smith, Oxford: Basil Blackwell.

Lefebvre, H. (2009), *Dialectical Materialism*. Trans. J. Sturrock, Minneapolis: University of Minnesota Press.

Letts, Q. (2013), ' "People cheered at the end, possibly because we'd finally reached the end": Quentin Letts' first night review of Port', *Daily Mail*, 29 January. Available online: http://www.dailymail.co.uk/tvshowbiz/article-2269949/Port-review-Royal-National-Theatre-People-cheered-the-end--possibly-wed-finally-reached-it.html (accessed 7 February 2018).

Little, R., and McLaughlin, E. (2007), *The Royal Court Theatre: Inside Out*, London: Oberon Books.

Love, C. (2016), 'New Perspectives on home: Simon Stephens and authorship in British theatre', *Contemporary Theatre Review*, 26(3): 319–27.

Love, C. (2017), 'Rita, Sue and Bob Too today: Andrea Dunbar's truths still haunt us', *Guardian*, 14 September. Available online: https://www.theguardian.com/stage/2017/sep/14/rita-sue-and-bob-too-andrea-dunbar-austerity-council-estate (accessed 1 February 2018).

Love, C. (2018), ' "Power has to be grasped": British theatre is tackling its class problem', *Guardian*, 13 March. Available online: https://www.theguardian.com/stage/2018/mar/13/british-theatre-class-problem (accessed 16 March 2018).

LovesTweedyx (2010), 'Cheryl Cole hits back at Wagner about council estates'. Available online: https://www.youtube.com/watch?v=YQ9599F-9WI (accessed 31 March 2017).

LSE/Guardian (2011), *Reading the Riots: Investigating England's Summer of Disorder*. Available online: http://eprints.lse.ac.uk/46297/1/Reading%20the%20riots(published).pdf (accessed 31 March 2017).

Lubiano, W. (1997), ' "But compared to what?" ' Reading realism, representation and essentialism in School Daze, Do the Right Thing, and the Spike Lee discourse', in V. Smith (ed.), *Representing Blackness: Issues in Film and Video*, London: Athlone Press.

Lux (N.D.), 'Estate, a reverie', lux.org.uk. Available online: https://lux.org.uk/work/013429-estate-a-reverie (accessed 15 May 2018).

Mackey, S. (2007), 'Performance, place and allotments: *Feast* or Famine?', *Contemporary Theatre Review*, 17(2): 181–91.

Malone, C. (2008), 'Force low-life to work for a living', *News of the World*, 7 December, 3.

Martin, A. (2014), 'Mark Duggan, the man who lived by the gun: arms draped around two violent gangsters, the thug whose death sparked riots – but who his family insist was a peacemaker', *Daily Mail*, 8 January. Available online: http://www.dailymail.co.uk/news/article-2536197/Mark-Duggan-Arms-draped-two-violent-gangsters-thug-death-sparked-riots.html (accessed 31 March 2017).

Martin, C. (2012), 'Introduction: Dramaturgy of the real', in C. Martin (ed.), *Dramaturgy of the Real on the World Stage*, 1–14, Basingstoke: Palgrave Macmillan.

McAuley, G. (1999), *Space in Performance, Making Meaning in the Theatre*, Michigan: University of Michigan Press.

McCarthy, L. (2010), 'The agency of the applied body', Theatre Applications, 21–23 April, Central School of Speech and Drama: London.

McCarthy, L. (2018), 'The Performance of Waste: Dismantling Spaces of Neoliberalism in Site Specific Art Practices', PhD thesis, Queen Mary University of London.

McConnell, J. (2014), ' "We are still mythical": Kate Tempest's *Brand New Ancients*', *Arion*, 22(1): 195–206.

McCracken, S. (2007), *Masculinities, Modernist Fiction and the Urban Public Sphere*, Manchester: Manchester University Press.

McGarvey, D. (2017), *Poverty Safari: Understanding the Anger of Britain's Underclass*, Edinburgh: Luath Press.

McKenzie, J. (N.D.), *Jordan McKenzie*. Available online: http://www.jordanmckenzie.co.uk (accessed 15 May 2018).

McKenzie, L. (2009), 'Finding Value on a Council Estate: Complex Lives, Motherhood and Exclusion', PhD thesis, University of Nottingham.

McKenzie, L. (2015), *Getting By: Estates, Class and Culture in Austerity Britain*, Bristol: Policy Press.

McKenzie, L. (2016), 'Poor women have never had "privacy". So why should those who bank offshore?', *Guardian*, 19 April. Available online: https://www.theguardian.com/society/2016/apr/19/working-class-women-privacy-tax-havens (accessed 30 March 2017).

McKenzie, L. (2017), ' "It's not ideal": Reconsidering "anger" and "apathy" in the Brexit vote among an invisible working class', *Competition & Change*, 21(3): 199–210.

McKinney, J. (2013), 'Scenography, spectacle and the body of the spectator', *Performance Research*, 18(3): 63–74.

McKinnie, M. (2012), 'Rethinking site-specificity: Monopoly, urban space, and the cultural economics of site-specific performance', in A. Birch and J. Tompkins (eds), *Performing Site-specific Theatre: Politics, Place, Practice*, 21–36, Basingstoke: Palgrave Macmillan.

McLaughlin, R. (2017), 'Laura Oldfield Ford: "I map ruptures, such as the London riots"', *Studio International*, 9 February. Available online: http://www.studiointernational.com/index.php/laura-oldfield-ford-interview-i-map-ruptures-london-riots (accessed 12 May 2018).

Merrifield, A. (1999), 'The extraordinary voyages of Ed Soja', *Annals of the Association of American Geographers*, 89(2): 345–47.

Miller, D. (1988), 'Appropriating the state on the council estate', *Man*, 23(2): 353–72.

Ministry of Housing, Communities and Local Government (2017), *English Housing Survey 2015–2016: Private Rented Sector*. Available online: https://www.gov.uk/government/statistics/english-housing-survey-2015-to-2016-private-rented-sector (accessed 15 May 2018).

Ministry of Housing, Communities and Local Government (2018), *A New Deal for Social Housing*. Available online: https://assets.publishing.service.gov.uk/government/uploads/system/uploads/attachment_data/file/733605/A_new_deal_for_social_housing_web_accessible.pdf (accessed 21 August 2018).

Minton, A. (2017), *Big Capital: Who Is London For?* London: Penguin.

Montgomery, W. (2011), 'Sounding the Heygate estate', *City: Analysis of Urban Trends: Culture, Theory, Policy, Action*, 15(3–4): 443–55.

Moore, R., Harewood, D., Walsh, T., Hanley, L., Adonis, A., Bird, J., Scott, S., Hudson, K., and Barnes, M. (2017), 'Decent homes for all … has the social

housing dream died?', *Observer*, 25 June. Available online: https://www.
theguardian.com/society/2017/jun/25/dispossession-social-housing-crisis-
documentary-thatcher-legacy-right-to-buy (accessed 15 May 2018).

Moreton, C. (2008), 'Missing: The contrasting searches for Shannon and
Madeline', *Independent*, 2 March. Available online: http://www.independent.
co.uk/news/uk/crime/missing-the-contrasting-searches-for-shannon-and-
madeleine-790207.html (accessed 30 March 2017).

Mortimer, B. (2014), 'Documentary charts last days of the Haggerston estate',
East End Review, 7 November. Available online: http://www.eastendreview.
co.uk/2014/11/07/estate-a-reverie-haggerston-samuel-house/ (accessed 15
May 2018).

Mouffe, C. (2007), 'Artistic activism and agonistic spaces', *Art and Research: A
Journal of Ideas, Contexts and Methods*, 1(2). Available online: http://www.
artandresearch.org.uk/v1n2/mouffe.html (accessed 16 May 2018).

Muir, K. (2017), 'Film review: Dispossession the great social housing swindle',
Times, 16 June. Available online: https://www.thetimes.co.uk/article/
film-review-dispossession-the-great-social-housing-swindle-xrn22mrns
(accessed 15 May 2018).

Mullen, K. (2014), 'Before the stylist: Look back at Cheryl's worst ever outfits',
Daily Record, 3 November. Available online: http://www.dailyrecord.co.uk/
entertainment/celebrity/cheryl-cole-x-factor-worst-4559427 (accessed 31
March 2017).

Munjee, T. (2014), 'Appreciating "Thirdspace" alternative way of viewing
and valuing site-specific dance performance', *Journal of Dance Education*,
14(4): 130–5.

Murphy, P. (2012), 'Class and performance in the age of global capitalism',
Theatre Research International, 37(1): 49–62.

Murray, C. (N.D.), *DenMarked*. Unpublished.

National Council of Social Service (1938), *New Housing Estates and Their Social
Problems*, Community Centres and Associations Committee, London: NCSS.

National Housing Federation (2013), Bedroom Tax. Available online: http://
www.housing.org.uk/policy/welfare-reform/bedroomtax (accessed 3
June 2013).

National Theatre (2017), *The History of the National Theatre*. Available
online: https://www.nationaltheatre.org.uk/about-the-national-theatre/
history (accessed 7 February 2018).

National Youth Theatre (2017), *National Youth Theatre*. Available online: http://
nyt.org.uk (accessed 20 April 2017).

Nayak, A. (2006), 'Displaced masculinities: Race, youth and class in the post-
industrial city', *Sociology*, 40(5): 813–31.

Neelands, J., Belfiore, E., Firth, C., Hart, N., Perrin, L., Brock, S., Holdaway, D.,
and Woddis, J. (2015), *Enriching Britain: Culture, Creativity and Growth: The
2015 Report by the Warwick Commission on the Future of Cultural Value*,
Coventry: University of Warwick. Available online: https://warwick.

ac.uk/research/warwickcommission/futureculture/finalreport/warwick_
commission_report_2015.pdf (accessed 20 June 2018).

Nunn, H., and Biressi, A. (2010), 'Shameless? Picturing the "underclass" after
Thatcherism', in E. Ho and L. Hadley (eds), *Thatcher & After: Margaret
Thatcher and her Afterlife in Contemporary Culture*, 137–57,
Basingstoke: Palgrave Macmillan.

Oakley, K., and O'Brien, D. (2016), 'Learning to labour unequally:
Understanding the relationship between cultural production, cultural
consumption and inequality', *Social Identities*, 22(5): 471–86.

Ogbar, J. O. G. (2007), *Hip-Hop Revolution: The Culture and Politics of Rap*,
Lawrence: University Press of Kansas.

O'Toole, E. (2012), 'The Ethics of Intercultural Performance', PhD thesis, Royal
Holloway.

Out of Joint (N.D.), 'The company', *Out of Joint*. Available online: http://www.
outofjoint.co.uk/aboutus/company.html (accessed 1 February 2018).

Ovalhouse (2012), *Artistic Policy*. Available online: http://www.ovalhouse.com/
about/artistic-policy (accessed 31 January 2012).

Palmer, S. D., and Popat, S. H. (2007), 'Dancing in the streets: The sensuous
manifold as a concept for designing experience', *International Journal of
Performance Art and Digital Media*, 2(3): 297–314.

Parker, T. (1983), *The People of Providence: A Housing Estate and Some of Its
Inhabitants*, Exmouth: Eland.

Pearce, J., and Milne, E. J. (2010), *Participation and Community on Bradford's
Traditionally White Estates*, York: Joseph Rowntree Foundation.

Pearce, M. (2017), *Black British Drama: A Transnational Story*, London:
Routledge.

Pearson, M., and Shanks, M. (2001), *Theatre/Archaeology*, London and
New York: Routledge.

Pearson, M., and Turner, C. (2018), 'Living between architectures: Inhabiting
Clifford McLucas's Built Scenography', in A. Filmer and J. Rufford
(eds), *Performing Architectures: Projects, Practices, Pedagogies*, 93–108,
London: Bloomsbury.

Peirse, A. (2016), 'Speaking for herself: Andrea Dunbar and Bradford on film',
Journal for Cultural Research, 20: 60–72. Available online: http:dx.doi.org/10.
1080/14797585.2015.1134060 (accessed 16 February 2018).

Performance Space (2014), 'Post Poplar: Politics people place & performance'.
Available online: https://ymlp.com/zpjP6M (accessed 17 May 2018).

Pitches, J. (2011), 'Introduction', in J. Pitches and S. Popat (eds), *Performance
Perspectives: A Critical Introduction*, 1–19, Basingstoke: Palgrave Macmillan.

Porteous, D., and Smith, S. E. (2001), *Domicide: The Global Destruction of Home*,
McGill: Queens University Press.

Power, A. (1999), *Estates on the Edge: The Social Consequences of Mass Housing
in Northern Europe*, Basingstoke: Palgrave Macmillan.

Power, M. J. (2015), 'Book review: Lisa McKenzie *Getting By: Estates, Class and Culture in Austerity Britain*', *Critical Social Policy*, 35(4): 118–31.

Pritchard, S. (2016), 'Hipsters and artists are the gentrifying foot soldiers of capitalism', *Guardian,* 13 September. Available online: https://www.theguardian.com/commentisfree/2016/sep/13/hipsters-artists-gentrifying-capitalism (accessed 18 April 2018).

Pritchard, S. (2017a), 'Artwashing: Social capital and anti-gentrification activism', *Colouring in Culture*, 17 June. Available online: http://colouringinculture.org/blog/artwashingsocialcapitalantigentrification (accessed 1 February 2018).

Pritchard, S. (2017b), 'A brief history of art, property and artwashing', *Colouring in Culture*, 13 October. Available online: http://colouringinculture.org/blog/artpropertyartwashing (accessed 18 April 2018).

Quinon, M. (N.D.), 'Chav', *World Wide Words*. Available online: http://www.worldwidewords.org/topicalwords/tw-cha2.htm (accessed 3 June 2013).

Ravetz, A. (2001), *Council Housing and Culture: The History of a Social Experiment*, Abingdon and New York: Routledge.

Reay, D., and Lucey, H. (2000), ' "I don't really like it here but I don't want to be anywhere else": Children and inner-city council estates', *Antipode*, 32(4): 410–28.

Reddit (2015), 'Everyone treats Cheryl Cole like the peoples [*sic*] princess and forget she beat up a toilet attendant in a nightclub', 30 August. Available online: https://www.reddit.com/r/britishproblems/comments/3izits/everyone_treats_cheryl_cole_like_the_peoples/ (accessed 31 March 2017).

Reeves, P. (2005), *An Introduction to Social Housing*, Oxford and Burlington: Elsevier Butterworth-Heinemann.

Reinelt, J. (1986), 'Beyond Brecht: Britain's new feminist drama', *Theatre Journal*, 38(2): 154–63.

Rendell, J. (2006), *Art & Architecture: A Place Between*, London: I.B Tauris.

Rhodes, J. (2011), 'Fighting for "respectability": Media representations of the white "working-class" male boxing "hero" ', *Journal of Sport and Social Issues*, 35(4): 350–77.

Richardson, C. (2012), 'Making "changes": 2pac, Nas and the habitus of the hood', in C. Richardson and H. A. Skott-Myhre (eds), *Habitus of the Hood*, 193–214, Bristol: Intellect.

Richardson, C., and Skott-Myhre, H. A. (2012), 'Introduction', in C. Richardson and H. A. Skott-Myhre (eds), *Habitus of the Hood*, 7–25, Bristol: Intellect.

Roberts, D. (2018), 'Housing acts: Performing public housing', in A. Filmer and J. Rufford (eds), *Performing Architectures: Projects, Practices, Pedagogies*, 125–42, London: Bloomsbury Methuen.

Roberts, P., and Stafford-Clark, M. (2007), *Taking Stock: The Theatre of Max Stafford-Clark*, London: Nick Hern Books.

Rogaly, B., and Taylor, B. (2011), *Moving Histories of Class and Community, Identity, Place and Belonging in Contemporary England*, Basingstoke: Palgrave Macmillan.

Rose, M. E. (1972), *The Relief of Poverty 1834–1914*, London: Macmillan.

Rose, T. (2008), *The Hip Hop Wars*, New York: Basic Civitas.

Royal Court (2010) 'Off the Endz Resource Pack'. Available online: http://www.royalcourttheatre.com/education/educational-resources (accessed 30 March 2017).

Royal Court (2017), 'Our Story'. Available online: https://royalcourttheatre.com/about/ (accessed 1 February 2018).

RT.com (2017), *The Great British Housing Sell Off*. Available online: https://www.rt.com/shows/renegade-inc/406107-free-market-economic-uk/ (accessed 1 February 2018).

Sachs Olsen, C. (2016), 'Materiality as performance', *Performance Research*, 21(3): 37–46.

Sachs Olsen, C. (2017), 'Collaborative challenges: Negotiating the complicities of socially engaged art within an era of neoliberal capitalism', *Environment and Planning*, 36(2): 273–93.

Savage, M. (2015), *Social Class in the 21st Century*, London: Pelican.

Scarry, E. (2006), *On Beauty and Being Just*, London: Duckworth.

Schechner, R. (2013), *Performance Studies: An Introduction*, London and New York: Routledge.

Seymour, R. (2017), 'What's the matter with the "white working class?"', *Salvage*, 2 February. Available online: http://salvage.zone/online-exclusive/whats-the-matter-with-the-white-working-class/ (accessed 31 March 2017).

Sharpe, G. (2015), 'Precarious identities: "Young" motherhood, desistance and stigma', *Criminology and Criminal Justice*, 15(4): 1–6.

Shildrick, T. (2018), 'Lessons from Grenfell: Poverty propaganda, stigma and class power', *Sociological Review Monographs*, 66(4): 783–98.

Shohat, E., and Stam, R. (1994), *Unthinking Eurocentrism: Multiculturalism and the Media*, London: Routledge.

Sierz, A. (2011), *Rewriting the Nation: British Theatre Today*, London: Methuen.

Singh, A. (2011), 'Cheryl Cole. From nightclub brawler to nation's sweetheart', *Telegraph*, 5 May. Available online: http://www.telegraph.co.uk/culture/tvandradio/x-factor/8495217/Cheryl-Cole-from-nightclub-brawler-to-nations-sweetheart.html (accessed 31 March 2017).

Skeggs, B. (2001), 'The toilet paper: Femininity, class and misrecognition', *Women's Studies International Forum*, 24(2–3): 295–307.

Skeggs, B. (2005), 'The making of class and gender through visualising moral subject formation', *Sociology*, 39(5): 965–82.

Skinnyman (2004), 'Council estate of mind'. *Council Estate of Mind* [CD]. London: Low Life Records.

Slater, T. (2018), 'The invention of the "sink estate": Consequential categorisation and the UK housing crisis', *Sociological Review*, 66(4): 877–97.

Smith, M. (2014), *Jordan McKenzie: An Englishman Abroad*, exh. cat., Isantbul: Kasa Gallery.

Smithson, R. (1967), 'The monuments of Passaic', *Artforum* (December), 52–57, as 'A Tour of the Monuments of Passaic, New Jersey', in J. Flam (ed.), *Robert Smithson, Collected Writings*, 68–74, Berkeley: University of California Press, 1996.

Snow, A. (2018), 'Critics of colour collective launches to promote theatre writers from diverse backgrounds', *The Stage*, 20 April. Available from https://www.thestage.co.uk/news/2018/critics-colour-collective-launched-increase-theatre-critics-diverse-backgrounds/ (accessed 21 June 2018).

Soans, R. (2000), 'A State Affair', in A. Dunbar and R. Soans (eds), *Rita Sue and Bob Too/A State Affair*, 83–134, London: Methuen.

Social Housing Regulator (2011), *A Revised Regulatory Framework for Social Housing in England from April 2012: A Statutory Consultation*. Available online: http://www.citywesthousingtrust.org.uk/sites/default/files/resource/A%20revised%20regulatory%20framework%20for%20social%20housing%20from%20April%202012.pdf (accessed 4 June 2013).

Soja, E. W. (1996), *Thirdspace: Journeys to Los Angeles and Other Real-and-Imagined Places*, Malden: Blackwell.

Solomos, J. (2011), 'Race, rumours and riots: Past, present and future', *Sociological Research Online*, 16(4): Available online: http://www.socresonline.org.uk/16/4/20.html (accessed 31 March 2017).

Southbank Centre (2012), *Press Release*, 11 July. Available online: https://www.southbankcentre.co.uk/s3fs-public/press_releases/Roger_Hiorns_Seizure_ACC_Press_Release_FINAL.pdf (accessed 16 May 2018).

Space Syntax (2009), *London, Wenlock Barn Estate*. Available online: http://www.spacesyntax.com/project/shoreditch-wenlock-barn-estate/ (accessed 16 May 2018).

Spencer, C. (2001), 'Rita, Sue and Bob Too; A state affair', *Telegraph*, 24 December. Available online: http://www.telegraph.co.uk/expat/4180044/Rita-Sue-and-Bob-Too-A-State-Affair.html (accessed 1 February 2018).

SPID (2009), *Business Plan 2009–2012*. Unpublished.

SPID Theatre Company (2017), 'About'. Available online: http://spidtheatre.com/about/ (accessed 1 February 2018).

SteelTVonline (2012), 'National Youth Theatre of GB performing SLICK at Sheffield's Park Hill'. Available online: https://www.youtube.com/watch?v=5nx2ju-vdEw (accessed 18 April 2018).

Stephens, S. (2013), *Port*, London: Bloomsbury Methuen.

Stripe, A. (2016), 'Writing Andrea Dunbar: Framing the Non-Fiction Novel in the Literary North', PhD thesis, University of Huddersfield.

Stripe, A. (2017), *Black Teeth and a Brilliant Smile*, London: Fleet.

Strudwick, L. (2017), 'Is Arts Council England abandoning the working classes?', *Heads Together*. Available online: http://www.headstogether.org/perch/resources/ace-portfolio-articlev3.pdf (accessed 1 February 2018).

Swartz, D. (1997), *Culture and Power: The Sociology of Pierre Bourdieu*, Chicago: University of Chicago Press.

Takako, D. (2014), 'The making of Menace II Society', *Dazed*. Available online: http://www.dazeddigital.com/artsandculture/article/16699/1/the-making-of-menace-ii-society (accessed 2 December 2014).

Taketwoimages (2012), 'National Youth Theatre. FLOOD – elements only'. Available online: https://www.youtube.com/watch?v=mIrdDVHLC7c (accessed 18 April 2018).

Tate (N.D.), 'Minimalism'. Available online: http://www.tate.org.uk/art/art-terms/m/minimalism (accessed 15 May 2018).

Taunton, M. (2009), *Fictions of the City: Class, Culture and Mass Housing in London and Paris*, Basingstoke, Palgrave Macmillan.

Taylor, A. (2008), 'Estate is nastier than Beirut', *Sun*, 6 April.

Taylor, L. (2013), 'Voice, body and the transmission of the real in documentary theatre', *Contemporary Theatre Review*, 23(3): 368–79.

Taylor, M., and O'Brien, D. (2017), ' "Culture is a meritocracy": Why creative workers' attitudes may reinforce social inequality', *Sociological Research Online*, 12 September. Available online: http://journals.sagepub.com/doi/abs/10.1177/1360780417726732?journalCode=sroa (accessed 1 February 2018).

Telegraph Reporters (2017), 'Shannon Matthews trial: The 'pure evil' of mother Karen Matthews', *Telegraph*, 14 February. Available online: https://www.telegraph.co.uk/news/2017/02/13/shannon-matthews-trial-pure-evil-mother-karen-matthews/ (accessed 16 May 2018).

Tenant Services Authority (2009), *Regulatory Framework for Social Housing in England from April 2010*. Available online: http://www.tenantservicesauthority.org/server/show/ConWebDoc.20175 (accessed 7 February 2012).

Theartsdesk.com (2012), 'National Theatre 2013 season'. Available online: http://www.theartsdesk.com/theatre/national-theatre-2013-season (accessed 7 February 2018).

Theatre Royal Stratford East (2012), *Mission Statement*. Available online: http://www.stratfordeast.com/our_work/mission_statement.shtml (accessed 31 January 2012).

Thompson, J. (2009), *Performance Affects*, Basingstoke: Palgrave Macmillan.

Thompson, J. (2015) 'Towards an aesthetics of care', *Research in Drama Education: The Journal of Applied Theatre and Performance*, 20(4): 430–41.

Trivelli, E. (2011), 'A blue feeling in the gallery: Roger Hiorns' *Seizure* and the arts market', *Liminalities*, 7(1). Available online: http://liminalities.net/7-1/seizure.pdf (accessed 15 May 2018).

Tyler, I. (2008), 'Chav Mum, Chav Scum', *Feminist Media Studies*, 8(1): 17–34.

Tyler, I. (2013), *Revolting Subjects: Social Abjection and Resistance in Neoliberal Britain*, London and New York: Zed Books.

Tyler, I., and Bennet, B. (2010), ' "Celebrity chav": Fame, femininity and social class', *European Journal of Cultural Studies*, 13(3): 375–93.

Tomlin, L. (2013), *Acts and Apparitions: Discourses on the Real in Performance Practice and Theory, 1990–2010*, Manchester: Manchester University Press.

Tompkins, J. (2012a), 'Theatre's heterotopia and the site-specific production of Suitcase', *TDR: The Drama Review*, 56(2): 101–12.

Tompkins, J. (2012b), 'The place and practice of site-specific theatre and performance', in A. Birch and J. Tompkins (eds), *Performing Site-specific Theatre: Politics, Place, Practice*, 1–17, Basingstoke: Palgrave Macmillan.

Trueman, M. (2015), 'No Milk for the Foxes: The beatboxing show bringing "council estate rage to the theatre"', *Guardian*, 22 April 2015. Available online: https://www.theguardian.com/stage/2015/apr/22/no-milk-for-the-foxes-beatboxing-theatre-council-estate-class-beats-elements (accessed 7 February 2018).

Tucker, P. (2017), 'The astonishing neglect of Grenfell survivors is part of a national malaise', *Guardian*, 7 December. Available online: https://www.theguardian.com/commentisfree/2017/dec/07/neglect-grenfell-tower-survivors-tory-housing-policy (accessed 18 April 2018).

Turner, C. (2004), 'Palimpsest or potential space? Finding a vocabulary for site-specific performance', *New Theatre Quarterly*, 20(4): 373–90.

Turner, C. (2015), *Dramaturgy and Architecture: Theatre, Utopia and the Built Environment*, Basingstoke: Palgrave Macmillan.

Upchurch, A. (2016), *The Origins of the Arts Council Movement: Philanthropy and Policy*, Basingstoke: Palgrave Macmillan.

Urban Splash (2011), *Park Hill*. Available online: http://www.urbansplash.co.uk/residential/park-hill (accessed 5 December 2011).

Urban Splash (2018), 'About Us', *Urban Splash*. Available online: http://www.urbansplash.co.uk/about-us/our-story (accessed 18 April 2018).

Urbandictionary.com (N.D.), 'White trash'. Available online: http://www.urbandictionary.com/define.php?term=white%20trash (accessed 30 March 2017).

Vanden Heuvel, M. (1992). 'Complementary spaces: Realism, performance and a new dialogics of theatre', *Theatre Journal*, 44(1): 47-58.

Vincent, B. (2014), 'Viewpoint: Escape from the 'sink' estate', *BBC News*, 20 February. Available online: http://www.bbc.co.uk/news/magazine-26254706 (accessed 31 March 2017).

Virtanen, M., et al. (2013), 'Perceived job insecurity as a risk factor for incident coronary heart disease: Systematic review and meta analysis', *British Medical Journal*. Open Access. Available online: http://www.bmj.com/highwire/filestream/656953/field_highwire_article_pdf/0/b mj.f4746 (accessed 31 March 2017).

Wallis, M. (2009), 'Performance, complexity and emergent objects', in K. Alexiou, J. Johnson and T. Zamenopoulos (eds), *Embracing Complexity in Design*, 143–60, Abingdon: Routledge.

Wallpaper (2009), 'Seizure by Roger Hiorns reopens in London', *Wallpaper*, 3 August. Available online: https://www.wallpaper.com/art/seizure-by-roger-hiorns-re-opens-in-london (accessed 18 May 2018).

Watt, P. (2006), 'Respectability, roughness and "race": Neighbourhood place images and the making of working-class social distinctions in London', *International Journal of Urban and Regional Research*, 30(4): 776–97.

Watt, P. (2008), ' "Underclass" and "ordinary people" discourses: Representing/ re-presenting council tenants in a housing campaign', *Critical Discourse Studies*, 5(3): 345–57.

Watt, P. (2009), 'Housing stock transfers, regeneration and state-led gentrification in London', *Urban Policy and Research*, 27(3): 229–42.

Watt, P., and Minton, A. (2016), 'London's housing crisis and its activisms', *City: Analysis of Urban Trends, Culture, Theory, Policy, Action*, 20(2): 204–21.

Wacquant, L. (2008), *Urban Outcasts: A Comparative Sociology of Advanced Marginality*, Cambridge: Polity Press.

Welsh, I. (2002), *Porno*, London: Cape.

Wenlockbarntmo (2018), *Wenlock Barn TMO*. Available online: http://www. wenlockbarntmo.co.uk (accessed 18 April 2018).

West, E. (2010), 'The man with 15 kids by 14 women. The welfare state has turned back the clock – to one million BC', *Telegraph*, 22 September. Available online: http://blogs.telegraph.co.uk/news/edwest/100054718/the-man-with-15-kids-by- 14-women-the-welfare-state-has-turned-back-the-clock-to-one-million-bc/ (accessed 21 November 2013).

Williams, G. (2008), 'Roger Hiorns: Artangel at Harper Road', *ArtForum*, 47(4). Available online: http://www.mutualart.com/OpenArticle/Roger-Hiorns/49333F041E3A27AB (accessed 18 April 2018).

Williams, R. (1977a), 'A lecture on realism', *Screen*, 18(1): 61–74.

Williams, R. (1977b), *Marxism and Literature*, Oxford: University of Oxford Press.

Wilson, E. (1992), 'The Invisible Flâneur', *New Left Review*, I/91. Available online: https://newleftreview.org/I/191/elizabeth-wilson-the-invisible-flaneur (accessed 12 June 2016).

Wilson, W. (2017), 'Under-occupying social housing: Housing benefit entitlement'. Available online: http://www.parliament.uk/briefing-papers/ SN06272 (accessed 22 August 2018).

Winlow, S., Hall, S., and Treadwell, J. (2016), *The Rise of the Right: English Nationalism and the Transformation of Working-Class Politics*, Bristol: Policy Press.

Wood, A. (2009) ' "Original London style": London Posse and the birth of British Hip Hop', *Atlantic Studies*, 6(2): 175–90.

Wray, M. (2006), *Not Quite White: White Trash and the Boundaries of Whiteness*, Durham and London: Duke University Press.

Wright, K. J. (2011), 'Participant Perspectives on Participation: A Case of a Housing Estate in Leeds', PhD thesis, University of Leeds.

Zimmerman, A. L. and Johansson, L. (2010), 'Some time in utopia?', in Fugitive Images (eds), *Estate*, 2–16, London: Myrdle Court Press.

Index

220 *Index*

sensuous manifold 128–31, 140, 185
sexual excess/sexuality 46, 47, 83
Shameless 35, 40, 61
Sheffield 6, 115–16
Shoreditch 143–4
sink estates 1, 27, 41, 49, 169
site-specific 9, 19, 115–51
Skepta 153–4
Slick 124–33
Slung Low 177
Smith, Sheridan 41
Soans, Robin 80, 83–4, 93
social cleansing 117–19, 135, 140,
     150–1, 156–7, 188, 193 n.1
social inclusion 9, 55, 77, 95, 98, 127
  social exclusion 47–9, 55, 120
social mobility 53–4, 56, 95, 184, 187
social realism 24, 41, 84–5, 99, 183
  see also realism
Soho Theatre 84, 88
Soja, Edward 20–2, 23–4
spare bedroom tax 2, 6–7, 190 n.9
SPID Theatre Company 78–9
St Ann's estate 35
Stafford-Clark, Max 81, 83, 84,
     85, 88, 89
Stephens, Simon 93–4, 95, 97, 101–3
  Port 93–103
stereotypes 32–3, 37, 40, 46, 62, 92,
     99, 106
stigma 3, 7, 9, 11, 13, 29, 41, 44–9, 56,
     67, 104, 123, 154–6, 187
Stockport 93–103
stop and search 67–8, 166
Stormzy 154–5
Stripe, Adelle 82, 91
  *Black Teeth and a Brilliant
     Smile* 92–3
subversion 146, 148–50, 159, 167–8

taste 11, 43, 57, 76, 97
Tempest, Kate 72, 93
  Brand New Ancients 111

tenancies 2, 6–8
The Westbridge, Rachel
     De-lahay 11
Theatre Local/Beyond the
     Court 79–80
Theatre Royal Stratford East 79
time/temporality 141–2
transnational 4, 67, 155–6, 184
trialectics 23–34
tucker green, debbie 63
Tyler, Imogen 32–3, 46–7,
     56–8, 75

underclass 2, 10, 59
Urban Splash 115–16, 124–6,
     129–30, 132–3
Utopia 14, 96, 131–3, 140, 163–4,
     168–70, 174, 191 n.13

Vasseur, Roman 150–1
verticality 161
Vicky Pollard 46, 99
Victoria and Albert Museum
     117–19
voice 144, 150, 156–60, 177
  see also authentic voice

Welsh, Irvine, *Porno* (novel) 189 n.5
Wenlock Barn estate 116, 142–50
white trash 41, 47–9, 60, 99
whiteness 48, 60

X-Factor 51

yearning 159–60, 173–4
Yorkshire (county) 39, 44, 75,
     81, 124–6
Yorkshire Sculpture Park (YSP) 116,
     134–8, 141
  see also Seizure

Zimmerman, Andrea Luka 168–74
  see also Fugitive Images